| DUS | CHINA | MESO-AMERICA | CENTRAL ANDES |
|---|---|---|---|

CLASSIC  POST-CLASSIC

MAYA

MEXICAN

*INCA*

*Late Kingdom*
*Tiahuanaco*

*CLASSIC*
*CULTURES*

*Chou*
*and Later*
*historic China*

FORMATIVE

OLMEC

CHAVÍN

*asions*

*S*

*vilization*

SHANG

*Black*
*Pottery*

*Painted*
*Pottery*

— **Cultural Continuity**

— **Trade**

*Chinese*
*Neolithic*

— **Conquest**

*es*

— **Intermittent Trade**

# THE
# ORIGINS OF

*Carroll L. Riley*

# CIVILIZATION

*Carbondale and Edwardsville*

SOUTHERN ILLINOIS UNIVERSITY PRESS

FEFFER & SIMONS, INC.

*London and Amsterdam*

Copyright © 1969, by Southern Illinois University Press
All rights reserved
Printed in the United States of America
Designed by Andor Braun
Standard Book Number 8093–0361–2
Library of Congress Catalog Card Number 69–10036

*To Brent*

In this present era of specialized knowledge, writing a general survey on civilization is a chancy thing, for no one person can control more than a segment of the basic data. In a book which, hopefully, will have a diverse audience, the author must avoid both the Scylla of facile generalization and the Charybdis of overdetail. Inevitably, at one point, he will choose the theory fashionable yesterday but discounted today, or he will fail to read that key article that changes a whole perspective. His charts and maps will attempt to synthesize the ideas of various experts and will satisfy none. In areas where he has firsthand knowledge his own strongly-held ideas, as if by their own volition, will parade themselves as fair-minded consensus.

Still and all I do believe that writing a book such as this can be rewarding. We students of human culture—anthropologists, historians, cultural geographers or whatever we wish to name ourselves—all too often count trees and call this simple statistical operation a forest. We busy ourselves with detail, but lack an overview, an attempt to fit the human experience into some general framework. I attempt such an overview in this book.

★  ★  ★

I have had much and generous help in the preparation of this work. Special thanks go to Robert L. Gold, J. Charles Kelley, Campbell W. Pennington, Robert L. Rands, Philip C. Weigand, and Gordon R. Willey for their helpful comments. J. Cary Davis advised on various classical materials and Richard V. Lee on medical details, while Basil C. Hedrick read the finished manuscript in detail, giving me both mechanical and substantive criticisms. My thanks also go to Tullio Tentori of the Museo Nazionale Delle Arte, Rome, to A. T. Lucas and the staff of the National Museum of Ireland, to Fr. Feichin O'Doherty of University College, Dublin, and to the officers of the Royal Irish Academy, the latter having provided me with working facilities for an extended period of time. Gloria Bowring, Marie M. Doenges, Lawrence Dusek, Lisa Ferree, Ellen A. Kelley, Louis C. Kuttruff, Tso-Hwa Lee, C. S. Lien, Jon D. Muller, George E. Mylonas, and Jonathan E. Reyman helped in supplying and preparing illustrations, as did the personnel at the Oriental Institute and Field Museum, Chicago. D. Kathleen Abbass and Diane K. Zinkhon did yeowomanly service in retyping and proofing the manuscript.

The shortcomings of the book are my own.

Carroll L. Riley

*Southern Illinois University*
*June 4, 1968*

# Contents

# List of Illustrations

# THE ORIGINS OF CIVILIZATION

THE WORD civilization is ultimately derived from the Latin civilis and closely connected to the word civis, that is, citizen. Also related are such words as city, civil, civilian, and civility. Such a derivation may seem farfetched at first, but if we consider the implications of the word citizen in the Greco-Roman world, the connection may be much clearer. A citizen in the ancient Mediterranean world was first and foremost the inhabitant of a city, thus an urbanite (compare also Greek—politicia, polity or method of government; polis [city], politics, politician, police, policy). Even under the massive imperialism of the Roman Empire the important unit was the city. In early Greek and Roman times we hear little of the pagani (pagans), the country-folk, but much about citizens.

There are certain implications of town or city living that will be important to our definition of civilization. Cities first of all demand specialists; in fact, cities might be thought of as aggregates of specialists who live in convenient proximity to each other. In order to feed these specialists, there must be a surplus of basic food. To assume the collection and distribution of these supplies and to control both the primary producers and the specialist consumers, political authority is needed and so a political organization of considerable complexity must appear. The religion of the civilized group generally—probably always—tends to follow this same trend to complexity.

The history of civilization, as such, is a short, recent phase in the long and slow development of man. It is true that once certain basic inventions were made, civilized societies swiftly followed, but these basic inventions or discoveries came very late in the history of man. They are primarily the several techniques that gave man control over food supply by food production (agriculture and animal husbandry). Associated with these tremendous discoveries came certain other inventions: new tools, methods, and attitudes to cope with the plentiful life.

These basic discoveries seem to have been made independently in the Old World and the New. Yet the civilizations that grew from them are remarkably similar—so similar that many specialists feel that they cannot represent parallel growth and one area must have

*The Meaning of Civilization*

greatly influenced the other. However, given certain basic factors of food surplus and environmental conditions, it does seem that the superstructure of civilization will be roughly the same whatever the area. Partly this is due to the remarkable similarity of the human species. The physical range of human beings is considerably less than that of some other domesticated animals—this is due in part to the restlessness of man and his strong inclination to mix his genes with those of other groups, and in part to the fact that the appearance of modern man (*Homo sapiens*) was probably rather recent. Presumably all human groups have much the same mental processes and abilities so that given certain conditions they can be expected to channel events in certain ways.

In addition, humans have a base of very similar culture. This is particularly true of language, perhaps the most humanizing aspect of the human animal. Often we become so interested in the obvious diversity of human language that we overlook the amazing underlying similarities. Briefly, it can be said that all languages and thus probably all thought processes of modern man are very much alike. Flexible, symbolic ideas are created by forming and reforming some few dozen basic sound groups called phonemes—made by breath escaping the lungs and being shaped in the throat and mouth.[1] Conceptualizations such as morphemes, words, phrases, follow certain regularized patterns which, however, may show striking specific differences from one language to another. For example, in English and certain other western European languages there is a relatively simple grammar or arbitrary arrangement of the linguistic patterns—most utterances following a subject / action / object pattern. Meaning is carried by manipulating phrases and sentences, that is, by syntax. In some such languages, say, German, there appears a considerable amount of deadwood with such things as useless (non-informative) gender indicators, but even German follows the general pattern of western European language. Latin, on the other hand, has a highly complex series of grammatical forms in which the change is one of morphology—that is, within the word itself. Other languages show, from our point of view, even more exotic variations. A number of the languages from Negro Africa have a gender prefix that extends throughout most of the words of an utterance—thus giving a fine alliterative quality to speech.

Languages may also differ in the innate and subjective values they place on the external world. Language is a window to reality for human beings and different languages may allow us to observe different segments of reality. In western European languages all events and actions are presented in terms of mass and of rigid time-categories with time itself representing a kind of object. For example, in English we say "ten nights went by" using exactly the same grammatical structure as if we were saying "ten knights went by." Abstractions are represented as a kind of concrete object—with mass. We say, "Her heart was filled with love," in exactly the same way as we would say, "Her mug was filled with beer." Love here is a kind of liquid and the heart a hollow vessel.

In certain other languages, this kind of structure is not used but other modes of expression, alien to us, are employed. In the American Indian language, Hopi, an important part of speech has been called a "tensor," that is, an indicator of the intensity of a situation.

Language was not the only part of culture formed early in human history. A rough idea of the essential unity of human beings can be gained by looking at traits and patterns that are universal—that is to say, part of the cultural heritage of all men. These include not only such wide categories as language, family structure, and religious organization but also a number of the more specific restrictions, the "shame" sense and many others. Most of these traits (possibly all) go back to a very early level of humanity and are actually implicit in any realistic definition of what is "human."

In spite of the many changes in human life produced by civilization—changes in mere numbers of human beings, in complexity of social, political, and religious organization, and in technology—in spite of these things it must be realized that the whole of mankind has more similarities than dissimilarities and civilization may be looked upon as a delectable but thin icing on the thick cake of human culture. It is the way of life of only part of the human species and has been for a relatively short time, roughly five to six thousand years.

Yet, because of the immense technological advances

possible only to civilized communities, man has for the first time really achieved some control over his environment. Only yesterday, as the earth counts time, man was seriously challenged by fellow predators among the mammals. Today he is in partial control of his total environment and is on the threshold of leaving the planet altogether. If man can avoid self-destruction, who knows what the future may hold.

THE STUDY of civilization should properly begin with some consideration of that immense period during which men struggled toward a civilized state. Indeed, it might be well to look even farther back to a time when there were no men but, rather, animals in the process of becoming men.

## II

*In*
*the Beginning*

It comes as no shock today to say that man is a mammal, genetically related to the other warm-blooded, large-brained, furry or hairy animals that have come to dominate the earth's surface in the past sixty to seventy million years. This is more than idle knowledge, for much that is unique to man—the great superstructure of learned behavior or culture, invented by him—has a firm foundation in his mammalian heritage.

Like other mammals, man has a large brain, especially that portion known as the forebrain, almost certainly the seat of generalized mental activity. In man this forebrain is vast in size and very complex and is, we all presume, the physiological basis of culture—but it is still a good mammalian brain.

Another general mammalian physical trait—the production by females of a nutritive liquid called milk to feed the young—is a basis of the family. In man, the institution of the family becomes far more complex than in any other mammal (involving as it does, kinship, mating taboos, and rudimentary political organization), but basically the human family unit is like that of other mammals. It is not only the mammary aspect of mammals that necessitates a family structure; also important is the fact that young are born helpless. This early protection by adults gives the infant time to learn, to choose from alternative patterns of behavior. Such generalized activity is essentially denied lower life-forms that must function reasonably well from birth. Such creatures as reptiles, fish, and the various nonvertebrates rely on instinctive, or built-in, patterns of behavior. To put it another way, the mammals sacrifice immediate efficiency for a far greater potential in later life.

Even the sexual specialization of mammals affects human culture. Because mammals bear their young alive, the mother (in general we can say any nubile female) must spend a great deal of her time in the difficult and vital task of carrying, bearing, feeding, and caring for young. Male mammals remain more generalized in their activities, freer to range; on a human level, freer to innovate. It is probably correct to say that, in general, men have taken more active roles in human invention and in the direction of cultural systems while women have had enormous influence as cultural transmitters due to their direct influence on the young.

The subgroup of mammals to which humans belong is called Primates and our closest primate relatives are the apes and monkeys. We human beings share a great deal with other primates; a very large brain, the important prehensile hand, and many other structural features including vocalization—which in humans becomes speech—and the high level of sex drive (as opposed to a cyclic arrangement) that adds such zest and poignancy to human existence. We differ from these primate poor-relations in total overall brain size, and in a specialized foot which, with attendant bone changes throughout the body, allows us to stand and walk upright. On these two things, plus the primate hand, is based much of humanness.

It is not known when man first appeared. A reasonable guess would put his debut in the Pliocene period— say at some point between ten million and perhaps two million years ago. There is fossil evidence from Italy, dated about ten million years ago, of a manlike but probably nonhuman primate named Oreopithecus. Sometime between one and two million years ago there appeared in South and East Africa, in the first part of the geological period known as the Pleistocene, rather small animals known collectively as Australopithecinae. These creatures (they include such forms as Zinjanthropus, Australopithecus, and Paranthropus) have body forms that are reasonably humanlike. For example, they probably stood more or less upright; they are still rather apelike, or at least nonhuman, in head features, but had a brain larger in relation to body size than that of any known ape past or present. An additional crucially important point is that they seem to have been tool users and tool makers.[1]

This at once puts them out of reach of the apes, for behind the crude stone pebble tools we see shadowy aspects of other parts of culture, a rudimentary language and some sophistication of social organization. It

1

*Hunting scene? Prehistoric rock art, Libyan Sahara, Mesolithic or early Neolithic*

**Courtesy Istituto Italiano di Cultura, New York**

is dangerous to go too far on the scant evidence of crude tools and skeletal remains but if we were asked to reconstruct the origin of man the tentative and timid reconstruction might go something like the following.

At some point in the past one of the higher primates began to develop the specialized feet and changes in long bones, pelvis, vertebral column, and skull that led to the upright stance.[2] Possibly this occurred when a tree-living animal was forced by gradual shrinkage of forests to go to the ground for food—the human hand and other primate hands and feet do seem to have developed for tree living. Change in the bony structure may have stimulated the head changes that led to a larger brain, while walking upright certainly left the hands freer for manipulative purposes—leading first perhaps to random use, then eventually to invention of tools. Actually we can only speculate on the sequence of events that led to the origin of humanity. Probably flexible hand and brain were only two in an interlocking nexus that in time created man.[3]

One factor, however, discussed to some degree in the first chapter, must have been of overriding importance. This was language, an invention peculiar to man. Language involves the symbolic representation of experience, or of (as Mischa Titiev so aptly expresses it) algebraic mentality. The invention of language was probably a function of a brain that had reached a "crossover" point in size and complexity, a point that none of the other primates, much less the lower mammals, has reached. Whatever the specific history of language it becomes the focal point for human culture. Almost certainly it underlies the forward leaps in technology that we see in the early Pleistocene epoch and was basic to every other aspect of culture. So important is language that we can fairly say it marks the real dividing line between human and nonhuman.[4]

Speech probably developed as an evolutionary survival mechanism. With language, the events and objects of the external world could be transmitted into arbitrary symbols and manipulated in the mind. One of the things then possible is that hypothetical actual situations can be created and hypothetical solutions for them worked out within the mind. This is a roundabout way of saying that we think with language; that is, we communicate with ourselves as well as with others.

The advantages of this form of mental activity can hardly be overemphasized. Language means that the human group can cooperate in ways impossible to other animals; it can plan future projects and can carry them through with precision and detail. Man started his journey into humanhood at a considerable disadvantage among other animals — he is a carnivore without specialized equipment, fangs, claws, great muscular power, or speed, to compete for prey. However, through language he more than made up for this lack, utilizing the novel idea of the flexible, foreplanning, interacting group.

Along with language, probably both stimulating it and being stimulated by it, came the invention of tools. These first tools were likely both offensive and defensive weapons of stone or wood, used in the primary task of food collecting. Some of them may have had several functions — for example, a common early tool is a heavy core of flint or other fracturable material, which in later stages became known as a "fist axe" or coup de poing. This was probably a hunting tool but it may have been also used for such diverse activities as digging roots, cracking nuts, and chopping wood.

The parts of culture which leave no physical remains are, of course, harder to reconstruct than technology. We can say that language probably was extremely early because it seems unlikely that tool traditions could be established without linguistic communication. For certain other major aspects of human culture there is less evidence. In spite of its fundamental and universal importance today we have no idea when religion began, though it is probably an early aspect of human culture. At any rate, man was surely a language-using animal before he was a religious animal, for religion (at least in its conceptual aspects) is a part of man's symbolic universe. The symbols used in identifying things religious do not directly represent the outside environment. For example, the phonetic elements that go into the word tree represent, by algebraic shortcut, an ideal tree, or the concept of trees in general, or a specific tree. The ideal tree of course does not exist, but its specific prototype does. The phonetic combination of the word spirit, or ghost, may also be general or specific in nature but (at least as far as objective proof is concerned) it has no counterpart in the physical world.

Many years ago the English anthropologist Edward B. Tylor suggested that religion appeared as a direct result of men's first dealings with a symbolic universe. Tylor considered religion an attempt by man to explain the puzzling phenomena of dreams and death. The curious adventures a man had in his dreams, when he might visit far places and see distant people without ever leaving his bed, surely demanded explanation. Equally puzzling was the sudden loss of animation in death with no other immediate body change. Tylor felt that the simplest way for primitive man to explain these events was to assume a body / soul dualism out of which grew the secondary idea of souls for nonhuman and even nonliving things (stones, streams, and so forth). A powerful leader might be expected, after death, to continue his influence; out of such conjecture might have developed the idea of gods.

Certainly, with the invention of a symbolic system man began to consider for the first time questions that other animals never ask. An ape or a dog probably dreams and certainly dies, but neither animal can construct symbols to represent, communicate, and ponder these puzzling events. To become human—that is, to become a language-using animal—meant for man the eating of fruit of the tree of knowledge and expulsion forever from the paradise of perfect animal innocence.

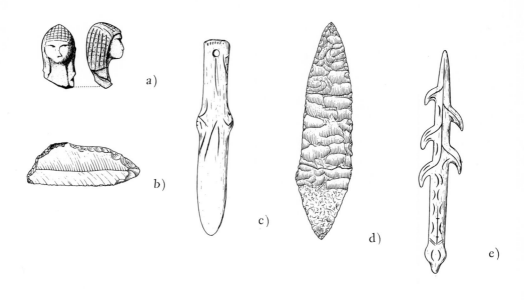
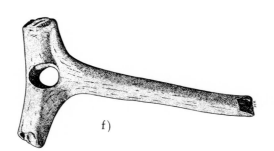

2
Artifacts, Upper Paleolithic, France

a) Female figurine head of ivory    e) Antler, harpoon point
b) Endscraper    f) Lance shaft straightener
c) Bone dagger    g) Ivory baton
d) Knife, "laurel leaf" shape

WE ACTUALLY know all too little of man in this first age of slow groping toward humanity. We do know that by the middle of the Pleistocene epoch, say by a quarter of a million years ago, man was becoming larger-brained and presumably more intelligent. His tool traditions (hardly more is left of his culture) were now quite elaborate and we find tools for hunting, for scraping and cutting, and probably for a number of other uses. Meanwhile, physical evolution continued. Some one hundred thousand years ago the big-brained group known collectively as the Neanderthals appeared in the Old World, humans perhaps as efficient as ourselves in brain use, and with quite elaborate cultures. For the first time we have direct evidence of religion: careful burial in caves, with grave offerings.

The Neanderthals continued to flourish through the initial phase of the fourth, or last, of the great glacier periods that make up most of the Pleistocene, a period called the Würm in Europe, the Wisconsin in America. The Neanderthals then disappeared, displaced or absorbed, and the history of the last thirty to fifty thousand years has been that of *Homo sapiens*, our own species of man.

Anthropologists are still undecided as to when modern man first appeared. One group considers him to be descended from an early Neanderthal stock (the first Neanderthal men were somewhat more "modern" than later "classic" Neanderthals). Others feel that the antecedents of *Homo sapiens* must extend back to the middle Pleistocene or beyond.[1] At any rate, it is clear that from mid-Würmian times he spread throughout the world, undertaking man's last major migrations, and becoming the dominant primate in all habitable areas. The long developmental history of pre-*sapiens* man takes place in the Old World heartland, with North America, South America, Australia, and much of Oceania unoccupied by human beings. However, modern man has been characterized by a willingness to explore abroad and so the New World was entered, probably via the Bering Straits, perhaps more than thirty thousand years ago. Man invaded Australia, an isolated continent, home of kangaroos and other marsupials, at some point in the late Pleistocene and also began his slow spread into Oceania.

# *Enter* Homo Sapiens

3
*"The Sorcerer," Upper
Paleolithic painting from Les
Trois Frères cave, France*

Several of the cultures of early man are well known.
In Europe, during the height of the Würm glacier,
when a large part of the continent was ice-covered,
groups of big game hunters lived south of the ice fields.
They have left us records in the form of finely chipped
implements: spear points, scrapers, gravers for carving
and etching, and other stone tools. Their burials provide a great deal of information about the physical type
(completely modern) and some incidental insight as to
their taste in the decorative arts and their technical skill
in making necklaces and other costume items. But
most impressive are the great galleries of paintings on
the walls of western European caves.

These paintings, mostly of animals, were begun perhaps as early as thirty thousand years ago. The latest
ones, and some of the best, date from no more than
10,000 B.C., near the end of the ice age itself and the

beginning of recent times. During these many thousands of years several techniques were developed. In fact some were probably forgotten and rediscovered, for ice, animals, and human groups were restlessly fluctuating over those thousands of years and such a situation makes unlikely a simple cultural progression. Nevertheless, the early paintings do tend to be simple line drawings of animals, while the full flowering of cave art, with magnificent polychrome techniques, was generally later in time.

The cave art seems to have been, at least in part, for purposes of magic; attempts by trained magicians to ensure capture of large game animals (bison, deer, horse, perhaps the woolly mammoth and woolly rhinoceros). It is clear that we are dealing with groups that have a food surplus and are willing to spend some of it in tasteful but economically useless pursuits. Useless, that is, from our point of view; the ancient hunters surely felt that the magician, by painting or drawing magical pictures, played an essential role in increasing and helping capture the animals.

One other indication of the mental life of man in the late Pleistocene comes from small figurines of nude women found in various places in Europe. These usually emphasize sexual characteristics, with scanty detail paid to features of face, arms, and lower legs. The tiny statuettes (they are only a few inches high) have been called Venuses and it is suggested that they were used in fertility rites. There seems a good chance that they represented chthonian or earth deities and are related to, perhaps are directly ancestral to, the earth goddesses of historic times.

We know far more of European early modern man than of his fellows in other areas of the world. This partly is because a great deal of prehistoric archaeology has been done in Europe, particularly western Europe. There is, however, another reason. European cultures of this period, the Upper Paleolithic (that is, later part of the Old Stone Age), were indeed quite brilliant. Apparently the vast supply of large food animals grazing in the grass or tundra country south of the ice sheets meant surplus food and large human populations. We have seen how some of this surplus was used to support specialists for the splendid cave art; probably

4
*Upper Paleolithic Venus figure*

*Enter* **Homo Sapiens**

15

the rest was expended in festivals or rites of which we have almost no knowledge today.[2]

Many of the first peoples in the New World, possibly all of them, were big game hunters and they, too, seem to have been very successful. The American hunters (often called Paleo-Indians) left delicately chipped spears or dart-points and other stone tools. They hunted bison and the mammoth as well as smaller animals. Unfortunately, they do not seem to have been artistically inclined—at least we have nothing to match the great cave paintings of Europe.

In other parts of the world late-Pleistocene man made varying adjustments to his environment. For most of these areas we have little or no information, but it is certain that by the end of the ice age (about ten thousand years ago) man had spread into every habitable continent. In fact a Carbon-14 date from a man-made hearth shows that our species had reached the very tip of South America by eighty-five hundred years ago. Almost certainly he spread there from the north, and descended from pioneers who had originally entered at the Bering Straits.

In this period the minor changes in body form which allow us to distinguish races may have been taking place. The environmental pressures produced by fluctuation of ice in the northern parts of the world and/or rain patterns and sea levels elsewhere must have presented early *Homo sapiens*, as it did his predecessors, with sharp challenges. His response to these challenges eventually produced the human being of today, sculptured, so one might say, by ice, wind, and rain.

THE WÜRM and Wisconsin ice sheets began their final retreats some ten thousand years ago and by eight thousand years ago had largely disappeared from the earth. Today we find glaciers only in the very northern and southern portions of the world, and even much of the Arctic region, though cold, is very dry. The past ten thousand years have seen several periods of temperature and rainfall variation though never enough temperature fall to produce continental ice sheets. These variations have been charted by analysis of pollen deposits in ancient lakes or bogs in various areas; especially in northern Europe and in eastern and southwestern United States.

The end of the glaciers brought wide-scale changes to many parts of the earth. In northern Europe and Asia and probably also Canada and the northern United States, the land rose slowly following its release from the weight of the glacial mass. Meanwhile the sea also rose as glacial ice melted and drained into the oceans. In Europe a thick tangle of forest matted the countryside, choking out the great herds of animals that depended on this terrain. In North Africa moisture-bearing winds were gradually shifting northward leaving behind an increasingly dry land and, in fact, a belt of desert on semidesert lands that stretched to central Asia. The great Sahara or desert of North Africa, is a product of this recent or post-Pleistocene period.

Eventually the rising ocean covered thousands of square miles of southeast Asian land until finally that continent attained its present contours. The sea also encroached onto the north European plain, creating marshes and lakes and finally turning Great Britain into the island she has remained ever since. In the New World the Great Lakes, among others, were formed by water from melting glacial ice.

There was, during the post-Pleistocene period, a general shrinkage of the areas inhabited by vast animal herds and a number of animal species disappeared. These included, in Eurasia, the woolly mammoth and rhinoceros, and in America the mammoth, the great *Bison antiquus*, the ground sloth, and the horse. In Europe the highly successful Upper Paleolithic period came to a close and its peoples were gradually transformed into squalid bands of small game hunters and

# IV

*Setting the Stage, Old World and New*

collectors of seeds and roots. The great art disappeared with the surplus that had supported it, and Europe became a backwater, a cultural appendage to Asia and Africa.

Even before the end of the Pleistocene, in both the Old World and the New, there appeared certain peoples whose life, though not as spectacular as that of the big game hunters, had far greater potential for the future of mankind. In the Old World they seemed to thrive best in the belt of, at that time, relatively well-watered land from North Africa to India where lived the small animals they hunted and the variety of food plants they gathered. They have been given a series of names: in North Africa, Oranian, Dabba, and Capsian; in West Asia, Natufian, and Karim Shahir, among others. At the risk of some oversimplification, we can group them under the name Mesolithic ("Middle" Stone Age). These peoples probably differed considerably from one another in culture, but they had in common the fact that they intensively utilized their various environments. The plants they gathered included certain wild cereals, the ancestors of domesticated wheat, barley, and millet; and these wild cereals were harvested by bone or wood sickles which were set with tiny flint flakes called microliths. The microlithic tradition (and presumably the economy it implied) may actually have evolved in central Asia. In postglacial times it spread to Europe where carriers of it mingled or competed with the descendants of the older big game hunters of Pleistocene times. The heartland of these Mesolithic cultures, however, was in the great belt, steadily growing more arid, south and east of the Mediterranean.

In the New World, peoples of this same general economic tradition also date back to Pleistocene times. Most of the data on these early groups are from North America, particularly the United States and Mexico. There seem to have crystallized quite early (ten thousand or more years ago) certain groups in the eastern and central United States called the Archaic, and others in the western United States and Mexico collectively known as the Desert Culture. In general, these and similar cultures in Central and South America can be referred to as an American Mesolithic.[1] Unlike their

5
*Human figures, prehistoric
rock art, Libyan Sahara,
Mesolithic or early Neolithic*

predecessors, the hunting peoples, they concentrated on a variety of plant foods and on small game.

In both parts of the world the cultural equipment of the Mesolithic peoples had been largely bequeathed them by earlier Pleistocene man. The main hunting weapon was the spear or lance, though probably by the end of the Upper Paleolithic a simple mechanical device, the atlatl, or spear thrower, had been invented. This is a flat piece of wood, or some other resilient material, one end of which is held in the hand. The other end is notched or scooped out, so that the butt end of a short spear can be fitted into the notched end of the atlatl, the shaft and point of the spear projecting forward along the body of the atlatl. The spear is then cast, much as a stone is cast from a sling; it has a short range but great penetrating power.

A whole series of skin scrapers, knives, gravers, and other stone tools had been invented in the Pleistocene

*Setting the Stage, Old
World and New* 19

and were spread over the entire world by man in his wanderings. At some point toward the end of the Pleistocene, the dog became the first domesticated animal. This event happened early enough for dogs to travel with their human owners to Australia and to the Americas.

Certain technical inventions were made by the Mesolithic groups in the New World and Old. In the Old World the bow seems to have been a Mesolithic invention. It was probably especially adapted for the hunting of smaller, more agile animals because of its long range and great accuracy. The bow is, perhaps, man's first tool in which energy is stored for sudden release when needed. The use of microlithic flints set in sickles was a contribution of Old World Mesolithic man, while in both the Old and the New World ways of grinding the wild seeds were invented or adapted—the mortar and pestle as well as the more efficient hand grinder (in which seeds are placed on a flat stone and scrubbed with another stone). This latter device, called a metate by New World archaeologists and a quern by those in the Old World, was especially useful to early agriculturists and is still found in simple agricultural societies.

At this point we might describe an actual group from each hemisphere in order to give some idea of the kind of people we are dealing with. Of course, no given Mesolithic people can be called "typical" if by the term we mean that they contain similar cultural assemblages as other groups hundreds or thousands of miles away. They are typical only in the sense of giving an idea of the general level of culture of the time.

In the southwest United States, the Cochise complex represents one area where Desert Culture peoples lived for several millennia with relatively little change in the general level of culture.[2] The oldest Cochise remains, the Sulphur Springs Phase (named for a southern Arizona valley in which artifacts are found), show a people who were settling down to grub out an existence from what they could find among the plants of their region. The presence of projectile points indicate that they still hunted large game animals with spear or atlatl. They prepared the hides with stone scrapers and knives, then thriftily split open the bones for the marrow. Metates and associated hand grinding stones, called manos in

America, tell us something of the use of plants, especially of seeds and nuts. Sulphur Springs is generally estimated as being eight thousand to ten thousand years old and is representative of a quite early population of diversified hunters and gatherers. Later periods in the Cochise complex show an increasing dependence on gathering and small animal hunting—in fact many of the larger species, the mammoth and the horse, were becoming extinct.

We can say very little about the social and political life of the Cochise peoples. Obviously they lived in small groups and (arguing by analogy from modern primitive peoples) probably were grouped in extended families of only a few dozen people: a man and his wife, certain of their married children, a sprawling brood of grandchildren, and a scattering of other relatives. However, it was from such small bands—though probably far south of Arizona—that American agriculture eventually came.

In the Old World a comparable culture, on about the same time level, might be the Natufian of Palestine, one of a large number of Mesolithic peoples living in an elongated area that extended from North Africa across western and southwestern Asia. Like many of their contemporaries, people of the Natufian reaped crops of cereal grains using sickles set with microliths, tiny stone blades, and ground the grains with pestles in stone mortars. This diet was supplemented by game, as proven by archaeological finds of scrapers and projectile (possibly arrow) points. The Natufians also used bone in quantity and ate fish as well as other animals and plants. They lived both in the open and in caves; the open site at Eynan, north of the Sea of Galilee, contained the stone lower courses of circular houses, the largest about thirty feet in diameter. These are especially interesting, for we have rather scanty evidence of housing in most parts of the world during the Mesolithic period.

At some unknown point in the past, in both the Old World and the New, one or the other of these Mesolithic societies took the fateful step of planting and domesticating particular plants and so became the first agriculturists.

The period of early agriculture is, rather illogically,

called the Neolithic (New Stone Age). The terms Paleolithic, Mesolithic, Neolithic, incidentally, referred originally to certain styles of stone work. It must be remembered that the archaeologist, the student of cultures of the past, works mainly with material remains, and in pre-metal ages much of the material was of stone. The sequence of stone ages, worked out a hundred years ago, agrees well enough with the environmental changes and basic discoveries that shaped human prehistory. As we have said, the term Mesolithic here refers to groups whose diversified economy allowed them to survive the changes brought about by the end of the Pleistocene. Some of these people eventually evolved an agriculture and so became Neolithic, this term having taken on the meaning of simple agriculturist.

In favored areas certain of these simple agricultural peoples went on to develop civilization. We will consider first the events of the Old World, tracing man's slow evolution from the technologically simple hunter-gatherers of the Natufian or Capsian type, to the great river valley civilizations of the Nile, Tigris-Euphrates, the Indus, and the Hwang Ho. From these primary areas there grew secondary centers in the Mediterranean region and elsewhere.

After tracing the course of civilization in the Old World, we will turn our attention to the New World where, from Archaic groups of Central and South America, came the first impulses toward the civilization of Mesoamerica and the central Andes. The New World development was later than that of the Old World and was largely independent of it.

Some ten thousand years ago man was poised on the edge of his great adventure. A million years before, the first hesitant steps had been made. Now, after the slow incubation of the Stone Age, man was nearing civilized life. In certain areas, both in America and in Afro-Asia, the human animal made certain basic discoveries and in so doing he transformed the world.

ABOUT ten thousand years ago the amazing discoveries that were to change and rechange human history were made somewhere south or east of the Mediterranean Sea. The archaeologist V. Gordon Childe has referred to these events as "revolutions"; but this brings visions of rapid violent change, so perhaps some other word or phrase would be better.

The discovery of agriculture and the domestication of animals were likely a result of slow, painful experimentation on the part of some seed-gathering Mesolithic culture. Such cultures generally have barely a subsistence economy and very little incentive to experiment. So, even though simple to us, the step from reaping wild cereal grains to sowing them on prepared soil for a future harvest was actually a large one. The notion of selecting and storing seed grain represented a considerable innovation on the part of gatherers and considerable self-discipline too, for it subtracted from the supply immediately available for food.[1]

As a matter of fact, we do not know for certain whether particular known cultures were or were not truly agricultural. The Natufian of Palestine discussed in Chapter IV may actually have sown as well as reaped, at least during one part of their existence. Recent discoveries at Jericho on the Jordan River make the Natufian peoples serious claimants to this crucial "first" in the history of post-Pleistocene man.[2]

The first domesticated grains were wheat and barley, both of which in various forms grow wild in the Afro-Asian area. We do not know whether there was one center for the domestication of plants, or if different species were independently domesticated in various parts of North Africa and western Asia—or, for that matter, if the same species was independently domesticated by more than one group.

Very early, perhaps before glacial ice had completely melted from the face of Europe and Asia, emmer wheat (*Triticum dicoccum*), barley (*Hordeum* sp.), and club wheat (*T. compactum*) were being cultivated in or near the Mediterranean basin. Flax, the seeds perhaps originally used for food, seems to have been one of the first, but millet, another popular cereal grain, may have come later. In fact an old suggestion is that millet long existed as an impurity in wheat.[3] When the idea of

# V

## The First Farmers of the Old World

agriculture was slowly diffused northward from its Mediterranean homeland the hardier millet began to crowd out wheat. At any rate, by the time agriculture reached China, probably in the fourth or third millennium, it was mainly a millet agriculture.

It is not known whether domestication of animals was stimulated by agriculture or whether this idea was contributed by other, nonagricultural, peoples. A classic hypothesis (now largely discounted) was that as the Sahara dried, following the last glacial period in the north, man and animals were more and more forced together in restricted water holes, and out of this may have come animal domestication. Regardless of the origin of animal husbandry, however, it can be said that the ecology of agricultural peoples is especially fitted to domestication of certain animals. The by-products of agricultural crops, straw or stubble, can be used in feeding animals, and the animal manure is a ready-at-hand fertilizer. Mesolithic and early Neolithic groups depended on wild game for skins and meat. Agriculture, by increasing the total food supply, causes a rise in population thus making advantageous a dependable supply of animals.

Three of the earliest domesticated animals were the cow, the sheep, and the goat.[4] All of them fulfill the requirements for meat and skins listed above. In addition, the sheep soon became important for another reason. As population grew, the new agricultural communities must have felt a pressing need for certain raw materials, not the least important being those connected with clothing.

Earlier hunting man had clothed himself with skins, but larger populations meant that there were no longer enough wild animals to go around, and even with domesticated herds it must have been uneconomical to slaughter large numbers of animals. Clearly some substitute was needed. It is interesting that in both the Old World and the New the same series of basic inventions led to the introduction of cloth. Spinning or twisting of fibers to produce cord or rope was probably known from Paleolithic times, as was basket weaving. Elaborating on these techniques, man produced an invention called a loom which mechanically intertwines threads to produce cloth.

The loom appeared, independently invented as far as we know, in both New World and Old because there was an obvious basic demand for cloth in both hemispheres. In the New World most cloth was made from the fibers of the cotton plant. In the Old World flax was soon utilized, for the fibers of this plant produce the satisfactory cloth, linen. Probably the most important single fiber, however, was wool. The first sheep were presumably domesticated in Asia where present-day wild breeds live. Ancient varieties of mouflon (*Ovis musimon, O. orientalis*) and the urial (*O. vignei*), the latter a longer-tailed sheep, were probably the first domesticated. Interestingly, these did not produce wool but were used for meat, milk products, and hides. The secondary selection of sheep for wool was a human innovation and gives us some inkling of the skill, knowledge, and imagination of these early populations.

Several other animals were domesticated at the beginning of agricultural times. The goat probably appeared about the same time as the sheep; in fact it is difficult to distinguish between skeletal remains of these two animals.[5] The ass or donkey also was domesticated early as a beast of burden, and the pig as a food animal.[6] The area south of the Mediterranean was becoming drier, however, and animals that prefer forest land never prospered in those parts. The pig, in fact, eventually became taboo in the diet of many western Asian and North African peoples. Europe, with its extensive oak forests, proved more receptive to the pig, and the animal has a basic place in the diet to this day.

It is interesting to note that the horse, so important to later cultures, was not to be domesticated for some thousands of years, and the camel also seems a latecomer. Certainly the early high cultures of Mesopotamia and Egypt did without horse or camel transport. On the other hand, there were experiments in domestication that failed; the gazelle is an example.

A very early agriculture comes from the site of Jericho in the valley of the Jordan River north of the Dead Sea.[7] Here Kathleen Kenyon found a large town, dating about 7000 B.C., whose buildings showed considerable architectural skill. Evidence for agriculture is not conclusive but it seems highly unlikely that the people of Jericho could have maintained a permanent habitat

Courtesy The Metropolitan Museum of Art, Purchase, 1955. Joseph Pulitzer Bequest

6

Bronze sistrum
(musical rattle
used in religious
ceremonies) from
central Anatolia,
2300–2000 B.C.

without a dependable food supply based on regular food production.[8] Parenthetically, the early Jericho culture was without pottery, an experiment in practical chemistry so often linked with agriculture.

The first "city" of Jericho may owe its exuberant growth to an excellent environment produced by adequate rainfall in this zone south of the vanishing glacier. The experiment in premature civilization was repeated elsewhere. At Çatal Hüyük in the Konya Plain of central Anatolia there was, by 6000 B.C., town life with agriculture, animal domestication, weaving, pottery making, and, apparently, also the beginnings of religious and political specialization.[9] The Anatolian area may have been extremely important in the rise of early agricultural cultures. Even earlier than Catal Hüyük is the nonpottery Neolithic at Hacilar in southwestern Turkey, and both Hacilar and the site of Mersin in Cilicia have long sequences that extend into metal-using periods. However, much work needs to be done before the influence of early Anatolia can be properly assessed.

From present evidence, the sequences of culture that were to lead to civilization seem to have begun in Egypt and Mesopotamia perhaps seven thousand years ago. In the middle Nile valley a people called Tasian [10] cultivated emmer wheat and barley and had already domesticated sheep or goats or both. The Tasians were undoubtedly hunters and fishers as well as agriculturists. Unlike the first settlers at Jericho, they had pottery; thus in Egypt, as in Anatolia, man had added another great basic invention. Pottery is made by molding vessels of clay and firing them at a sufficient heat to produce chemical change. The resultant product will not disintegrate when wet and can be placed directly on fire. Because of its fragile nature pottery is not popular with nomadic groups. It is especially suited to settled agriculturists, allowing them to efficiently boil cereal grains and protein-rich legumes. Tasian pottery is quite well made and must have had a cruder ancestor, still undiscovered. The Tasians also had weaving, for traces of linen cloth have been found, though the type of loom is unknown.

A second, probably related culture, called Fayumian, appears in Lower (northern) Egypt at about the same period as Tasian. Flint sickles were used to harvest emmer and barley. Cattle and pigs appear as domesticated animals, as well as sheep and/or goats. In both these early cultures are found palettes of stone, usually of alabaster, and similar palettes in historic Egypt were used by ladies to hold eye paint. We might consider this an example of ancient frivolity but, at least in historic times, painting the eyelids with a lead or copper compound had some therapeutic value as a specific against eye disease. A somewhat later culture, the Merimdian of the Nile delta area, combined agriculture with enthusiastic hunting and fishing, and if the finds of mace heads are interpreted correctly, the Merimdians also experimented with warfare. A related culture at El Omari, east of the delta, shows traces of the Asiatic wheat, einkorn (*Triticum monococcum*).

Beginning sometime after 4500 B.C., the widespread Badarian culture extended throughout much of the Nile valley. The Badarians traded widely, their boats voyaging up and down the Nile and probably beyond, for they imported such luxury goods as turquoise, cedar, and ostrich shell from outside Egypt. Copper appears for the first time, though it may have been cold-hammered and neither smelted nor cast.[11] Badarian craftsmen made excellent pottery and also exquisite vases of alabaster.

Like the other early Egyptian cultures, the Badarians buried their dead, often in desert graves, and occasionally with a female figurine of ivory or clay. Possibly such statuettes are wife substitutes, but they may also link with the Upper Paleolithic "Venuses" and be mother or earth goddesses.[12]

The Badarians and their predecessors farmed the sides of the Nile valley gradually increasing the amount of available land on the edge of the flood plain. From present evidence it looks as if they also utilized high natural levees near the actual river. The Amratian culture, an outgrowth of the Badarian, began the slow and exacting task of controlling the river itself through irrigation canals. We are now near to civilization in Egypt. The historically known statelets, or nomes (see Chapter VI), are forming—at least designs and drawings on Amratian pots show animals that are known to be associated in some way with the nomes. One suggestion is that the nomes were originally totemic clans strung out along the Nile. A totem is a symbolic representation of the clan or some other social or political unit (the American Eagle is a kind of national totem). It may be, then, that the Amratian animals painted on pottery vessels are totems. Certain pictures of this type suggest traditional gods and goddesses of Egypt; one is the cow-headed female (later Hathor, goddess of fertility), while another is the as yet unidentified animal (possibly a jackal) known to the later Egyptians as Set or Seth.

Pictures of captives suggest slavery and this, in turn, implies a rich and expanding culture. There is another reason to think so. Amratian peoples imported not only luxury goods but even some workaday materials such as flint for the beautifully made arrow points, knives, and daggers. Much of this material originated outside the Nile valley; for example, green malachite, shiny black obsidian, conifer wood, and sea shells for decoration (the flint was probably local and was traded up and down the Nile). Some of these goods may have come by boat from across the eastern Mediterranean; certainly serviceable boats were in use on the Nile itself. Cold-hammered copper implements are found in graves, but the smelting of ores was almost certainly still unknown.

The cult of the dead, so important in historic times, already had appeared. The burying of tiny figurines and clay animal models presumably represented real individuals that were to magically serve the dead person in an afterlife. A little later, at the beginnings of Dynastic Egypt, the early rulers were buried with numbers of actual human attendants, including members of the royal harem. Later still, Egypt returned to the highly practical use of statuettes instead of real persons.

Judging from the unearthed figurines it would seem that men wore a penis sheath—thus providing a tie with the culture of prehistoric Crete. This costume item is also called the "Libyan sheath" and points up the fact that one element of Amratian culture may have come across the desert from the west. The new ideas were carried by people of Mediterranean stock who mixed with the indigenous Badarians, the latter already a blend of Mediterranean and Negroid racial types.[13]

The archaeological findings seem to indicate a wide

contact in Amratian times and very probably Egypt was brought into touch with the slightly more advanced cultures of the Fertile Crescent to the east. At any rate, at the end of Amratian times (3600 B.C.) a wave of Asian influence reached Egypt, and the succeeding Gerzean period represents the assimilation of new traits from abroad, and the literacy that in a few centuries was to produce Pharaonic Egypt.

The Fertile Crescent, so named by James H. Breasted, founder of Chicago's Oriental Institute, is the great arc of rich lands reaching from the alluvium of the Tigris-Euphrates to the west and then south through modern Syria and Israel. It was here that civilization first began and throughout ancient times the Fertile Crescent remained in the center for cultural transmissions, east and west, north and south. The earliest civilization of Egypt owes much to it; so, at several times remove, does China, India, Europe, and sub-Saharan Africa.

We have already seen an early expansion of culture at Jericho on the Jordan. Somewhat later, perhaps on roughly the same time level as the Tasian in Egypt, pottery-using agricultural cultures developed at Hassuna, a site west of the Tigris river in present-day Iraq. Inhabitants of the site of Jarmo on a tributary of the Tigris may have developed agriculture earlier, but Jarmo has not yet been firmly tied into the Mesopotamian sequence.[14] The dating at Sialk in modern Iran is also uncertain, though presumably Sialk is early. At Hassuna, villagers made crude pottery, cultivated grain, and domesticated cattle, sheep, and goats. Their techniques improved with time; before the end of the long Hassuna sequence there was excellent decorated pottery and elaborate houses.

At the end of the Hassuna period a new culture appears, best-known from the site of Tell Halaf on the Khabur (a tributary of the Euphrates). The Halafian period represented a considerable cultural advance; for example, metal appears for the first time. The Halafian used both emmer wheat and barley, and had a number of domestic animals: sheep, goats, swine, and cattle. Beautiful pottery, often elaborately decorated in checks, zigzags, rosettes, and animal figures, was molded in several colors by the Halafians; though still a

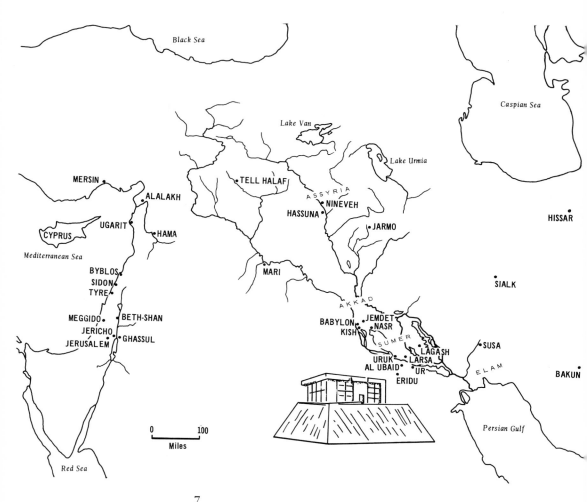

Black Sea

Caspian Sea

Lake Van

Lake Urmia

MERSIN

TELL HALAF

ASSYRIA
NINEVEH
HASSUNA
JARMO

HISSAR

ALALAKH

UGARIT
CYPRUS
HAMA

Mediterranean Sea

MARI

SIALK

BYBLOS
SIDON
TYRE

AKKAD

MEGGIDO
BETH-SHAN
JERICHO
JERUSALEM
GHASSUL

BABYLON
KISH
JEMDET
NASR

SUMER
LAGASH
URUK
LARSA
AL UBAID
UR
ERIDU

SUSA

ELAM

BAKUN

Red Sea

0        100
Miles

Persian Gulf

7
The Near East to 1500 B.C.

folk culture, Halaf had very considerable sophistication.

There was a great deal of trade and perhaps a certain amount of specialist production by various villages. One thing that foreshadows later Mesopotamian life is the appearance of the clay seal. Female figurines of clay are common to the Halafian culture—like those of Badarian Egypt they may represent a mother goddess.

Halaf was replaced by the widespread Ubaid culture, named for a site in southern Iraq near the ancient city of Ur. In the north this culture appears in a local, rather retarded, version, but in the south (the lower Tigris-Euphrates valleys) it represents a considerable advance over the peasant cultures of the past. As in Egypt, human beings were beginning to nibble at the edges of the swamplands created by floodwaters of great rivers and rich in alluvial soil. The Ubaid people of the south soon had the specialization and the surplus to create monumental temples to their gods. Casting of copper was now known and trade was widespread. A little later, at the beginning of history, we find the Mesopotamian peoples enthusiastic traders, so it is no surprise to find that there was trade in this formative period.

There were good reasons for trade. The lower Tigris and Euphrates valleys lack even stone for tools and implements, so deeply are the basic landforms covered by river mud. But the muddy rivers are a blessing, for as they spread out in the lowlands of Mesopotamia they deposit rich silt and renew the lands. At the same time, the rivers allow relatively easy and cheap transport of large amounts of goods. The ease and cheapness of river traffic was never so great, however, that the prehistoric and historic people of the two rivers could afford to build in stone as did the Egyptians. The river peoples found reeds and clay, especially the latter, in inexhaustible supply and adaptable to transformation by human ingenuity into many things (even sickles were sometimes made of clay). The Ubaid people imported flint and amazonite for tools; copper for weapons, tools, and jewelry; and wood for many purposes of building and decoration. A little later the semiprecious lapis lazuli from the mountains far to the east would become a standard import.

The Ubaid period was succeeded by that of the Uruk and full urbanization. This is the threshold of civilization; the technical names "Ubaid" and "Uruk" obscure the fact that the Sumerians were probably in residence.[15] We have described these cultures as impersonal archaeological units, but now we are in a period upon which the written mythologies and histories of later time already cast a dim and uncertain light.

8
*Statue of Sumerian Priest*

WE DO not know the name of the first king, the first high priest, the first city architect, or the inventor (or inventors) of writing. These things all help mark the beginnings of civilization, however, and we can say a great deal about the reasons for kingship, for elaborate religious organizations, and why cities and literacy appeared.

The transition in both Egypt and Mesopotamia to urban life, with its large number of specialists, its large-scale government, and its complex, priest-directed religion, took place between 4000 and 3000 B.C. Urbanism rests on the solid advance made by such earlier cultures as Amratian in Egypt and Ubaid in Mesopotamia; in both areas the transformation was slow, taking some centuries. As the peoples of these two areas were, at this time, still on the threshold of literacy, we cannot directly document the origin of the process. The evidence of archaeology and the historical writings of later times make the outline, if not the specifics, relatively clear.

The events that helped produce civilization in the Near East were also at work in the Indus, in the Hwang Ho valley of China, and in Central and South America. Man, under certain special circumstances, was reacting to a set of stimuli. He was, in Arnold Toynbee's terms, meeting a challenge. In the regions mentioned above he successfully met this challenge; in other areas, seemingly equally favored environmentally, he did not. It is doubtful that we will ever know all the reasons for the rise of high cultures; perhaps a major factor was simply historical accident. In the Nile and the Tigris-Euphrates valleys there were somewhat similar environmental conditions as far as human beings were concerned. In both places small agricultural communities clung to the edge of the river valleys, their backs to the desert, slowly clearing the river lands and planting in the rich alluvial soils. These rivers, unfortunately for the early farmers, were somewhat difficult for primitive agriculture. Much of the land was marshy, especially in the Tigris-Euphrates area, and useless for agriculture until drained. The great rivers fluctuated in size, the Nile with amazing regularity. While this always brought fresh silt to the valleys, it also might bring floods. In addition, both Egypt and lower Mesopotamia have an annual rainfall so low that dry farming is

## VI

# The River Lands: Egypt

impossible and river water itself must be used to supply the growing plants. In certain areas enough soil water is trapped during flood season to make subsequent planting practical, but for really efficient agriculture, irrigation is necessary.

Irrigation in the Nile valley represents a classic example of the need for, and the potential of, large-scale water control. The Nile, one of the world's great rivers, rises in the highlands of East Africa and flows northward across hundreds of miles of barren desert to the Mediterranean Sea. This river is navigable for a vast distance, from the delta to the area around Aswan where the first of a series of cataracts brings the river, its valley cut deep into earlier sedimentary deposits, to the North African coastal plain. It is within this elongated region that Egyptian culture developed—it later expanded southward to Nubia but such expansion was a by-product of national imperialism.

From prehistoric times there have been two Egypts within the area described above. The delta is a fan-shaped lowland where the Nile flows tortuously in many channels through its own deposited sediments. In ancient times it was a rank jungle, immensely rich in animals and fish. For the agriculturist it had many potentialities and it is unfortunate that we know all too little about early times in the delta. The material objects of early man are deeply buried and much of the prehistory of the delta is lost. We do know that the delta cultures were open to influences from the outside; the Libyan desert to the west, the Asian coast, Crete, and the Aegean. It is likely that much of the luxury goods traded from outside Egypt, found in Badarian and Amratian sites, came through the delta.

About Upper Egypt we have more knowledge. South of the delta and the nearby ancient lake basin, the Fayum, the Nile flows in a narrow trough normally not more than twenty miles, and sometimes only four or five miles, across. Beyond it on either side stretches the desert isolating the trough and forcing the settlers of the valley to look north and south for contacts. This combination of east-west isolation combined with easy navigability of the river makes understandable—in fact, almost inevitable—the essential unity of Upper Egypt. The distinction between north and south, between

Delta and River, was important throughout the history of Egypt. From earliest historical times Egypt was the "Two Lands." [1]

At some point around 3500 B.C. the small agricultural communities that were scattered up and down the river began to unite in extensive cooperation aimed at controlling the Nile and bringing more land into agricultural use. At about the same time a series of influences, probably transmitted through the delta from Mesopotamia, stimulated this process of organization. Copper appears in larger quantities and a true metal-tradition seems to be at hand. Other trade items including silver, lapis lazuli, and Mesopotamian cylinder seals make their appearance in Egypt, as do boats with high prows and high sterns of foreign (Mesopotamian) make. Also about this time the Egyptians began to experiment with a monumental brick architecture. More important, though less easy to demonstrate, there came new ideas of political organization, and of certain arts and crafts, especially that of writing. Egyptian writing is by no means a copy of Mesopotamian, but the idea likely came from the east. [2]

There must have been a gradual rise in population as greater amounts of land were won from the Nile by means of canals, dykes, and catch basins. These utilized, stored, and directed the waters that spread yearly across the Valley of the Nile as Abyssinian snows melted far to the south. The increase in population produced a cyclic situation, for more people meant land hunger. There was a ready solution, however, and this was to reclaim even more land, drain more swamps, and push the sown ever further into the valley.

All of this implies technological innovation and increasing skill in the applied arts. It means something which proved to be even more fraught with a potential for change. Canals must be kept clean, dykes and catch basins must be kept in repair, and eventually the magnitude of these tasks reached beyond the abilities of extended family heads or of clan chiefs. These new problems must be met by new specialists, for the alternative was death by starvation. [3] In these circumstances certain leaders extended their power, attracted to themselves technicians and artisans, and became the first ruling classes of the expanding society. In Egypt, as in all other areas of early civilization, the new rulers bolstered their power with supernatural sanctions—and one result was the creation of religious specialists, the first priesthoods.

In ancient times the Egyptians never succeeded in clearing all the rivers, for even in late historic times pictures on tomb walls show nobles hunting and fishing in thick papyrus swamps. It is difficult to estimate Egypt's population in early civilized time, but there may have been less than a million people. Even so, this represents a dense population, for settlement was strung out in small towns or villages along the river. As in modern Egypt, the desert, which makes up most of the area of the present-day country, was virtually uninhabited.

The structure of society in Egypt throughout much of her history was somewhat peculiar. Until relatively late times there did not seem to develop the intense urbanism that we see so early in Mesopotamia. In fact, it is not clear at all whether the Old Kingdom (2660–2180 B.C., Third Dynasty through Sixth) ever produced a real city in the Mesopotamian, or modern, sense. Such a state of affairs would suggest that Egypt was not really civilized in our technical sense of the word. However, transportation was so easy and the population so lineally distributed along the Nile, that the country itself might be described, even in earliest civilized times, as a kind of meta-city.

At any rate, in the archaeological period called Gerzean we began to see the first results of the quickening brought about by larger populations and more specialization. The Gerzean can be more or less equated with the period of the nomes: a series of independent statelets that ruled Egypt in the second half of the fourth millennium. These tiny territorial units, each with its own totem symbol (and each with its own god), controlled more or less contiguous stretches of river, no doubt to the annoyance of merchants and other travelers. Under the nomes the task of draining and reclaiming land went on and the new Mesopotamian ideas slowly diffused from one nome to another.

The new surplus and the new need for authority produced a ruling class further and further removed from the older clan or family chieftainship. It must

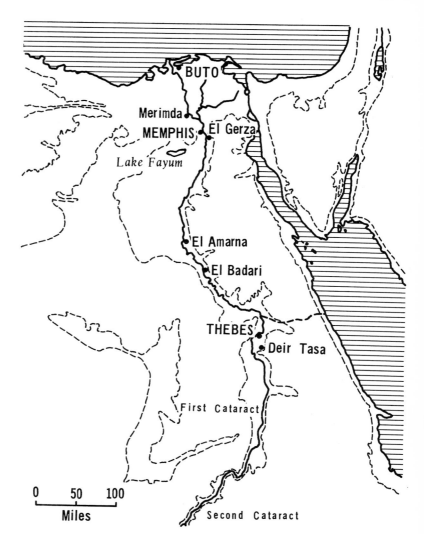

9
*Egypt to 1500 B.C.*

0    50    100

**Miles**

BUTO

Merimda

MEMPHIS    El Gerza

Lake Fayum

El Amarna

El Badari

THEBES

Deir Tasa

First Cataract

Second Cataract

have been these new rulers who eagerly accepted Mesopotamian ideas and so brought Egypt into a metal age
and an age of literacy. There is evidence for this from
archaeology. On the edges of the desert, tombs begin to
rise that are built in the Mesopotamian fashion and
clearly suggest social status. Writing, which appears in
the earliest dynasties as a crude and as yet only imperfectly understood system, must have had an incubation
period, for though the idea may have come from Mesopotamia, the symbols themselves go back to earlier
"picture-writing" and are completely Egyptian. By the
Third Dynasty (*c.* 2700 B.C.) a fully workable hieroglyphic script had been devised; it was, however, a
tangle of picture signs, rebus elements, determinatives,
plus the rudiments of an alphabet.

*The River Lands:*
*Egypt* 37

Narmer Palette, Archaic
Egypt

The nome chieftains were aggressive and there is
much evidence of war; mace heads and arrow heads in
the archaeological sites, mutilated bodies in the graves.
Eventually the more successful nome leaders unified
large areas of Egypt. There may have been, for a time,
two political Egypts, with one king residing in the
Delta and another in Upper Egypt. Whatever the case,
we do know that around 3100 B.C. (the date is to be
taken as an estimate only) some powerful chieftain
from Upper Egypt united both parts of the country and
so created the kingdom of the two lands.

According to a much later tradition this first king
was named Menes. Because of the incomplete nature of
contemporary documents we are not certain just who
he was, but he may possibly be identified with the
monarch Narmer or with Narmer's son, Hor-aha.[4] At
any rate, someone from Upper Egypt—whatever his
name—unified the country and from a capital at Mem-

phis, near the delta, began a dynastic period which was to last for three thousand years. The first four hundred years or so, embodying the First and Second Dynasties, were periods of experimentation and transition. The Old Kingdom, and dependable history of Egypt, began with the Third Dynasty, about 2700 B.C.

We know of certain things that happened in late predynastic times. A number of deities, who were probably originally worshiped by particular nomes or tribes, became very important in much of Egypt. One of these was the cow goddess, Hathor; another, the falcon god, Horus, who became especially connected with the early kings. The serpent goddess, Edjo, of Buto in the delta, clearly had special significance to the rulers of Lower Egypt. A sun god, given various names in different regions, was important and indeed natural in almost cloudless Egypt. Later he was syncretized as Amun-Re and much later (c. 1370 B.C., during Akhenaton's reign), as Aton, he made a bold attempt to replace all the other gods. A number of animals, among others the crocodile, the jackal, the ibis, appeared in divine form; in fact a remarkable number of the gods of Egypt appeared as animal deities and may originally have been clan totems.[5]

At the beginning of history, Egyptian religion had become very systematized and we can dimly see the work of an organized priesthood attempting to bring order to diverse and often conflicting tribal or nome traditions. One of the most important mythic cycles had to do with Osiris, supposed to have been an early divine king. This god is set upon and hacked to pieces by his evil brother Set, embodiment of the desert. His sister-wife, Isis, collects the parts of Osiris' body and magically reanimates him. However, the god / king goes to the underworld where he becomes a judge of human souls. Osiris' son, Horus, finally avenges his father in a great struggle with Set. Here we seem to have a reflection of an early political struggle, for Set was the deity of a large segment of the Egyptian people, at the beginning of Dynastic times. The struggle between Horus worshippers and Set worshippers was long and hard, and as late as Second Dynasty times at least one king deserted Horus in favor of Set. By the beginning of the Third Dynasty, however, the myth had reached its final form (Set had been crushingly defeated), and it gave the Horus kings a strong propaganda weapon in their attempts to unite Egypt. Later, during the Middle Kingdom (around 2000 B.C.) the Osiris doctrine became a method for extending immortality to the humblest citizen.[6]

Another mythic cycle, interesting because it has rather direct Mesopotamian parallels, tells how the goddess of the heavens, Nut, is torn from her mate, the earth-god, Keb, by the god of the air, Shu. Pictorially she is usually represented with her star-decorated nude body arched across the sky, supported by Shu, while her earth-bound mate lies at her feet. Sometimes Nut appears, not as a woman, but as a divine cow. The sun, then, is born as a child (or a calf) from this supernatural mother and sails each day across the sky, dying at day's end only to be reborn the following morning.

It is certain that the religion of Egypt shows considerable reworking during the predynastic and early Dynastic periods. We have already said that the emerging rulers in the early civilizations seem always to have employed religion to sanction their power and to have used the priesthoods which appear at the beginning of civilization as instruments for power. This, of course, is from our point of view; the early Egyptian or Babylonian certainly considered one of the prime functions of governments to be that of enforcing and directing the duties of man to his gods. As political bureaucracies developed to control the intensive work needed for large-scale agriculture and extensive specialization, so did religious bureaucracies rise to deal with the new complex of things religious. Normally these two sets of specialists were related, for one man could function in both spheres, the religious and political. Certainly they paralleled each other in structure and in function, the very organization of the gods being somewhat looked on as a supernatural political state. In addition, they supported each other; the priests gave the political rulers the sanction of religion and the political leaders acted, when necessary, as police agents and tax collectors for the religious organizations.

The question of why religious organizations appear cannot be surely answered, but on a primitive level religious control is probably in the hands of the old

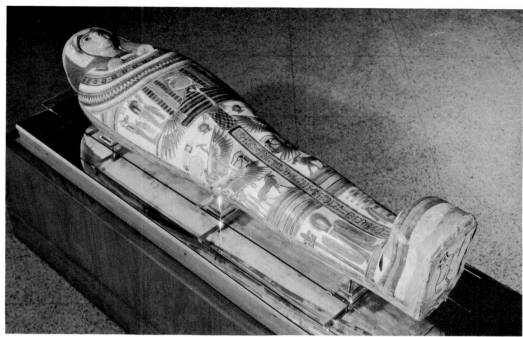

people of the group—that is, those who know the traditions and myths of the tribe or band. In many areas, however, especially in agricultural communities, there are semispecialists who dabble in magic and who are the medicine men as well as the religious leaders. Such individuals may innovate within certain limits and may gradually modify, codify, or explain the mythology that is part of the cultural heritage of every human group. When surplus, advanced technology, and specialization appear, these religious figures sometimes, perhaps always, band together to form priesthoods. Given man's avid interest in the awe-inspiring and the supernatural, the incipient priesthoods are in a good position to grow in power and prestige. In actual fact, in Egypt and elsewhere, they seem to have been able to drain off a great deal of the surplus and to capture the services of many of the artisans. The great works of early civilizations are not only those connected with production. Even more impressive are the temples and tombs; the first monumental architecture in most parts of the world was religious architecture.

We can study the activities of the priesthoods, their contributions—particularly that of writing—and their functions more clearly in Mesopotamia. Though she had multitudes of priests, vast temples and, at a much

11
*Egyptian mummy coffin,*
*c. 10th century* B.C.

12
Step pyramid at Saqqara

13
Pyramids at Gizeh (or Giza)

14
Sphinx at Gizeh (or Giza)

later date (*c.* 1000 B.C.), a priest-ruled nation, Egypt started with a rather atypical conception of the organization of religious and political power. Sometime in the period around 3000 B.C. the early Dynastic kings of Egypt managed to persuade the country that they were gods incarnate.[7] At first there was an identification with Horus (perhaps a totem of the original conqueror of Egypt), but by about 2500 B.C. the Egyptian kings were also considered to be sons of the sun god Re.[8]

Dealing with a divine king created certain problems for the priesthood and the bureaucracy, and in fact for the ruler himself. For one thing, it led to the idealized and occasionally practiced institution of brother-sister marriage—as it did in Peru, another area where this idea obtained—in order to beget divine heirs to the throne. It also put a great deal more emphasis on the person of the king even after his death. The Egyptians had, presumably in prehistoric days, noticed the mummifying effect of dry desert air on bodies. In the early Dynasties they began gradually to incorporate mummification into the death practices. This preserved the king's body as a focus to which his soul could return and it encouraged the construction of mortuary buildings.

Mesopotamian construction techniques had already entered Egypt and for a while during the Old Kingdom vast amounts of the nation's time and energy were lavished on construction of tombs for the god-kings. These structures, first in clay and then in stone, culminated in the awe-inspiring pyramids of the lower Nile. Inside these artificial mountains were placed, along with vast quantities of precious metals and other valuable grave goods, the bodies of the gods for whom they were built. Around the tombs of the pyramids were clustered those of the higher bureaucrats; presumably their only hope of an afterlife was in the afterworld service of the man-god.

In our time there remains little except the silent structures and fragments of the temples in which the dead god was to be worshiped. Indeed, no culture can really afford to lock up vast amounts of its surplus wealth, especially hard-to-replace metals, in the service of the dead. The Egyptians soon became proficient grave robbers, and the gold, silver, and precious jewels flowed openly into the tombs only to be surreptitiously removed and allowed to reenter the blood stream of the nation.

Some catastrophe overcame the Old Kingdom for reasons now unclear. It has been suggested that a desire on the part of the lowly Egyptian peasant and artisan to share immortality led to class bitterness and finally to revolt. It is true that in Middle Kingdom times (*c.* 2000 B.C.) and later, the Osiris cult was liberalized and salvation democratized. However, other factors may have been operating. The exactions for tomb and temple surely overtaxed a peasantry that, at best, had little margin. Possibly the old rivalry between the two Egypts, Delta and River, broke out again, or possibly the outlawed Set cult revived for a time, throwing the country into religious strife.

Order was eventually restored in the country and factors of cohesion still proved very strong, for the Egypt of the later Dynasties followed the basic pattern of government invented at the beginning of Egyptian history.

While the forms of government remained much the same, the actual function changed with changing times. The Middle Kingdom was followed by an unprecedented event, a conquest of Egypt by Asiatic groups collectively called the Hyksos, who entered the country about 1750 B.C. and ruled for almost two centuries. When they were expelled, Egypt, seemingly shaken by the breakdown of her secure isolation, entered a period of imperialistic expansion. This too ended, by about 1300 B.C., and the nation began its centuries of slow decline.

WE LEFT the Mesopotamians of Ubaid culture on the very edge of civilization at about the beginning of the fourth millennium B.C. There is some evidence of extensive contact with the outside world, with new pottery styles and perhaps a new ethnic element entering at this time. The period known conventionally as Uruk (from the town variously called Uruk, Erech, or Warka) is marked by unpainted red-slipped and gray pottery that was sometimes made by the potter's wheel. The importance of Uruk was in the change from village to urban patterns of life; it was, in V. Gordon Childe's words, the "urban revolution" in Mesopotamia.

It might be well to turn back and describe this region at the beginning of the urban revolution. Mesopotamia means "the land between the rivers," the rivers being the Tigris and the Euphrates. At present these two great streams unite just north of the town of Basra and then flow together for, roughly fifty miles to the Persian Gulf. Actually, a great deal of this lower Mesopotamian plain is built from river mud swept from the highlands of Kurdistan by the two rivers. In early times the delta had not progressed so far. The present speed of deposition of the rivers is estimated at one and a half miles per century and when the Sumerian cities were built (some already begun by Ubaid times) the gulf extended in some places a hundred or more miles further north and west. Five thousand years ago many of the Sumerian centers lay near salt water; today their ruins are far inland.[1] In the Uruk period the various elements that were to make up Dynastic Sumerian life began definitely to appear.[2]

A number of settlements grew into cities during this period: Ur, Lagash, and Uruk, among others. The Uruk culture people were probably Sumerian-speaking, at least those who lived in the south portion of the two-rivers country. Nevertheless, there is some indication (in pottery types for example) of peoples from the outside—Semitic-speaking, if we project back known linguistic distributions of historic times—sifting into the middle valleys. In fairly early times a Semitic-speaking land known as Akkad had risen just to the north of Sumer. In the Uruk period, however, we are still in protohistoric times and are actually witnessing the birth of Sumerian civilization, and soon we will be

# VII

*The River Lands: Mesopotamia*

| | EGYPT | | PALESTINE | SYRIA – LEBANON | MESOPOTAMIA | |
|---|---|---|---|---|---|---|
| | Upper | Lower | | | North | South |
| 1500BC | 18th Dynasty | | Late Bronze I | | Early Assyrian | Old Babylonian |
| | Hyksos interlude | | Middle Bronze II | Local Traditions Byblos, Ras Shamra, Amq sites, Hama — 12th Dynasty Egyptian Contacts | | Ur III |
| 2000 | 12th Dynasty | | Middle Bronze I | | | Akkado-Sumerian |
| 2500 | Old Kingdom | | Early Bronze III | Sargonid influence (?) | | Sargon I / Sumerian |
| | | | Early Bronze II | Jemdet Nasr influences | | Early Dynastic |
| 3000 | 1st Dynasty | | Early Bronze I | Khirbet Kerak | | Jemdet Nasr / Late Uruk |
| | Late Gerzean | | | Uruk influences | | Early Uruk |
| 3500 | | | | | Late Ubaid | Late Ubaid |
| | Early Gerzean Amratian | El Omari | | | | |
| 4000 | | Merimdian | Ghassulian | Ubaid influence | | |
| | Badarian | | | | Late Halaf | |
| 4500 | | | | | | |
| | | | | | Early Ubaid Early Halaf | |
| 5000 | Tasian (Early Badarian) | Fayumian | | Early Halaf | Late Hassuna | Early Ubaid |
| 5500 | | | | | | |
| 6000 | | | Jericho Pre–Pottery Neolithic B | | Early Hassuna | |
| 6500 | | | | | Jarmo | |
| | | | Jericho Pre–Pottery Neolithic A | | | |

dealing with history and can talk with some assurance of actual people and recorded events.

Certain advances in technology can be readily seen from the archaeological record. The potter's wheel has already been mentioned and this implies a certain professionalism in pottery making. Metallurgy came into its own among Uruk people of lower Mesopotamia though it may have had its origins in the preceding Ubaid. The Ubaid pattern of farming villages surrounding temples, however, was definitely changed; the temples retained their importance but the villages grew, first into towns, then into small cities.

The Uruk priests and political leaders in fact became quite ambitious in their temple construction. The "white" temple at the site of Uruk stood on a high platform over 200 feet long and more than 150 feet wide. On this was built the imposing temple, itself more than 60 by 50 feet. The temple substructures are becoming ziggurats the "artificial mountains" of later times. Like earlier Ubaid temples (for example, the one at Al Ubaid excavated by Sir Leonard Woolley) those of the Uruk people were decorated with frescoes. Inward-sloping platforms were made of earth and rubble and faced with brick. Skilled masons built the temples, laying their tile-shaped bricks not only for geometric decorations but also for recessing and buttressing. The Uruk temple has its analogy in the "Mesopotamian style" mastabas (tombs) of early Dynasty Egypt in that period before the Egyptians evolved their own massive stonemasonry.

Other things have been found that show Uruk to be a part of the classic Mesopotamian life. In late Uruk times cylinder seals, often works of art in miniature, replaced the simple stamp seal that we have already seen in Gerzean Egypt. The Uruk seals pictorially represent organized war. That the Uruk people were engaged in this lucrative business is also suggested by mace heads and by representations of bound captives, possibly slaves.

There are certain other features that became standard in historic times. For example, though there seems to have been a basic decimal system of numerical notation, there is also the beginning of sexagesimal (using 60 as a unit) notation.[3] We still have this system in our clocks and compasses. Wheeled vehicles were in use by Uruk times, at least for military purposes, for war chariots are represented on seals, while from Dynastic Sumer we see four-wheeled, ass-drawn war chariots. Another use of animals, in this case probably oxen, was for pulling a plough.[4] Several animals, long domesticated (the cow, sheep, and goat), were now, presumably, utilized on a larger scale. Metallurgical experts cast copper and a copper and lead alloy, using the lost-wax method, making not only weapons but tools and implements. Trade was extensive, as witness the finds of such luxury goods as lapis lazuli. As time went on there was increasing dependence on river craft, especially to carry heavy trade items.

The culture that we saw developing in Ubaid times and elaborating in Uruk, continues in the succeeding Jemdet Nasr period. New cities are built; presumably population pressure was beginning to tell. The site of Jemdet Nasr itself is in the middle Euphrates valley very near the later city of Babylon. The culture was an elaborate one with considerable metal in use for tools and weapons, and a number of luxury goods including faience vessels (possibly the result of Egyptian influence). The principal metal is still copper; techniques of alloying this metal with tin to produce bronze do not appear until Dynastic times. Writing is now employed. Though still crude, it was no longer pictographic but had rebus elements—of this, more later. Jemdet Nasr culture can be readily identified by certain innovations

16
*Early picture writing, Mesopotamia*

*Courtesy* Oriental Institute, University of Chicago

which include conventionalization of art in seals, minor changes in burial customs, and changes in metal and ceramic forms, especially a revival of painted decoration on pottery. There seems to be no serious break and we have, broadly speaking, a continuation from Uruk— very possibly from Ubaid—to historic Sumer.

East of the Tigris around the historic site of Susa the same urban revolution was going on, differing in detail from that of Sumer but obviously influenced by and influencing it. The Elamites of Susa worked out their own script, somewhat different from that of Mesopotamia proper. It is not until Sumer, and then Akkad and Babylon, launched military adventures in its direction that Elam became thoroughly Mesopotamized. Meanwhile, this eastern outpost of high culture may have had a part in the transmission of civilization to the Indus, as it clearly did to parts of Iran.

The actual events that led to urbanism in Mesopotamia, and in Elam to the east, were generally similar to those of Egypt. One major difference lay in the attitude toward national organization and power in the two areas. From a political organization based on a series of contiguous villages along the river (that is to say, the nome), Egypt went on to large-scale political structure and soon to a single kingdom. Unification became the normal state of affairs for Egypt from late prehistoric times, and the periods of breakdown, when the central authority was suppressed, were looked upon by Egyptians as times of disaster. Along with this rigid centralism went a rather slow development of cities, partly because of the rapid transit up and down the river as suggested in Chapter VI. In fact it may be that true cities did not really develop in Egypt until after the Hyksos invasions. By that time urban life was many centuries old in its homeland of Mesopotamia.

The Mesopotamian area was much less homogeneous than was Egypt. For one thing, instead of a narrowly contained river valley there was a series of branching rivers and great stretches of potentially usable land between the two main arteries of the system, the Tigris and Euphrates. For another thing, Mesopotamia was much more open to outside influences than was Egypt. It formed only the eastern horn of the great Fertile Crescent, and farther east Susa and the plateau of Iran were easily accessible while the Persian Gulf gave a sea outlet to the south. This was a far cry from Egypt where, from the Delta to Aswan and beyond, people spoke dialects of the same language (a Hamitic language distantly related to Semitic) and had much the same culture. In Mesopotamia, the southern region was taken up by speakers of Sumerian, a language that seems to have left no descendants and whose relatives are unknown.[5] Surrounding the Sumerians were speakers of Semitic languages, the most important of whom lived in Akkad.[6] Customs of the Sumerians and Akkadians differed considerably, though the later Semitic-speaking civilization of Mesopotamia was an amalgam of the two.

For these and perhaps other reasons Mesopotamia never had a concept of continuous imperial rule though large kingdoms and even empires do appear on occasion. In addition, the idea of the god-king was probably absent.[7] The early unit of political power in Mesopotamia was the city with its surrounding lands and villages.

17
*Ram in thicket, Sumerian*

The first kings of the Dynastic (early historic) period of Sumer ruled over city-states and if a king, exceptionally energetic or exceptionally lucky, managed to subdue some of his neighbors, his reign over them seldom lasted very long. Even the later Babylonian and Assyrian kingdoms and empires of the region were really cities writ large. In fact so pervasive became this pattern that it was exported throughout the Western world and became the model for later peoples: the Greeks, Phoenicians, Carthaginians, Etruscans, and Romans. This political domination by a particular city or cities may have been the pattern for the Indus valley (the situation there is less clear) and seems to have been true for early civilized China. In addition, it is the essential pattern of civilization in the New World.

Because of the importance of cities it might be well to consider the rise of cities and of other uses of civilization in the Mesopotamian homeland. We saw how the Ubaid people had already established large temples in the farming villages, somewhat like the cathedral villages of medieval Europe. It is a safe guess that already there were elaborate priesthoods serving in these temples; in fact Woolley's data from Al Ubaid itself, makes this almost certain. The Ubaid populations were already skilled in technology and the land was being cleared, drained, and watered on a large scale. Once launched, these projects paid the same tremendous dividends that they did in the Nile valley. In the area between the two rivers, canals could bring ample water to the rich alluvial soil and canals could also drain pest-ridden and agriculturally unusable marshes. As in Egypt, population began to rise; the massive mounds, substructures for temples, that appear in Uruk times is evidence that a large supply of manpower was at hand. Draining and irrigating operations soon produced that cyclic situation where a food surplus led to population growth, then to new demands for more land and more food. This in turn led to even greater efforts to control the rivers and to increase the supply of grain.

There were tragic moments. In deposits at Ur, between Ubaid and Uruk deposits, Woolley found an eleven-foot deposit of river sediments, obviously left by a great flood. This may be the origin of the Sumerian

18
*Gold vessels, early Sumerian*

flood story and of those later flood legends including the one in Judeo-Christian tradition in which Noah played such a dramatic role. Flood legends are widespread in the world, however, and the Sumerian story may have been hundreds or thousands of years old before this great protohistoric disaster.[8]

In spite of occasional floods and other natural setbacks it is clear that the process of land-clearing went on at a rather rapid pace. Certain favored villages became towns and then small cities, containing the priests of the local temple, merchants, and many craftsmen: metal workers, weavers, brickmakers, and others. In addition, the peasants who worked nearby lands lived within the shelter of city walls, as did a new kind of specialist, the city bureaucrat. The latter was necessary because the tasks of administration grew with the cities. Walls and streets must be kept in repair, the honest citizens must be protected from those less fortunate or less enterprising, regularized dependable relations must be maintained with other cities, and the flow of agricultural goods from the outlying farms must continue undisturbed.

By Dynastic times kings had already appeared; their origins going back to the earliest urban life. The king was not, as in Egypt, a god, but rather the god's representative on earth; later Sumerian texts would refer to him as the "tenant farmer of the god." The early political organization must have drawn heavily on priestly organizations already set up, and, as in Egypt, the political and religious power went hand in hand.

If not actually divine, the king seems to have been surrounded with an almost supernatural aura and it is fairly clear that the Sumerians believed in his continuation as a very important person in the afterworld. At least this is the best explanation for the elaborate "royal tombs" at Ur in Early Dynastic times. Here a king or a queen would be buried in a brick or stone tomb built in a great pit. The royal personage was surrounded by a number of servants, male and female, and chariots or wagons, with the asses or oxen that pulled them. Great riches in precious metals, elegant vessels and jewelry, were also heaped in the tomb and, as it was filled in, more individuals were killed and thrown into the pit. The most obvious reason for burying serving maids, musicians, and men-at-arms with a king is that their services will be needed in another world. In historic times the Mesopotamian peoples were gloomy about the possibility of personal resurrection; perhaps in early days dying with the king represented the best chance for a dancing girl or a common soldier to obtain life beyond the grave.

The religion of the protohistoric Sumerians, like that of the Egyptians, involved a number of local deities. Each city seems to have had its own god or goddess; for example, the temple of Sin, or Nanna, the moon god, was at Ur, that of An, the heaven or sky god, at Uruk.

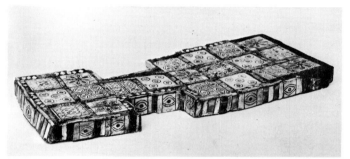

19
Gaming board, early
Sumerian

Courtesy University Museum, University of Pennsylvania

By Dynastic times there was a more or less coherent cosmology. The origin of things dates to the union of the sky god An and the earth goddess Ki, whose offspring, the air god Enlil, thrust the two apart. Enlil later raped the beautiful maiden goddess Ninlil, who then bore Sin, the moon god. Later children of Enlil and Ninlil became gods of the underworld. Another great deity was the culture hero Enki, who made the land and originated civilization. Less helpful to man was a goddess of war and love, Inanna.

The early Semitic-speakers retained many of these deities (possibly a parallel group had already developed in early Akkad). The goddess Inanna became Ishtar (the Greek Astarte) and An became Ana; other deities were given Semitic names but retained their Sumerian characteristics. One powerful god of later times, Marduk, the local deity of the city of Babylon seems, however, not to have been known to the Sumerians.

The great gloomy legend of the Sumerian culture hero Gilgamesh, tells us something of the Mesopotamian attitude toward the supernatural. The struggles and failure of this magnificent hero to attain immortality seem to have held the imagination of Sumerian and Semite alike and was told and retold for two thousand years.[9] Man in the Fertile Crescent was clearly convinced of the futility of human hopes and human endeavor. Many centuries after the fall of Sumer, and when even Babylonia was nearing its final decline, this sentiment is wonderfully echoed in the Biblical Book of Job(14:1–2).[10]

> Man *that is* born of a woman *is* of few days, and full of trouble.
> 2. He cometh forth like a flower, and is cut down: he fleeth also as a shadow, and continueth not.

The early priestly corporations contributed to later societies one of the most signal advances in human culture. As the temple establishments grew ever larger the need of keeping accounts became critical. At first such accounts were scribbled on clay tablets with a sharp stick and were simple in the extreme. Even in early times, however, there were certain conventions. For example, the picture of a jar with marks scratched beside it represented the number of jars of beer or grain received by the corporation. This type of ideographic notation had obvious limitations and so in the times of Uruk and Jemdet Nasr there appeared refinements that allowed the priests and their helpers to note down abstract ideas. It is probably an early stage of this writing that kindled Egyptian interest and produced Egyptian hieroglyphics.

In the Uruk period a considerable number of pictographs were invented; some of them, such as the plough and boat, quite recognizable. However, in a further development, some of these signs took on secondary phonetic meanings and as such could be used in a number of contexts, for example, the symbol for arrow (pronounced ti) attained a secondary meaning, "to live" or "the process of living." The picture of a man's body ⌑ became associated with the syllable lu, man, while woman, munus, was represented by a picture of the pudendum, sal ▽. A mountain (kur) was drawn as a series of semilunar figures ⌂ which also had the

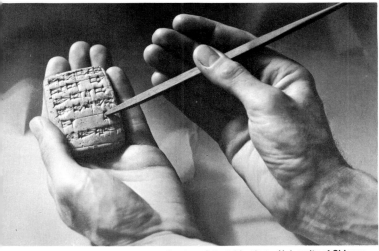

20
*Cast of cuneiform tablet,
with hand holding stylus in
proper position*

sound value of kur. The word geme, slave girl, was shown by combining the signs kur and sal (munus) thus giving the literal meaning of "mountain woman." The sign for mouth, ka also had the meaning dug, to speak.[11] Probably the most important technical advance in Mesopotamian writing was the introduction of a reed stylus with a wedge-shaped end to impress rather than scratch the clay. This avoided smearing the tablet and with this innovation we can speak of cuneiform (wedge-shaped) writing.

Though probably invented by the priests, this new tool soon became popular with king and merchant alike. In historic times we have not only temple accounts and myths but also political documents, private letters, bills of sale, wills, law codes, contracts, and the various other written records proper to a vigorous trading community.

The dates for these early civilizations vary somewhat from area to area. For southern Mesopotamia, estimates based on such diverse factors as the rate of temple reconstruction, Carbon-14 dating, cross ties with other areas, and the later king lists give the beginning of Ubaid before 4500 B.C. It was a long period, ending around 3500 B.C. Uruk takes up the period 3500–3100 B.C., and Jemdet Nasr from 3100 B.C. to 2900 B.C., the latter date marking the approximate beginning of Dynastic Sumer.[12] The Dynastic period eventually brings us fully into history and we see a series of city-states,

*The River Lands:
Mesopotamia* 55

including among others, Ur, Eridu, Lagash, and Uruk in south Mesopotamia; and Agade, Kish, and Nippur in the central valleys. The southern peoples spoke Sumerian as they may have done from Ubaid times; in the north there was probably already an infiltration of Semitic speech. In the third millennium, one city-leader after another gained temporary power over his neighbors, that is, created a dynasty, only to fall and then bring about uneasy peace among equals till another adventurer seized power.

The Sumerian cities were walled and were built around a temple that normally topped a large stepped mound or ziggurat. Streets, except for large throughways, were little more than alleys. Probably from very early times the Sumerian cities tended to group artisans in particular areas so that metal workers, potters, jewelry makers, and other craftsmen lived near one another and in places of easy access to their clientele. Some of the towns contained regular cemeteries either inside or outside the walls. Beginning very early in time, however, there was a practice of burying the dead, especially children, under the house floor and archaeologists now excavate many burials from what were once residential areas. Houses, originally of reeds, became flat-roofed structures of adobe or sun-dried mud. The better houses had several rooms surrounding a center court and some may have had a second story. The Sumerian builders originally used a rectangular adobe brick, but in Early Dynastic times a brick with rounded tops, technically called planoconvex, was introduced. These bricks were far from optimal shape though they could be used to give a herringbone pattern to monumental structures.

The basic Mesopotamian mud brick house had its counterpart in Egypt and in the Indus valley. Later it spread across north Africa, its distribution being roughly that of the desert or semidesert belt in Afrasia. In more humid areas, especially on the north shore of the Mediterranean, this particular arrangement of rooms enclosing a central court was copied in materials other than adobe. Much later the Spaniards brought this house type to the New World but found it already in use in a number of areas, independently invented many centuries before the Spanish conquest. Even the common word adobe (from Arabic al dobe) is old, going back to an ancient Egyptian word *d-b-* with the identical meaning of sun-dried brick.

Originally some of the Mesopotamian settlements may have been founded on the flat lowlands near the Tigris or Euphrates. However, as the centuries passed each succeeding town was built on the ruins of the one before. This might be a gradual process, individual householders over the years leveling their adobe structures and erecting new houses on the ruins of the old. It might also be the result of a catastrophe; fire, invasion, plague that left the town deserted till adobe walls had fallen and the whole was rubble. Then the returning inhabitants, or a new group, would smooth over the site and erect a new settlement. Over a long span of time many of these settlements became high artificial hills, or tells. Once a tell was established in the flat lowlands of the lower rivers it became a choice building site, for it lifted habitation and temple well above water at flood stage. In addition such a tell was easier to defend than would be a city on the plain. As a result some of these tells were occupied for hundreds or even thousands of years.

At least as early as Uruk times the Sumerians needed defense against invading armies. By the beginning of the Dynastic period war for loot and especially for personal power was commonplace. The desertion, or near desertion, of certain smaller sites such as Uqair and Jemdet Nasr suggest that agricultural workers did not find it safe to leave their families in villages outside the protecting city walls even if they themselves must go out to cultivate the crops and repair canals.

One of the best documents of war surviving from early Sumer is the wooden plaque covered with shell and stone mosaic known as the "Standard of Ur." There are three panels showing clean-shaven Sumerian warriors armed with spears and dressed in the typical kiltlike Sumerian garment, some with overcloaks. Interspersed with the lines of infantry are four-wheeled war chariots pulled by asses. Naked prisoners and the naked bodies of the fallen indicate that the battle is over. The opposite side of the plaque shows a victory celebration and a representation of spoil and of prisoners.

We know only a few individuals from the very early

Sumerian Dynastic period, and they are at first faceless names from the king lists. As times goes on, individual ideas and more and more details of individual lives appear. A few really noteworthy persons briefly take their turn on the Sumerian stage. One of these from the city of Lagash, a king (or perhaps an usurper) named Urukagina, made a bold attempt to reduce the power of the political and priestly bureaucracy. He did this by instigating a series of social reforms, and drafting a law code to protect the poor in their dealings with rich neighbors and with greedy officials. The moral outrage of this king was recorded in cuneiform tablets and he seems to have acted directly in the name of the city god, Ningirsu. The reforms of Urukagina failed and the king himself was deposed, seemingly a victim of reactionary forces in his own city who betrayed Lagash in a war with nearby Umma. For all his failure, and in spite of the small scope of his operations, Urukagina will always interest us. He represents a new kind of thinking in the ancient Near East, and in his reforms he gropes toward a new moral system that places high value on the human individual.[13] We get only brief glimpses of these ideas in the Mesopotamian documents but, much later, the Hebrew prophets make this morality the center and heart of their doctrine. Their code of ethics was more systematic, more imaginative, and bolder, but it is the fruition of ideas that go back at least to Urukagina.

Around 2300 B.C. the city of Agade in Semitic-speaking Akkad, north of Sumer, began a period of rapid expansion under a king named Sargon. This man is surrounded by legend; one story tells how Sargon, as a baby, was found floating down the Euphrates in a basket and was rescued by a woman in the household of the king of Kish. This risky but dramatic voyage to greatness seems to have been highly regarded in the Near East; we will see it again with Moses. At any rate, Sargon became cupbearer to the king and eventually usurped the throne. From his new capital at Agade he conquered an area that reached to the Persian Gulf and may have extended as far west as the Mediterranean. The empire of Sargon lasted for only a century then Sumer again became powerful and Ur, then Larsa, then Ur once more, ruled southern Mesopotamia. But in

spite of all this the twilight period had come to Sumer. Outsiders from both east and west, the Elamites and Amorites,[14] took advantages of the intercity struggle and swept into the valley. There seemed also to be decay from within. Even during the third and last dynasty of Ur it is reasonable to believe that Semitic speech was slowly replacing Sumerian, and Akkadian customs in general were seeping into the lower valley. After the barbarian invasions Sumerian was lost as a language of everyday life. Interestingly, it survived for many centuries as a priestly language and religious texts in Sumerian were written and read by priests in Babylonian days. Slowly the Sumerian cities dwindled and died. Even Ur was reduced to a village and finally disappeared, probably in the eighth century B.C.

The Akkadians had adopted Sumerian script, using it to write their own Semitic language, and so cuneiform continued to be written for two thousand years after Sargon. When the barbarian invasions had spent their force, a New-Akkadian civilization came into being, centered at Babylon (Bab-ulani, Gate of God(s); in Sumerian, Ka-dingir-ra) a city just east of the Eu-

21
*Ancient Babylon*

phrates in the middle valley. The fluctuation of power between desert and valley continued. A mountain people from western Iran, the Kassites, swept down on Babylon and established a barbarian dynasty. They were eventually expelled, but the balance of power was shifting northward where, on the Tigris, the Semitic-speaking Assyrians were beginning to expand. A little later the Assyrians became the scourge of the Fertile Crescent and beyond; became, indeed, one of the most feared and hated peoples of antiquity.

Roughly we can say that the fourth and third B.C. millennia in Mesopotamia was Sumerian, the second millennium, Akkado-Babylonian, and the first millennium, Assyrian. However, from about 500 B.C. new groups and new ideas entered the Near East, old patterns were disrupted and old languages disappeared. Mesopotamia lost its premier position, and in the wider world of the past two thousand years has never regained it.

THE AREA between the Tigris and Euphrates Rivers and the Indus is for the most part plateau land, dry except in the higher elevations, and lacking large areas of alluvial soils so important to both the forementioned areas. The Iranian plateau rises to the southwest to form the mountain backbone of modern Afghanistan. The high, rugged country extends eastward into Baluchistan (part of present-day Pakistan) and then drops off to the plain of the Indus river. The Indus originates in the Punjab as a fan-shaped series of smaller rivers which unite and flow southwesterly through the Sind to the Arabian sea. At present the area of the lower and middle Indus is very dry, though the Punjab has considerable rainfall. Indications from archaeology, however, suggest that the Sind was better-watered as recently as three or four thousand years ago; perhaps a minor shift in the monsoon winds has seriously changed the climate.

The importance of the Iranian plateau lies in the fact that it was the presumed region for transmission of high culture from Mesopotamia to the Indus. That the major impulses traveled west to east can hardly be doubted, and the suggestion that Iran itself may have contributed significantly to early civilization does not seem very likely. Not till the first millennium B.C., with the coming of the Medes and the Persians, does Iran proper become a real center of power and influence.[1]

Nevertheless, there was early agricultural occupation in parts of Iran. At the site of Sialk, near Kashan in central Persia, a village of food producers goes back perhaps to Hassuna times. The type of culture represented at early Sialk may have gone far afield; some analogies can be seen in the far-north site of Anau near Merv in modern Soviet Turkmen east of the Caspian Sea. A later occupation at Sialk shows striking similarities to the tell of Hissar near Damghan, directly east of Tehran. The first phases of Sialk culture show a pottery-making Neolithic community, with domesticated cattle and sheep but also with considerable hunting, using the sling rather than the bow. Later there is considerable evidence of trade, metal is introduced, and by the period known as Sialk III 4 (Hissar 1 B), metallurgy was practiced locally and pots were made on the wheel. This period at Sialk seems related to the Uruk phase

## VIII

*Civilization Spreads to the Indus*

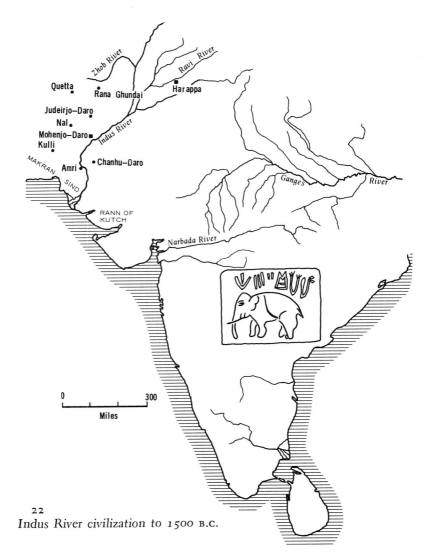

22
*Indus River civilization to 1500 B.C.*

further south and was presumably influenced by it. The last phase of Sialk III shows violent destruction, apparently by a group of proto-Elamites on an imperialistic venture. The succeeding town on the Sialk oasis is roughly contemporary with Jemdet Nasr. The obvious trade carried on by the Sialk people suggests that this town was on the main route, probably for lapis lazuli.

In southern Iran, near the later royal city of Persepolis, the site of Bakun shows a more fragmentary sequence but still an important one. The earlier portions of the site are probably Neolithic, but in the upper levels sophisticated pottery, seals, and such luxury goods as lapis lazuli are found. Like other prehistoric Iranians the people of Bakun used the sling for hunting and probably for warfare. The art styles suggest a connection with early Susa and Elam at a time-level equivalent to late Uruk or Jemdet Nasr.

Though little is known of eastern Iran archaeologically, several early cultures have been identified in Baluchistan. The archaeologist Stuart Piggott has schematically grouped these into two major categories using pottery as a criterion; a series of buff-ware cultures mainly in the center and south, and red-ware cultures in the north. This delineation follows an earlier division of Iranian cultures into these same two large divisions.

The earliest of the buff-ware group of cultures has been identified in the neighborhood of Quetta in central Baluchistan. This Quetta culture is known from fragmentary finds of a richly decorated buff-ware which Piggott feels to be related to early Susa and Sialk III (dating it then as equivalent in time to late Ubaid or Uruk, thus probably well after 4000 B.C.).

The Amri-Nal culture is more clearly defined; it is named for two sites, Amri on the Lower Indus, and Nal south of Quetta in Baluchistan. These sites probably represent either the early and late phases of the culture or possibly a regional division, east and west. Amri-Nal sites are on tells and are no more than village size. Some of the villages were surrounded by defensive walls, though there is relatively little evidence for warfare. Houses were of stone or perhaps mud brick, separated by narrow alleyways. Pottery was elaborately decorated and the vessels come in a number of forms. The Nal phase pottery is polychrome, and stylized animals and plants are common motifs. Amri pottery is characterized by curvilinear and geometric abstract designs. One interesting aspect of the culture is the complete lack of figurines, animal or human. Specimens of copper objects, including axes and chisels, have been found at the Nal cemetery. An analysis of one metal fragment shows that the copper is a natural alloy, with about 5 per cent nickel. Piggott reported only one stamp seal in the Amri-Nal culture. The Amri-Nal people buried, rather than cremated, their dead.

The place of Amri-Nal in the archaeological sequence of the Indus is far from clear. It seems to antedate the Indus civilization but also to be, in part, contemporary with it. Possibly the Amri-Nal peoples lived on the outskirts of the Indus civilization and were in fact displaced from some areas by the latter.

Another of the buff-ware cultures is that of Kulli, found in southern Baluchistan. Like the Amri-Nal folk, the Kulli villagers built houses of stone and mud brick on tells. Kulli differs from Amri-Nal in pottery types, a red-ware appearing alongside the buff-based pottery. There is a great variation of ceramic forms and the pottery decoration is dominated by grotesquely stylized humped cattle and felines (possibly tigers) sometimes interspersed with plant forms. Mixed with this distinctive pottery are sherds of Harappa style and, in fact, the Kulli pottery itself seems influenced by Harappa.

Very common in Kulli culture are figurines of cattle and women. Some of the cattle figures may have been toys; occasionally we find them with legs pierced for mounting on wheels. Clay models of carts from the Kulli sites, however, may belong to the Harappa culture. The female figurines are quite distinctive; they terminate at the waist, and the faces are grotesquely formed by clay appliqué. Their hair is shown elaborately dressed, and over the breasts (which may or may not be shown) are sometimes modeled thick strings of beads. Bangles on the wrists and arms (which are usually akimbo) suggest those still worn by girls in India and Pakistan. The meaning of the figurines is not clear, but they are probably religious in nature.

Copper objects are found in Kulli sites, and from the general evidence of pottery, Kulli seems to have been contemporary with the Indus river civilization. An indication of this comes from the city of Harappa itself. One of the art treasures from that site is a small copper statuette of a dancing girl. This nude maiden not only has the typical Kulli hairdress (as seen on the statuettes) but the Kulli arrangements of bangles on the arms.

It seems that the Kulli people may have been on one of the trade routes between the Indus valley and the west. This is suggested by the fact that sites in the Persian Makran, the part of Persia directly between the lower Indus and Sumer, have Kullilike ceramic wares. There is a good chance that merchants from the Indus penetrated the coastal areas of the Arabian Sea, perhaps

23
Dancing girl,
Indus civilization

following this route all the way to Sumer. On the other hand, the Kulli people may have acted as middlemen between the two areas of high culture. At any rate, they received a considerable number of items from the Indus; in return they exported, at least girls.

In north Baluchistan there is an important "red ware" culture, perhaps with ultimate ties to northern Persia. In the valley of the Zhob river and in the region north and west of the Bolan Pass there are tells of the Zhob culture. The site of Rana Ghundai, near the Zhob valley, has been most systematically explored and a long sequence of culture has been worked out.[2] In the very early level there appears to be largely a herding culture, with sheep, the humped cow, the ass, and the domestic horse (!). Later, presumably more sedentary, users of the site constructed painted pottery with animals in friezes around the vessel sides. Still later Zhob people (Rana Ghundai III) introduced refinements on this pattern and eventually the figures become mere designs on the pottery surfaces.

At various of the Zhob sites (probably dating from Rana Ghundai III though not found at the type site) there are curious female figurines, cut off near the waist-

24
*Mohenjo-Daro figure, l.,
closely resembles figurine, r.,
used by modern aborigines
of Orissa, Indus Valley*

**Courtesy** American Museum of Natural History

line like the Kulli group. These tiny figures have hooded or cauled heads with circular holes for eyes and beaks for noses. In a few cases this face becomes frankly a skull, perhaps a representation of a death goddess. The historian of religions E. O. James feels that these figures also had a fertility significance, and it is true that other Zhob figurines with vastly exaggerated female genitalia appear at about this time.[3]

Rana Ghundai III may well be (like Kulli to the south) contemporary with the Indus civilization, but the earlier levels of the site seem to have ties with Sialk and Hissar. The Zhob sequence, then, began considerably earlier than that of the Indus sites. The Zhob valley people very likely lived through the long centuries of Indus civilization as barbarian neighbors; finally the Zhob culture was swept away in the massive invasions that destroyed the Indus civilization itself.

The Indus, or Harappa, civilization presents us with one of the most striking enigmas of ancient times. The very fact that there was such a civilization went unrecognized until a few decades ago. As late as World War I prehistorians confidentially equated the rise of high culture in India with the arrival of the cattle herding, Indo-European-speakers from the west and north, the famous Aryans of the Rig-Veda. Even today the full geographical extent of the Indus river culture is not known for certain, but at any rate it stretched from Rupar in the upper Sutlej river valley throughout most of the Punjab and the Sind. It also extended westward to Sutkagen-Dor in western Pakistan near the Arabian Sea, southward at least to the Gulf of Cambay and eastward almost to Delhi. At present two very large cities are known, Harappa (wherein the culture received its alternate name) on the Ravi river of the Punjab, and Mohenjo-Daro, four hundred miles south and west, on the main Indus River. Each of these cities covers a square mile or more and is far larger than the other known Indus sites. These latter, however, are often impressive; such settlements as Chanhu-Daro, and recently discovered Judeierjo-Daro, west of the Indus, are as large as some of the Sumerian cities.

The enigma of the Indus culture lies in the fact that it seems to have sprung full-blown, or at least to have developed with amazing speed in the Indus river valley.

The fringes of Indus civilization, that is, the region along the Persian Sea (especially south of the Indus), may have been settled later than the valley area, but this is difficult to say because of the curious lack of change in the culture as a whole. The ties of this high culture with its barbaric neighbors to the west, with antecedent peoples in the Indus valley, and with the Sumerians of Mesopotamia are tantalizingly vague. In some ways the contacts with the future, with historic India, are clearer. Much that was to be typically Indian has its origins in Indus river culture. Probably these early Indus peoples, even more than the flamboyant but barbaric Vedic invaders, were the molders of Indian culture. We cannot be sure; the period from about 1500 B.C. (when the Aryans entered India) introduces a "dark age" for India, and the events of the next thousand years are, to say the least, obscure.

But to return to the Indus people. This much is known: the Sind and Baluchistan to the west had a series of flourishing peasant cultures, some of which must date from the fourth millennium B.C. There were

25
*Excavated area, Mohenjo-Daro*

obviously impulses from Mesopotamia, though most culture items were reworked rather than merely copied. During the third millennium B.C. (2500 B.C. is a convenient date if not taken too seriously) some of these villagers rapidly became civilized.[4] They did this by the selfsame method we have seen used in Egypt and Mesopotamia; farming groups moved into the rich plain of the Indus river, established irrigation systems and other control measures, and soon had the population and food surplus to build cities and to expand over a vast region.

The Indus civilization, however, has two elements that are conspicuously lacking in both Egypt and Mesopotamia. One is a monotonous regularity of culture (insofar as it can be reconstructed from archaeology), even in sites a thousand miles apart. This involves not only the larger items of house type and town plan, but also such minutiae as weights, measures, and size of building bricks. The second thing is a conservatism (perhaps stagnation is the better word) that almost defies belief. Although the civilization may have lasted for centuries, possibly for a thousand years, and though it obviously welcomed trade contacts with the outside, there is an amazing sameness from one end of the temporal range to the other. Copper and bronze implements of an inferior type, the flat ax, the spear and dagger without midribs, were made the same way in both early and late times. Mohenjo-Daro, built as it was in the river bottoms, had a series of floods, some of which seriously damaged the city, yet each rebuilding stage strictly copied the street arrangement of the previous city. A script, unlike, though probably influenced by, that of early Sumer, shows little or no change through time or space. Even the Egyptian, with his ideal of the static universe, was a wild and reckless innovator compared to the citizen of Harappa or Mohenjo-Daro. But of course no culture is completely changeless, and as more knowledge accumulates it may be possible to delineate clear subperiods within the Indus civilization. After all, it was discovered only in 1921 and much work remains to be done.[5]

In the absence of decipherable documents one cannot say too much of the political organization of the Harappa people. Nevertheless, it is hard to avoid the belief

26
Great bath, Mohenjo-Daro

that the Indus civilization was a tightly cohesive political unit, probably a kingdom or, better, an empire. Some central authority not only enforced a remarkable similarity of culture over a wide area, but indulged in city planning of a type that the world was not to see again until relatively modern times.

Although our knowledge of the origins of the civilization lacks greatly in detail, much can be reconstructed of the life of the times, and a great deal guessed of the decline and fall. Ceramics, that indispensable tool of the archaeologist, does give some hints even as to origins. Pottery decoration of the Indus people basically relates to the Zhob culture, and under the city of Harappa there is a small Zhoblike site. The Indus pottery, however, also has affinities with Kulli in south Baluchistan. It seems possible that the Indus civilization rose when diverse peoples trickled out of the Baluchistan hills and pooled their different traditions and different ideas. Out of such a merger came a vigorous new culture that began—possibly with outside help and advice via already opened trade routes—enthusiastically to drain swamps and construct canals, dykes, and revetments. Most experts believe that the Indus valley of this time (2500 B.C.) was wetter than now and supported extensive forests filled with wild animals.[6] In a short time the forests were pushed back, cities and towns were built, and the ideas of foreigners from distant Mesopotamia were absorbed and reworked. There may have been an explosive rise of population as the river lands were brought under cultivation. Presumably

*Civilization Spreads
to the Indus* 69

27
*General view of citadel area,*
*Mohenjo-Daro*

*Courtesy* Department of Archaeology, Government of Pakistan

the capital of this new land was either at Harappa or at Mohenjo-Daro, or possibly at both; the dual capital idea has analogies in historic India. In the large cities there is evidence for prosperity which would be suggested in any case by the very spread of the culture. Rows of large houses, built in the basic Near Eastern pattern of rooms around a court, indicate a large number of well-off individuals. Perhaps they were merchants, bureaucrats, or priests, or possibly all of these groups, and others, were represented.

The Indus people lived well in many ways. They cultivated bread wheat (*Triticum compactum*), two varieties of barley, and legumes. Bread wheat is a hybrid of other forms, one probably being emmer. There is some suggestion, though no certainty, that this rich variety of wheat may have originated somewhere near the Indian subcontinent. A number of animals were domesticated. They include, besides the ubiquitous dog, the zebu, or humped cow (*Bos indicus*), already encountered in the Zhob culture, the buffalo, and sheep, pigs, and goats, the latter related to the Kashmir, wool-bearing, goats. The Indus people seem to have had the cat, perhaps the earliest domestication of this animal—earlier even than in Egypt where the animal was sacred. Both the ass and horse appear; we have already seen evidence of the horse in early strata at Rana Ghundai. Possibly this was a wild species, but the horse may well be earlier in India and Baluchistan than in Sumer where the name, the "mountain ass," implies that it was an import (compare "mountain woman,"

*Origins of Civilization*
70

28
*Street drain, Mohenjo-Daro*

slave, with the obvious implication of foreignness).
Egypt did not receive the horse until the Hyksos invasions of the second millennium B.C.

There is evidence that the Indus people tamed the
elephant (it has never been truly domesticated).
Camel bones are found in the Indus cities and possibly
this is the origin point of camel domestication. Firm
evidence for such domestication, however, does not
come until around the beginning of the first millennium B.C., and the Indus camel bones may come from
wild species, though wild camels do not exist today.

It has already been suggested that considerable city
planning went into the construction of at least the
major sites. At both Harappa and Mohenjo-Daro there
is evidence of a north-south, east-west grid of streets. In
each case, inside the city proper there is an elaborate
structure called a "citadel," perhaps representing a governmental or religious center, or both. An important
feature at Mohenjo-Daro is a huge bath, or tank, built
of fired bricks and sealed with bitumen, arranged with a
system of drains. Such tanks in historic times were
associated with Hindu temples and we seem to have
here another example of the "Indian" character of the
Indus civilization. The complex of ruins in the citadel
areas are made up of terraces with flights of stairs or
ramps, and rooms. The descriptions sound curiously
like the great ceremonial complexes in the Mayan area
of the New World. It is hard to believe, in spite of
"defensive" walls, that there was any serious military
use of these areas, except perhaps at the end when the

Indus civilization was fighting for its life. The walls were immense in size; the one at Harappa, for example, forms a mound 1,200 feet by 600 feet. Originally the citadels were flanked by great arterial streets that dissected the cities. Other smaller streets formed a grid system that divided Harappa and Mohenjo-Daro into a series of blocks from which smaller streets and lanes radiate.

The Harappa people built elaborate drains under the major streets; these have covered manholes so that they can be entered and cleaned. The drains not only carried off excessive rain water, but were connected to individual house sewers. The larger houses were built with separate bathrooms fitted with drainpipes that led to the main city sewers. These better-class houses were built with baked bricks and in many cases were two-storied. The houses surrounded a courtyard and were usually entered from a side street. There is little evidence of fireplaces so, presumably, heating was by means of charcoal braziers, a widespread custom in the ancient world. One rather modern feature of the Indus house was the rubbish chute that penetrated the walls and emptied into an outside collection bin.

Some of the private houses had their own wells, but there were also public wells of baked brick. These are generally surrounded with vast numbers of potsherds from rough clay cups that were presumably used once and then thrown away, again suggesting Hindu India where there is a ritual taboo on drinking twice from the same cup. But perhaps we are going beyond our data here—after all, the litter of paper cups around an American water cooler has no obvious ritual significance.

The upper classes lived well, in fact luxuriously, and even the average citizen may have been quite comfortable. Rows of workers' houses have been excavated at Harappa and Mohenjo-Daro; at Harappa associated with large-scale wheat- and barley-grinding areas and with metal-working smelters. The houses are in parallel rows and remarkably standardized, each with two rooms, one larger than the other. Like the highly standardized pottery, the elaborate sewers, the rubbish collecting, and the rigid building regulations, this suggests the strength of the city authority and the high degree of systemization that had been obtained. One human

Courtesy **American Museum of Natural History**

touch is the find, from under one of these cottages, of a vast hoard of gold and jewels. This collection, the contents of a rich jewelry chest, must have been stolen, perhaps by one of the mill or smelter workers. In any event, the thief was unable to "fence" his fortune; it remained undiscovered for four thousand years.

Models of oxcarts are common in the ruins. Usually they are children's toys and, in fact, the clay toy cart remained a favorite in historic India. The carts resemble modern Indian and Pakistani ones very closely and measurements of cart ruts from Harappa show that the width (approximately three and a half feet) has not changed to the present day. Curiously, there are few representations of boats in spite of the obvious use of them.

The Indus civilization people wrote with a script that has, to date, not been deciphered. Most examples are from seals and are usually only a few symbols in length. There is no Indus "literature" extant; if it ever existed it was probably written on perishable materials. The script must have been difficult to use as there were two hundred and fifty or more distinct symbols. Probably the writing was a mixture of rebus elements, determinatives, and pictographs. Modern experts have been unable to demonstrate any significant evolution of the script in all the long history of the Indus civilization; this in direct contrast to both Egypt and Mesopotamia

30
*Main street, Mohenjo-Daro*

where changes and simplifications continued to be made for thousands of years. The fact of a static script in itself suggests limited use of writing, but whether this use was commercial or religious we do not know.

Nor is the language of the Indus people known. It was very likely non-Indo-European and may have been an ancestor to one or another of the Dravidian languages, now spoken mainly in south India but probably with a wider distribution in ancient time. Perhaps there was more than one language, as in Mesopotamia. At least the Indus people were racially mixed, having Mediterranean, "proto-Australoid," and possibly Mongoloid elements.

One dramatic example of standardization lies in the elaborate system of weights based on the unit 16 (compare the historic Indian 16 annas to a rupee). Another is in the two standard measuring units, one of about 13 inches, the other a little over 20 inches.

Our knowledge of Indus religion comes in large part from stamp seals. They show an earth goddess, or mother goddess, probably like those that exist in village India today. More significant, is a fairly clear indication of the god Shiva, three-faced, enthroned in Yogi position, and associated with animals. The god enthroned with deer at his feet suggests to us the much later representations of the Buddha who had the same animals placed in the same position. In addition to these items there is some indication that the cow was on its way to obtaining the sacred status it has in modern India.

*Origins of Civilization*
74

Though there certainly were trade contacts between the Indus and the Tigris-Euphrates areas, there is relatively little evidence from either region that conclusively shows such contacts. It is very likely that the Indus people got the idea of writing, of massive architecture, and probably of elaborate irrigation agriculture from the west—though it should be stressed again that these ideas were reworked in typically Indian forms. The archaeologist Sir Mortimer Wheeler points out that early buildings at Mohenjo-Daro show reinforcing with timbers that proved impractical in the wet climate and were later replaced by baked brick. This suggests, though only as one possibility among others, that initial direction and advice about large-scale construction had come from builders who were used to drier climates.

However that may be, there is evidence of both Sumerian and later Akkadian trade influence into the Indus. The use of faience was, in all probability, introduced from abroad, and other scattered items, cylinder seals, a few metal implements, and a few jewels show, or seem to show, direct connections. There are also Indus seals in Mesopotamia. The trade contacts may have been via the Island of Telmun, or Dilmun (probably to be identified with Bahrein in the Persian Gulf),[7] in later times and perhaps directly from Sumer in the earlier period. Goods traveled to Mesopotamia from Makkan and Meluhha and included ivory, precious metals, copper, lapis lazuli, and animals.[8] Ivory was doubtless one of the important trade items, for it was widely utilized in the Indus area for carving. Other cargos, such as slaves and cotton, may have gone from east to west. Domesticated cotton was, parenthetically, a distinctive Indus contribution to civilization. The plant was independently domesticated in the Americas where it had a very wide distribution.

The vast unnamed empire of the Indus collapsed at some time in the second millennium B.C. (a convenient estimate is 1500 B.C.). There is already some evidences of decline, perhaps from the weight of centuries of stagnation, but the final blow was given by Aryan barbarians who, with their horse-drawn war chariots and herds of cattle, swept into India from the west and north. The Hindu religious book of a later time, the Rig-Veda, describes in highly mythicized form the conquest of the Indus area, a conquest that led to a long period of turmoil and decline in India. When the curtain lifts again (around 500 B.C.) we can see that the center of things has shifted to the Ganges river, and much of north India has adopted the Indo-European languages of the Aryans. Nevertheless, the Indus civilization contributed its share to historic India. The exact debt that India and Pakistan owe the Indus civilization must be calculated by future archaeologists and historians.

The Aryans were only one of a group of Indo-European-speaking, cattle-raising, nomadic peoples who were beginning to spread from some original Asian homeland. There they had long been the recipients of high culture impulses from Mesopotamia, the idea of animal domestication being one of these borrowed techniques. Beginning possibly as early as 2000 B.C. these groups, for reasons now unknown, began a series of vast migrations that led them across thousands of miles. As Aryans they entered India. As Greeks and Illyrians, Slavs, Germans, and Celts they reached Europe, while distant kinsmen far to the east were pressing on China. The migrations of these and other peoples were to upset the balance of power in the Ancient World. In fact, the period from 2000 to about 1000 B.C. might be looked upon as one of those catalytic periods when long-established traditions and customs were shattered, a period when the groundwork was being laid for new dominant cultures in new areas. None of the ancient centers of civilization had achieved the changelessness and rigidity attained by the Indus people. But rigidity implies the inability to survive change, and certainly the Harappa culture suffered far more than Egypt and Mesopotamia. The wreckage on the Indus was so complete that the Indus river civilization literally disappeared from the records and minds of men, to be rediscovered only after thirty-five hundred years.

THOUGH THE peoples of the region now occupied by Syria, Lebanon, Israel, Jordan, and extreme southern Turkey were relative latecomers in the pageant of civilization, they nevertheless made two signal contributions. One of these was the alphabet, which was invented, or simplified from Egyptian models, somewhere in the southern part of the area and later spread by the adventurous seagoing Phoenicians. The second was the reworking of religious ideas long current in the Near East into a coherent ethic. This was the contribution of the Jews and it represents the most important basis of the widespread faiths of Christianity and Islam. The evolvement of the idea of a universal ethic is not, in fact, peculiar to the Jew; it may have been an integral part of Akhenaton's reforms in Eighteenth Dynasty Egypt, and certainly it can be seen in the reworking of traditional Hinduism made by Gautama, the Buddha, and in the gently skeptical humanism of the Chinese philosopher, Confucius. But the system of the Jews, especially when transferred to later religions, had a direct and deep impact on a large segment of mankind. A belief in the essential humanness of all men and the idea that man is indeed his brother's keeper springs from Jewish sources. It has made both Christianity and Islam fervently evangelical religions and has contributed to their dynamic spread across the world.

Both of these contributions came relatively late, long after civilization had appeared in the areas of the Tigris-Euphrates and the Nile. There was another, much earlier, significance to this western horn of the Fertile Crescent, however, for it was the region through which ideas trickled from one of the great river areas to the other. Later it became the battleground for ambitious nation-states: Egypt, Mitanni, Hatti, Babylonia, Assyria, and Persia.

The land west of the Euphrates in the Mediterranean drainage is fairly well-watered from winter rains in the Amanus, the Anti-Lebanons, and the mountains of Israel. Farther south it is drier and the Negev and Sinai regions are today virtual deserts. Nevertheless the Negev, at least, once supported a considerable population; the inhabitants cleverly utilizing all available sources of water.

There are two important rivers in the area. One is the

# IX

*Between the Euphrates and the Nile*

Orontes which rises in the Anti-Lebanon mountains, flows northward paralleling the coast, then turns westward into the Amq plain past the site of Antioch, and finally cuts across a spur of the Amanus to the Mediterranean. This area was one of the great crossroads of the ancient world, partly because of the fertility of the lower Orontes valley and partly because, from the Orontes to the upper Euphrates, the land is relatively open. Farther south is the long fault line stretching south from Lebanon to the Gulf of Aqaba. The central portion of this fault is occupied by the Jordan river, surely one of the most famous streams in the world. At about 1,500 feet above sea level the Jordan flows from its source near Dan into the Sea of Galilee, finally southward to drain into the great sink of the Dead Sea, 1,280 feet below sea level. The fault line continues south as the valley of the dry Wadi Arabah, to the Gulf of Aqaba.

In antiquity, parts of the rugged coast supported important trading cities. The traders in these cities acted as middlemen for the goods of the Tigris-Euphrates and the Nile, and other more distant places. They had local riches, however; copper in the mountains, gold in the rivers and, throughout the northern and central part of the area, great stands of mountain cedar. The cities were fortunately placed, in that the Nile delta was a short sail from the Syrian or Lebanese coast, the great copper-rich island of Cyprus even nearer, and Crete and the Aegean not beyond the reach of adventurous seamen. The Phoenicians became the greatest traders of antiquity, and sailed beyond the Aegean, to the western Mediterranean and into the Atlantic Ocean.

There were essentially two foci for early cultures in this region, one in the north and another in the south, in Palestine. Excavations on the Orontes and its tributaries and on the north coast of Syria have uncovered Neolithic settlements both along the river and on the Syrian coast, dating back to 5000 B.C. or even earlier. Some of the Neolithic pottery showed a peculiar type of decoration, a striped effect made with the burnishing tool. This technique is later found throughout much of the Mediterranean area and had a considerable distribution in time as well as in space. Other types of pottery, also with a westward distribution, are incised or impressed wares—the impressions often made with a cardium shell.

The Neolithic material in sites such as Hama (Hamah) on the middle Orontes, Ras Shamra (Ugarit) on the north Syrian coast, and Tell esh-Sheikh and others in the Amq plain still farther north, underlies deposits of Halafian culture. These advanced Neolithic peoples manufactured colorfully painted pottery. They originally used the bow for hunting and warfare, but then supplemented it with the sling. Copper, probably cold-hammered, began to appear.

During the fourth millennium cultural impulses seem to have come mainly from Mesopotamia. The Syrian area reflected reasonably well the changes in technologies, in styles and in ideas that produced Ubaid and Uruk. It may be that the areas of north Syria and south Turkey were already exporting cedar; certainly the cedar trade becomes tremendously important a little later. Again the strategic position of the Orontes valley should be stressed. It was near the divide that led to the Euphrates; the Amanus mountains were covered with conifer forests and the adjacent coastal areas look seaward to Egypt, to Cyprus, and beyond.

From sites in the Amq valley there is indication that the Uruk influence came suddenly to an end, probably due to the migration of a new people whose original affinities may have been with the north and east. They can be traced by a rather thick, black or red, handmade decorated pottery called Khirbet Kerak ware, named for a site south of the Sea of Galilee where the pottery was originally discovered. The evolution of this pottery from earlier Neolithic wares probably took place in the southern Caucasus, and the appearance of the Khirbet Kerak people suggests a mass migration in which they displaced or mixed with earlier settlers of the Orontes valley and possibly those in the Lebanon-Israel area to the south. They may have been members of the speech group known as Hurrian. At any rate, speakers of this language (perhaps related to historic languages of the Caucasus) were an important element in upper Euphrates populations by the second millennium B.C.

The date of this migration is not certain, but assuming that the Uruk period of Syria was somewhat later than that in the Mesopotamian homeland, we might place it at between 3000 B.C. and 2500 B.C. The Khirbet Kerak people were replaced in turn by new invaders, from the Aleppo plateau farther east, who brought such innovations as the potter's wheel, better metallurgy, and more elaborate techniques of building with mud brick. Whoever they were, these Aleppo migrants had been greatly influenced by the high culture traditions of Mesopotamia. The Khirbet Kerak people were forced west and south, and in the west may well have become one of the ancestors to the Hittites. If so, they are to return later to trouble Syria and Palestine.

The Aleppo settlers had contacts with the Nile valley; at least a slate palette similar to those of predynastic Egypt has been found at an early level in the site of Atchana in the Amq. This large site, the historic city of Alalakh, was very likely one of the places where Mesopotamian influences were channeled into Egypt. This would make the Orontes valley and adjacent coast a key area in the early spread of civilization. Certainly more systematic excavation is needed in the Amq.

The culture that overspread the Amq valley and surrounding regions had, like the pre-Khirbet Kerak, been influenced by Uruk, though it had developed its own local variant brand of culture. A little later it is possible to trace Jemdet Nasr connections. Still later, there is trade material from Early Dynastic Sumer in the form of engraved cylinder seals, either traded directly from Mesopotamia or copied from Sumerian models. The town of Alalakh had a considerable expansion in this period, quite possibly because of its control of cedar and other local products which were traded to the rich Sumerian city-states.

From the site of Byblos on the north Lebanese coast comes other indications of contact with the outside world. Overlying an earlier Neolithic village there was a small settlement of copper-using people who grew barley and olives (the olive tree was early in this region) and had a number of domesticated animals. The techniques of working copper and silver belonged to a local tradition, the same as that along the Orontes, and it may have influenced the early metal period in Crete and the Aegean. Before 3000 B.C., Byblos was trading with Egypt. A third phase at Byblos (the second period of metal-using peoples) saw the introduction of the potter's wheel with a distinctive "combed ware" which appears also in First Dynasty Egypt and in Early Dynastic Sumer. It is clear that Byblos was a port which continued to supply the Egyptians with Asiatic goods. Later the town became closely involved in international politics and was considerably influenced by Egypt.

In the third millennium there was probably actual physical expansion of Mesopotamia into the Mediterranean area. According to Akkadian records the great King Sargon I (see Chapter VII) extended his empire to the Mediterranean coast. There is a good possibility that Sargon actually overran the lower Orontes valley and captured the city of Alalakh. Just after 2000 B.C. there was an imperialistic expansion from another direction. Egyptian Pharaohs of the Twelfth Dynasty made an energetic attempt to control the Palestinian and Syrian coasts, reaching possibly as far north as the Amq, and certainly to Ugarit and Byblos on the coast. Egyptian influence lasted until, roughly, 1800 B.C. when Egypt's first empire faded and she was invaded in turn by the Hyksos.

The second millennium B.C. saw the Syrian area the pawn of great powers, north, south, and east. Less is known of relations with the west, but certainly the Cretan and Mycenaean civilizations owed a great deal to the coastal cities. A dramatic example of this was found at Alalakh in the Amq. In the period 1800–1750 B.C., the kings of Alalakh were building palaces with columned halls and frescoed rooms. Many architectural details and even the technique and subject matter of the frescoes (bulls, landscapes) is reminiscent of Minoan Crete. The various elements of palace architecture had a slow evolution in this area and, at least in their developed aspect, they appear rather suddenly in Crete. Undoubtedly there was contact between the Aegean and the Asiatic mainland and this contact was maintained for a very long period; broken pottery of Mycenaean origin, as late as the 1100's B.C., has been found near the port of Alalakh.

We see, then, the area reaching from southern coastal Turkey through Syria and Lebanon as a region of early high culture, originally influenced by Mesopotamia but in the second millennium falling more and more into the orbit of Egypt. The importance of this area was as a transmitter of civilization—it was at least one of the places through which early Mesopotamian influences trickled into Egypt. Later it was to influence the growing civilization of the Minoan West. Even later, part of the area was involved in the great adventure of the Phoenicians, a group of Canaanite-speakers who were established on the Syrian and Lebanese coast by the beginning of the third millennium. Here, on the narrow coastal plain, there grew up in the period 2000–1000 B.C. a series (perhaps a league) of commercial cities that traded throughout the Mediterranean and beyond. One of the early trading centers was Ugarit, directly across from the copper-rich island of Cyprus. It was one of the places through which Creto-Mycenaean influences passed to reach the Near East. Ugarit is often not considered with Phoenicia proper, whose best-known cities were Byblos, Tyre, and Sidon. The Phoenicians were probably the most valuable middlemen of the Mediterranean and influenced its life and its politics for a thousand years. Even after the decline of the home cities, the great Phoenician colony of Carthage in modern Tunisia remained powerful until it was destroyed by Rome, about 150 B.C.

Behind the Phoenician coast and beyond the coastal ranges the kingdom of Kadesh, which became a bone of contention between Hittites and Egyptians, grew up. This part of inland Syria eventually became a center for Aramaic speech and in the period after 1000 B.C. the Aramaic kingdom of Damascus was important in the power politics of the area.

Another powerful, though somewhat shadowy, state was that of Mitanni on the upper Euphrates. Mitanni may have been founded by wandering groups, some of them speaking Indo-European languages, who broke into the Fertile Crescent after 2000 B.C. These latecomers ruled over and eventually merged with non-Indo-European, non-Semitic, Hurrian-speakers who had been living on the upper Euphrates for a long period of time. Around the middle of the second millennium B.C. Mitanni engaged in international power politics with the Hittites, the Egyptians, and the Babylonians. The state was eventually defeated by the Hittites.

Though they must have spread much of the high culture of the Ancient World to distant Mediterranean shores, the Phoenicians are best-known for their gift of the alphabetic system of writing. It is interesting that they, rather than the literate, sophisticated Mycenaeans, gave a writing system to the later Greeks—and to us.

No one has ever accused the Phoenicians of morality. They were entrepreneurs whose lifeblood was trade, and piracy whenever possible; for this they received a bad name from their later rivals and imitators, the Greeks. Yet they gave more than they knew, for at their hands an easy literacy came to much of the world.

As we have seen, early writing, whether Mesopotamian or Egyptian depended on a skilled and jealous class of specialists. This was especially true in Egypt where the hieroglyphic and its derived hieratic were much too complex for the average person to learn. Mesopotamian writing eventually developed a fairly simple syllabary using signs for short syllables, normally a consonant and vowel. Even so, writing did not become really widespread in spite of the fact that an amazing number of people availed themselves of the services of professional scribes. The Akkadian-Babylonian cuneiform, though popular for thousands of years, was eventually displaced and forgotten.

Curiously, Egyptian hieroglyphic writing contained, practically from the beginning, elements of an alphabetic or phonemic system in which the few dozen individual sound-classes of the language were reproduced. The Egyptians never recognized, or perhaps never wished to recognize, the utility of these minimal sound units, and they continued to use ideographs, determinatives, and rebus (punning with pictures) elements, thus making a complicated and difficult script. However, at some time between 2000 and 1500 B.C. Semitic-speakers, probably from the Sinai, took over the phonetic portions of Egyptian writing, added other elements, and produced the first crude alphabetic writing. Presumably these innovators were in direct contact with the Egyptians. They may have been under Egyptian masters (Twelfth Dynasty) or had Egyptian scribes as servants (Hyksos period). The originators of this writing very likely used their script to represent the sounds, at least the consonants, of a local Canaanite dialect. From the very beginning there may have been introduced the handy acrophonic principle, whereby the

| | A | B | C | D | E |
|---|---|---|---|---|---|
| | Original pictograph | Pictograph in position of later cuneiform | Early Babylonian | Assyrian | Original or derived meaning |
| 1 | | | | | bird |
| 2 | | | | | fish |
| 3 | | | | | donkey |
| 4 | | | | | ox |
| 5 | | | | | sun day |
| 6 | | | | | grain |
| 7 | | | | | orchard |
| 8 | | | | | to plow to till |
| 9 | | | | | boomerang to throw to throw down |
| 10 | | | | | to stand to go |

31
Chart showing the development of cuneiform script

letters representing sounds in the language are named for words that begin with the letter in question and are represented by a drawing of the object represented by the word. It is as if we were to name our first letter *apple* and represent it by the drawing of an apple, the second letter *ball* with a representation of a ball.

Certain of these names appear in the early Sinaitic script. For example, a glottal stop (the stoppage of air in the throat, as in the break in the middle of *bottle* pronounced with an exaggerated Brooklyn accent) was called 'aleph, a word which began with such a glottal stop. Aleph means ox and was represented by an ox head. The labial stop, b, was called beth (house) and shown by the floor plan of a house; other sounds were given similar names and were similarly represented.

Variants of this script spread throughout the Canaanite area. It had a curious history in some places; at Ugarit, for example, it was adapted for writing on clay tablets using the typical wedge-shaped impressions of a reed stylus. This particular writing appeared not long after 1500 B.C. and was obviously influenced by Mesopotamia, as might be expected in that northern region. Still, it is alphabetic, with some thirty consonantal sounds being represented, and could hardly have been developed from the cuneiform syllabary of Babylonia. This latter system breaks up words in syllable units and, significantly, the only signs for simple sounds are for vowels (as if, in English, the word *interior* was written with the units, *in ter i or*). The Ugaritic alphabet is surely derived from the same source as those of Phoenicia and Israel, but rendered in cuneiform style by people who had long acquaintance with Mesopotamia.

The Phoenicians developed and began to diffuse their script before 1000 B.C. The great advantage of an alphabet is that it can reproduce the sounds of a language reasonably well with only two or three dozen symbols (in modern English, twenty-six are used). Additionally, if the symbols accurately represent the sounds of a language, the system can be learned in a few weeks, thus writing no longer becomes a monopoly of a small, highly-trained group of specialists.

The Phoenicians used their writing for commerce as well as for religion and probably it was this commercial use of the alphabet that recommended it to the Greeks. Earlier Mycenaean civilization had writing, but it was a clumsy syllabic system rather unfitted to consonant-clustering Greek and it did not survive the Dorian dark ages. In the ninth or eighth century B.C. the Greeks borrowed the Phoenician alphabet, changed it somewhat—mainly by adding vowel sounds—and passed it on to the Etruscans, the Romans, and eventually to us. The Greeks kept the Phoenician order of letters and the acrophonic principle, in fact even borrowed the Phoenician names, inevitably turning them into non-sense syllables. The Phoenician aleph becomes alpha though the sign α, eventually A, continues to have a vague resemblance to an ox head. Beth becomes beta β, later B, still the floor plan of a house. One letter goes back to early Egyptian; the sign for mouth (probably pronounced ro) was originally written ⬭ in hiero-glyphic, and ◁ in the more cursive hieratic. The Sina-itic people represented this as a human head, but later Phoenicians wrote the letter ◁. The Greeks turned it around to form P and called the letter rho. It is now written R.

In other forms this basic Canaanite alphabet spread eastward, modified by each people in turn until it reached eastern Asia. After 500 B.C. it replaced the cuneiform in Mesopotamia and a little later it su-perseded a late-Egyptian cursive form. Many centuries later, spread by Europeans, it replaced the evolving and still very inefficient writing systems of the American Indians. Only in eastern Asia, where the massive struc-ture of Chinese civilization grew up in isolation, has a nonalphabetic form prevailed to the present day.

The region that today encompasses the modern na-tions of Israel and Jordan did not receive the influences of civilization as rapidly as the Amq valley and nearby coast. It is interesting, however, to remember that the site of Jericho on the Jordan is the oldest known organ-ized town. At a date of perhaps 7000 B.C., or even earlier, a town tentatively estimated by Kenyon at two thousand inhabitants had grown up by the spring at Jericho, from Natufian forebears, as it now seems. Evi-dence for plant domestication is not conclusive, but the dense population suggests not only agriculture but irri-gation agriculture. In spite of this precocious begin-ning, the region failed to go on to full-blown civiliza-tion. Either Jericho was too exposed to attack or there was not enough cross-fertilization. At any rate, the Jordan valley was not destined to become the origin-point of civilization.

Following early Jericho, there were a series of crude Neolithic cultures which, like the earlier Natufians, often utilized the caves that literally dot this region. The Halafian influence did not spread so far south as

Palestine, but some dim reflections of it may have stimulated early Palestinians. At the site of Tuleilat Ghassul in Jordan near the Jordan river a distinctive culture called Ghassulian appeared by 4000 B.C. The Ghassulian people built mud brick houses and engaged in extensive agriculture, including the olive among their food plants. Pottery was thin and well-made and appeared in a number of forms. There was some copper, perhaps traded, but also a vast amount of flint work. The Ghassulian culture appears in a number of spots, from the Esdraelon and northern coastal plains to Beersheba and sites near Gaza in central Israel. Possibly this culture represented migrations of peoples from the north mixing with an indigenous Neolithic population.

The site of Ghassul itself seems to have been deserted before the end of the fourth millennium and there may have been a contraction of the whole Palestinian area at that time, possibly due to a climatic shift which produced slightly drier conditions. The area west of the Jordan, especially the Esdraelon plain, began to receive new settlements at about this time, representing either a shift of population from east of the Jordan, or new peoples coming in from outside Palestine, or both. At any rate, the Esdraelon plain soon became very important for natural reasons. It cuts across the north-south Israel highlands and serves as a highroad for peoples moving from the coast to the interior or vice versa. Sites on the plain or at the edge of it were in the position of controlling this corridor, hence the importance of such cities as Megiddo on the west and Beth-Shan, near the Jordan, on the east. From the Jordan it is possible to swing northeastward to the Damascus region or northwestward to the Phoenician coast. As an easy route from the coastal plain to the interior and to Syria, the plain was much traveled in later times by invading armies, especially Egyptian. The position of Palestine on the land routes between Egypt and the Orontes and Euphrates valleys was by no means an unqualified blessing.

For the south the third millennium B.C. was a period of general growth and development. It is taken up, archaeologically, by the period known as Early Bronze. Even before the beginning of this Bronze Age there is indication of a considerable contact with Mesopotamia; Jemdet Nasr cylinder seals are found at Megiddo, and Palestinian peoples, like those of the Orontes area and Syrian coast to the north, may have helped pass on culture impulses from Mesopotamia to Egypt. No significant cultural advances seem to have been made in the Palestinian area however. This is the age of what Kenyon calls "City States," small towns that were presumably independent. The level of technology was not particularly high; though the period is called Early Bronze, it is not entirely clear if bronze, rather than the softer copper, was used. There were, however, some technological improvements, such as, in the firing of pottery. There seems to have been intermittent warfare, probably between the city-states and between the city people and nomads of the badlands east of the Jordan.

A little before 2000 B.C. some of these desert peoples, tentatively identified by linguistic evidence and by Egyptian texts as the Amorites, invaded and conquered the area of Palestine. These same nomads seem to have been somehow involved in the obscure events that brought the Egyptian Old Kingdom crashing down and produced in Egypt what is technically called the First Intermediate Period. Linguistic cousins of the western Amorites were soon to plague lower Mesopotamia. In Israel and Jordan they caused the collapse of the Early Bronze city-states and heralded a kind of Dark Age.

Meanwhile, in the north of this area there was the beginning of the remarkable Phoenician civilization growing out of earlier high cultures of Syria. About 1900 B.C. some of these peoples spread southward and entered Palestine, beginning what is known as the Middle Bronze culture. The newcomers were called Canaanites and they had a tremendous influence on the later Hebrews as is indicated in the Old Testament. The Canaanites brought true bronze and other innovations, one being the fast wheel for making pottery. Perhaps even more important, they revived town life. Egypt, too, was making a recovery and beginning, with the Twelfth Dynasty, her first real expansion north into Palestine and Syria. As was said before, Egyptian influence reached as far as Ugarit, possibly even to Alalakh on the Orontes. It is possible that the group known as Habiru enter at this time. At any rate, some of these

32
*Obelisk of Queen
Hathshepsut, 18th
Dynasty Egypt*

diverse peoples swept into Egypt and imposed foreign
rule on the delta and the northern Nile valley. These
"Hyksos"—the name can be best translated as "rulers of
(foreign) countries" or just possibly as "shepherd
kings"—surely controlled much of the Palestinean area
as well as Egypt. They were driven out of the latter
country by the energetic Eighteenth Dynasty kings who
came to power around 1600 B.C. The victorious Egyptians soon advanced into Palestine and then into Syria.
Sometime in this general period wandering bands of
nomadic people appear, the Israelites of the Bible, who

perhaps are also the Habiru of contemporary records.[1] The Habiru are recorded as wanderers among the Canaanite cities during the troubles attending the Aton reforms of Akhenaton, who came to the Egyptian throne c. 1370. According to tradition, the Hebrews fled from bondage in Egypt, led by their culture hero Moses.[2] The entry of the Children of Israel into Canaan introduced more troubles to an already troubled land. The whole area beyond the Euphrates was now the battleground between Egypt and an aggressive Hittite power located in central Turkey. The appearance of hungry nomads as well must have seemed catastrophic to the Canaanites of Palestine.

The Hebrews, whatever their original point of origin, may have entered the Jordan valley from the east, attacking the fortified town of Jericho and reducing it. In general, however, the encroachment of the Hebrews seems rather gradual and the result of a number of separate tribes slowly infiltrating into the area. About 1200 B.C. another folk movement took place, this one on a vast scale, upsetting a great deal of the Near East. The restless groups known as "Peoples of the Sea" ripped the Hittite empire, then pushed southward through Syria and Palestine, finally to meet defeat at the hands of Rameses III in 1196 B.C. A number of tribes were involved including, possibly, some who are mentioned in Homer (the Danunu, for example, conceivably could be Homer's Danaoi). One such tribe that the Egyptians called the Peleset, and known to us as the Philistines, settled on the coastal plain of Israel.

The Philistines made little attempt to settle the interior; in general they occupied Canaanite coastal towns and their whole history is coastally oriented. Eventually they made an effort to control the Esdraelon plain, and traditional evidence indicates that by the eleventh century they held Beth-Shan. Megiddo does not seem to have been occupied by the Philistines and, in fact, must have been in ruins, for if it were in hostile hands Beth-Shan would be of no value to a coastal power. The chances are that the site of Megiddo was eventually reoccupied and rebuilt by the Hebrews, without fighting.

The struggle between these various peoples and the events that led to the united Israelite monarchy has been told and retold. By 1100 B.C. the Hebrews were strongly entrenched in the central hills of Palestine and seemed to have gradually absorbed the Canaanites around them who, after all, were linguistic kinsmen. A little before 1000 B.C., under the leadership of Saul, they challenged the Philistines, but after some initial successes Saul was decisively defeated and killed. His follower and rival, David, was allowed by the Philistines to set up a vassal kingdom, a serious miscalculation on their part. At that time the Israelites controlled the hills to the north and south of Jerusalem, but that city, the key to north-south movement through central Palestine, was in the hands of the Canaanites. In the year 995 B.C. David captured Jerusalem and thus united the two parts of Israel. He, and his son Solomon, created a strong, though not a stable, power in the Palestinian area. They never managed to completely overrun Philistia (perhaps because of Egyptian help to the latter) and thus were cut off from much of their own Mediterranean coastline. Nevertheless, the Hebrew kingdom had military successes to the east and north and eventually expanded beyond the Damascus area to the Euphrates river. Phoenicia like Philistia, however, remained independent.

The united kingdom of Israel was not to last. The centrifugal forces were so great that after the reign of Solomon it split into a northern Kingdom of Israel with a capital at Samaria, and a southern Kingdom of Judah with its capital at Jerusalem. Samaria, especially, was greatly influenced by the Phoenicians and for a time was a splendid and cosmopolitan center. Against this luxury and division of wealth, again and again were raised the voices of the Hebrew prophets. Often these voices were strident and cruel but slowly they forged the dramatic idea of one god, all powerful, eternal, and just. The Israelite prophets might be rough hillmen, unused to complex city life and city manners, but their idea of divinity towered far above the concepts of the Canaanites. The Canaanite nature gods and goddesses had their analogies (and perhaps prototypes) in Mesopotamia and Egypt, but were cruder; the rites were sensual and often brutal.

The origin of much of Old Testament cosmology seems to be Mesopotamian to which has been added the traditional history of the Israelites and the blunt simple morality of the Ten Commandments. But even as late as the united kingdom there does not seem to have been a full development of the idea of monotheism. The psalms popularly attributed to King David do speak, in lyrically beautiful passages, of a universal and personal god, but it is risky to assume monotheism on the basis of religious poetry. The urbane Solomon certainly had a considerable tolerance for the various Canaanite cults and for those of neighboring nations. He was strong enough and prestigious enough to escape with unscathed reputation, but later rulers had to deal with the increasing demands of prophets (largely self-appointed interpreters of the faith) for allegiance to Yahweh, the true God. Occasionally this led to ruthless murder as when the prophet Elisha induced an Israelite army officer named Jehu to revolt against Jehoram, king of Israel, and the queen-mother, Jezebel, because of their Phoenician-inspired religious tolerance. Jehu not only murdered the royal family, including their visiting kinsman Ahaziah, king of Judah, but slaughtered large numbers of local Baal worshipers. This particular adventure was unfortunate because Judah to the south and the Phoenician cities to the north were completely alienated. At this date, mid-ninth century, the prophets and their followers were still confusing city life with the evil life, and the peasant ways of the hills with virtue.

The confused and brutal conditions, produced by the Assyrian wars, and the Babylonian captivity softened the attitude of the Hebrew prophets toward cities, but sharpened their conception of Yahweh as a universal God. It is likely that it was in this period that much of the monotheism found or implied in the Pentateuch had its origin. Many latter-day political leaders, for example Ezra and Nehemiah, were much concerned that traditional Hebrew dogma be maintained, but they also championed the poor and the oppressed, thus following a tradition that goes back to the early days of Israelite power. Even later, certain teachers began to talk of the universal love and justice of Yahweh. Such a one was Hillel, another was Jesus of Nazareth.

THE ISLAND of Crete had a very advantageous position in the ancient Mediterranean. It is about equally distant from the Greek mainland and from Asia Minor and is not too far from Libya in North Africa. It is big enough to support large Neolithic populations, for it extends a hundred and fifty miles east and west and, at its greatest width, more than thirty-five miles north and south. The island is quite mountainous, the southern shoreline presenting a stern appearance because of the rapid rise in elevation. On the north, the mountains taper off more gradually but present a series of transverse spurs that break up the island into segments. The roughest country is in the west where summits go to 8,000 feet and more. Two breaks in the mountains, one between the western White Mountains and Mount Ida, and another east of Mount Ida, allow for north-south movement. Originally the island was probably heavily forested and these forests may have been one of the bases of Cretan naval power in the Minoan period. The country has a generally pleasant Mediterranean climate, with dry summers and winter rains.

*Crete*

Crete seems to have had little or no occupation in Paleolithic and Mesolithic times. It was fairly late in the Neolithic, as things went in the Near East, that farming people first moved into Crete. Two sources for these migrations have been suggested, Asia and North Africa, and perhaps both were represented. The region loosely called "Libya," that is, North Africa west of the Nile and east of modern Tunisia, is one of the possible sources. Some of the culture traits that are usually identified as Libyan also sifted into the Nile Valley and, in fact, some of them may have originated there, or even have spread from West Asia. The most obvious connections of Crete with the area west of the Nile were in items of costume, the penis sheath and the fashion of wearing hair with a side-lock falling in front of the ear. Our evidence for these items in Crete is post-Neolithic but they are part of a Libyan element in the early cultures of the Nile delta and may well have been introduced to the island in Neolithic times. In addition, skeletal remains from Crete are reminiscent of Libyan ones, but this is not very meaningful, for both areas were populated by the same statured, olive-skinned Mediterranean type of man. Certain ties with

X

the Nile are more definite: these include fragments of stone vases that may actually be Egyptian, the mace, and pottery that seems to be copied from predynastic or early Dynastic Egyptian models. It is possible that the ubiquitous double-axe was also derived from Egypt and was introduced at this period, though actual evidence of it does not appear until early Minoan times.

Evidence for contacts with Mesopotamia are specially noticeable in certain pottery types which in Crete are quite similar to those of early levels on the Syrian and Palestinian coasts. Figurines found in Cretan Neolithic deposits are also probably of Asian origin.

The Neolithic occupation was a relatively sparse one; people lived in scattered homesteads and farmed small tracts of land, though the particular crops are not definitely known. Stone celts (ungrooved axes) were used for clearing land, fighting, and perhaps hunting. A few houses, especially from the later years of the period, have been found; they are of mud and stone construction at the base but may have been built with sun-dried bricks in the upper portions. Architecture generally was rather crude. A similar Neolithic culture was spreading through the Cyclades, islands in the southern Aegean, north of Crete. Even before the Cretan settlement, Neolithic sites were beginning to appear on the Greek mainland. In the late third millennium this whole area became so strongly influenced by Crete that the Helladic cultures of Greece were in part a reflection of Minoan.

The date of the first Neolithic in Crete is still uncertain. We can conveniently use the figure of 5000 B.C. if we remember that there may have been a number of occupations at different times. The Neolithic peoples gradually spread over the eastern portion of the island, settling well-known places such as Knossos, Phaistos, Mokhlos, and Vasilike. The rugged west and even much of central Crete seems to have been largely uninhabited and the population pressure was probably quite low. Though Crete in later days considered the sea of utmost importance, we know nothing of sea voyaging in the Neolithic period. There must have been boats, not only to bring the settlers but also for the trade goods that have been occasionally found: obsidian from the Cyclades, copper axes from Mesopotamia or Egypt, and stone vases from Egypt.

The famous archaeologist Sir Arthur Evans who began his Cretan excavations and detailed explorations in 1900, continuing them for many years, has divided the preclassic period of Crete into three periods which he called Minoan after the King Minos of Greek legend. These periods are Early Minoan, Middle Minoan, and Late Minoan and each is divided into subperiods I, II, and III (actually even finer distinctions were made as time went on, for example, Middle Minoan IIa). In our broad outline of Minoan culture we will principally discuss the major divisions.

Early Minoan began around 3000 B.C. and originated in eastern and southern Crete, with the central portion of the island lagging somewhat behind. Actually, though some new influences were coming in, there must have been a period of some hundreds of years before the full implications of the Minoan period were realized. It involved the rise of towns, use of copper, and the appearance of specialists, among them, architects, metal workers, jewel makers, and merchants. New coastal towns were settled, Palaikastro in the extreme east, Pseira off the northeast coast, Gournia near Merabellou Bay, while Mokhlos, though originally a Neolithic site, now became much larger. There is some indication of actual migration of both Libyans and West Asians to the island and certainly trade was increasing. Especially in the latter part of the Early Minoan period, relations with the Cyclades were strong and constant and it is possible that Crete was already laying the foundation for the massive influence she exerted later over the Aegean islands and adjacent mainland. It is very doubtful if there was any island-wide unity in Early Minoan times—in fact three regional areas, central, southern, and eastern, can be defined, and even within these regions individual towns or townlets may have been autonomous. Religion in Early Minoan times is not well known but it seems an outgrowth of the Neolithic "nature worship." Actually the germs of the typical Minoan religion of a later period were surely present, though we have no really good evidence for it. There are long copper daggers, though organized warfare seems relatively rare. Some statuary appears but it is still rather crude; the most skillfully worked objects in Early Minoan times are seals; stamp

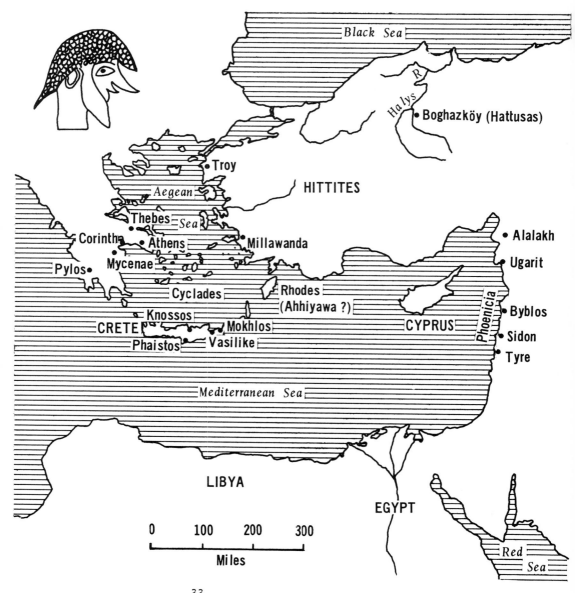

Black Sea

Halys R.

• Boghazköy (Hattusas)

• Troy

HITTITES

Aegean

Thebes

Sea

Corinth

Athens

Millawanda

Pylos•

• Mycenae

Cyclades

Rhodes
(Ahhiyawa ?)

• Alalakh

• Ugarit

Phoenicia

Knossos

CRETE

Mokhlos

CYPRUS

• Byblos

Phaistos

Vasilike

• Sidon

• Tyre

Mediterranean Sea

LIBYA

EGYPT

| 0 | 100 | 200 | 300 |

Miles

Red
Sea

33
The Minoan-Mycenaean world

seals, cylinder seals, three-sided seals (some of the latter may possibly be dice). Ivory was a favorite material for carving seals; in this regard we can recall that ivory was very popular in the contemporary Sumerian cities and, at least at a later date, was lavishly used at Alalakh on the Orontes. Some of the seal designs are abstract, geometric or curvilinear forms, while others reproduce native animals as well as apes or monkeys and lions; the former, at any rate, not native to the island. A series of Egyptian seals and scarabs from the First Intermediate Period (roughly, 2200 to 2000 B.C.) have been found, and these seem to have influenced Minoan art to some degree, although there was Asian influence as well, particularly in figurines. The Early Minoan individual was becoming a connoisseur of jewelry, and to this period must be dated the first work in gold, including gold appliqué. Pottery forms became stablized by the end of the Early Minoan; few new shapes were to be made throughout the rest of Minoan times. There was considerable experimentation with pottery decoration which led, probably for technical reasons of firing, to a light-on-dark ware that remained popular for many hundreds of years.

The Middle Minoan appears around, or perhaps somewhat after, 2000 B.C. and saw a definite shift of emphasis to the north coast and the central area of Crete. At the same time roads were beginning to connect the various towns, a very important one leading across the island from the emerging city of Knossos to the port of Komo near Phaistos on the south coast. It is impossible to tell the degree of unity of the island at the beginning of the period, but a standardization took place fairly rapidly. Early in the Middle Minoan there was the beginning of a palace at Knossos. If nothing else, this strongly suggests the growth of a wealthy class and indeed such a group is demonstrated by the fact that elaborate houses now appeared in the larger towns. Construction of these houses was usually in stone, in stone rubble with slab lining, or in sun-dried bricks. To the early part of the Middle Minoan probably belongs the first traces of the drainage system at Knossos. Even today Crete is remembered for its fine Minoan plumbing, but we must keep in mind that the Cretans were late; Harappa and Mohenjo-Daro had city-wide drains in the third millennium.

There is considerable evidence of costume and of other aspects of life from the graphic arts of the period. Figurines of men, naked except for the codpiece, and women with long skirts but bare-breasted, appear early in Middle Minoan. Later the Cretans were turning out figurines of female deities whose elegant costume doubtless copied that of upper-class Cretan women of the times. Skirts were full and a bodice reached from the skirt to the neck. It was, however, cut away in front to leave the breasts bare. Hats were very elaborate and the whole effect was one of high style.

Trade contacts were surely widespread and can be demonstrated by actual imports and exports. A Middle Minoan vase has been found in an Egyptian tomb while a statue from Twelfth Dynasty Egypt, or possibly Thirteenth Dynasty, was discovered at Knossos. These are but two examples of a series of cross ties with Egypt, dating mainly from the Twelfth Dynasty. Finds of Middle Minoan potsherds have also been made in Cyprus, on the Syrian coast, in the Cyclades, and in Greece. Crete gained considerably from these contacts. The potter's wheel was introduced, probably from Egypt or West Asia, and the wheel was also used for transportation—a model of a four-wheeled cart comes from this period. True bronze also appears as does the faience technique, the latter almost certainly introduced from Egypt. Another Middle Minoan invention, quite obviously due to Egyptian stimulation, was a hieroglyphic script. This was mainly a matter of idea diffusion, though a few signs—for example, the Egyptian ankh, or cross of life, ☥ —were clearly borrowed.

All too little is known about agriculture, but certainly wheat and other grain crops, the olive tree, and probably the vine were cultivated. Most of the Near Eastern domesticated animals had been introduced by Middle Minoan times: sheep and goats, the cow and pig; however, our first evidence for the horse comes from Late Minoan times. This animal was likely introduced to draw a chariot, a military weapon which came late to Crete, presumably because of the rough terrain. Probably oxen were used to draw carts and ploughs, but there is no definite evidence on this point.

The Cretans were active traders, employing ships of the basic high-prowed type that was widespread in the

34
*Cycladic marble statuette:*
*seated man with harp, c.*
*2500 B.C.*

Near East for thousands of years. These vessels had oars
and sails, were used in the lively import-export trade,
and may have formed the rudiments of a navy as well.

The religion of the Cretans by Middle Minoan times
is reasonably clear to us. Central to the religious beliefs
was a Mother, or Earth, Goddess shown in the courtly
bare-breasted costume of the Cretan lady. She has a
consort, a young boy, probably a son, and the two may
be the Cretan equivalent of the Syrian and Mesopotamian mother-son pairs in which the son, representing
the yearly seasonal change in vegetation, dies and is
reborn each year. It has been suggested that actual
Cretan youths chosen for this role were sacrificed at the
end of a year at which time a successor, representing

*Crete*

the rebirth of vegetation in spring, was chosen. This yearly sacrifice was carried out elsewhere, but we have no proof for it in Crete.

Sacred to the Mother Goddess was the dove; indeed, she may have absorbed an older dove goddess, derived from Egypt. The double-axe was her symbol, as was the snake; for example, one of the most famous statues of Crete shows this goddess with snakes wrapped around her arms. The snake was probably a house deity and "snake tubes" were found in Middle Minoan houses and shrines, presumably for communication with this friendly little daemon. The Mother is also associated with rustic shrines often in wild mountain settings where she appeared as mistress of wild animals and trees. At these shrines there was sacrifice of animals, their blood being poured on or into the ground, almost certainly a fertility rite. Her fertility aspect is also emphasized by phalli associated with these shrines.

One animal, the bull, was given vast importance, and was the object of elaborate bullbaitings, seemingly major social affairs in later Crete. The bull cult, wherever its point of origin, eventually spread to the far ends of the Mediterranean; the Spanish bullfight is a faint echo of it. It is also tempting to consider the bull a sky god as he was in other parts of the Near East, and to see a Cretan prototype in the bull aspects of the later Greek god Zeus. This may be the case, though the identification is by no means certain. The Mother, herself, was basically Asiatic in origin and her cult spread very early not only to Crete but to many other Mediterranean lands. We can only guess at the ceremonies held in her honor but they were surely diversified, for several later Greek goddesses took on various of her characteristics. One was the pre-Greek household deity Athena, whose association with serpents suggest the Mother, though the virgin aspects that were stressed in classic times were likely a Greek addition. In any event, her name is non-Greek even though she became the tutelary goddess of Athens, most famous of Greek cities. Aphrodite in all probability inherited the fertility aspects of the Mother Goddess and, to some degree, also represented the earlier deity in her maternal aspects. Artemis, the Roman Diana, was even more closely identified with the Mother Goddess, for she became the later Lady of the Wild Animals. In general, what seems to have happened in late Mycenaean and classic times was the replacement of the Earth Mother by elevation of the sky god Zeus to the center of the religious system. The Mother then became fragmented, her worship merged with that of subordinate or foreign female deities who finally took over most of her aspects and functions.

The second phase of Middle Minoan came to an end with a severe earthquake—Crete was, and is, very active tectonically. The succeeding period, the last part of Middle Minoan, is characterized by a dramatic rise of the palaces at Knossos and Phaistos. These were built on older foundations but have the full development of great halls, staircases, colonnades around interior courts, and decoration in fresco, that traditionally is associated with Minoan Crete. This is the type of architecture which Sir Leonard Woolley once suggested might have been developed at Alalakh in the Orontes valley and then transported as a complex to Crete, with Syrian architects actually directing Cretan palace construction. In this regard we should remember that Crete and the Orontes area had been interchanging ideas over hundreds of years, and the question of who influenced whom is probably a complicated one.

There is a good possibility that in this final phase of Middle Minoan, Crete was not only achieving political unity but was extending her influence throughout the Aegean. This is the time when the Mycenaean centers were beginning to develop and their ties with Crete can be seen in ceramic decoration and in wall paintings.

The Late Minoan period, beginning around 1550 B.C., brought the fruition of Cretan culture, with tremendous building programs especially at Knossos and Phaistos. A number of other towns were important, particularly in the eastern part of the island, and population was slowly spreading into the wild west of Crete. There is a fair chance that Knossos was the capital of a united Crete and that it controlled a great deal of the Aegean world. Certainly Crete had naval supremacy at this point and her commerce was far flung.[1] The palaces show something of the magnificence of life at great centers like Knossos and Phaistos. Frescoes, vases, and seals give glimpses of the very active life of the time.

The depicted scenes range from religious processions to naturalistic sketches; a famous one of the latter type, from Hagia Triadha near Phaistos, shows a cat stalking a pheasant through undergrowth. From this period also date the bull ring scenes where young men and women practice somersaulting onto backs of bulls by grasping the animals' horns. It has often been suggested that these youths and maidens were captives specially trained for the bull ring, and represented a tribute demanded by King Minos from his Aegean kingdom. Such at least is indicated by the later Greek story of Theseus. The legend, in brief, describes how the Cretans every nine years (or perhaps every year) exacted a tribute of boys and girls to be sacrificed to the Minotaur, a monster, half bull, half man, who roamed a specially constructed maze known as the labyrinth. With the Athenian quota of fourteen went the Athenian king's son, Theseus. The daughter of Minos, Ariadne, fell in love with Theseus, gave him a sword with which to slay the Minotaur and a ball of thread by which he could retrace his steps through the labyrinth. This being done, Theseus escaped with Ariadne to the isle of Naxos where he left her and sailed away with his companions.

The word labyrinth (place of the double-axe) suggests the palace at Knossos which, with its complex series of rooms, might be described as a maze. As the Cretan archaeologist J. D. S. Pendlebury (among others) has suggested, the victims, perhaps children of leading mainland families, might well have been brought to Knossos to be trained for the bull ring, as part of the imperial politics of Minoan kings.

Late Minoan contacts with various parts of the eastern Mediterranean were vigorous and widespread. At various times in Eighteenth Dynasty Egypt there appear pictures of Cretans (Kheftians) as well as material objects from Crete and from the mainland of Greece. There was contact with the Syrian coast and the Greek area proper had become quite Minoanized. One interesting example of this series of contacts is the appearance of Negro soldiers in Crete. There are various kinds of evidence for this, the most important being a Late Minoan painting at Knossos showing a double file of armed Negroes in military dress. The employment of mercenaries suggests the wealth and organization of a centralized Cretan state and also is another indication of contact with Egypt, for these soldiers probably came from the Upper Nile. This was the period in which Nilotic peoples were being drawn more and more into the cultural sphere of Egypt, and Nubians seem to have been in some demand as mercenaries. The effect of Nubian soldiers on the physical types and the cultures of the Aegean is unknown, but makes interesting speculation. At any rate, the appearance of exotic foreigners in the Cretan army gives us another of the fragments of data that suggest a Cretan empire.

The question of Cretan language has still not been solved. One line of evidence for language comes from the use of a script. Cretan hieroglyphics, even before the end of Middle Minoan times, were developing into the more cursive Linear A. By Late Minoan times Linear A inscriptions were found in many parts of Crete. It has not been deciphered, but the language of the Linear A, presumably that spoken by the Cretans, was not Greek. Some Cretan words survived into later Greek, mainly place names or names of plants; especially important are names that end in *ossos* or *assos* (Knossos, Halicarnassos) or in *nth* (Corinth, hyacinth). One important later word is thalassa (sea or ocean) which is presumably Cretan (at least it was originally non-Greek). If the Greeks moved to the Aegean from some continental homeland, it is logical that they would take over this name from seafaring indigenes. It is always risky to make definite language affiliations on the basis of a few words, but the *assos* names at least do suggest Luvian.[2]

From the site of Knossos and from two sites on the mainland, Mycenae and Pylos, come finds of another script obviously derived from Linear A, but distinctive; it has been given the name Linear B. This script is in the form of a syllabary of some eighty to ninety syllables (da, ro, pa, te, and so forth) an idea that perhaps diffused from Syria. Due to the work of M. G. F. Ventris, John Chadwick, Emmett L. Bennett, A. E. Kober, C. W. Blegan, and others we can say, with reasonable probability, that Linear B was the script of an archaic form of Greek.[3] Some uncertainty remains as to the dating of the Knossos Linear B tablets. Around

1400 B.C. there was a massive attack of some sort, in which many of the major cities of Crete were destroyed. It is very tempting to see this as a raid by Greek-speakers who had previously settled in southern Greece, picked up Minoan ways and Minoan overlords, and who now threw off Cretan hegemony. One difficulty is that Evans, who excavated the Cretan Linear B tablets, assigned them to the period before this systematic sacking of Knossos—thus indicating that Greek was being spoken in Crete during at least part of the period of Minoan power. This is quite possible of course; the Greeks may have been infiltrating the island for centuries. However, in 1960 Professor L. R. Palmer of Oxford University put forth another explanation. He suggests, on re-examination of field notes from the Evans excavations, that the Linear B tablets—mostly inventory or tax lists—should be dated later than the invasion, in other words, after 1400 B.C., at which time the Greeks presumably had settled the island in numbers and were becoming linguistically dominant. Palmer's ideas have been criticized by other experts and of course may not be valid. Nevertheless, certain mainland features appear in the later period, an important one being the popular tholos (tomb) which in Crete is probably an indication that a Greek aristocracy was now on the scene.

The later history of Crete is clearly related to the Greek Aegean, for it fell to the Doric barbarians in the twelfth century B.C. In classic times the Doric dialect was the standard Cretan language (though there remained non-Doric and non-Greek pockets of speech). Prosperity continued, for even in the time of Homer Crete is known as a rich island with many cities. But the Minoan glory has been forgotten; in Homer, Crete has truly entered the Greek world.

ONE GETS the impression that the Hittites came out of obscurity, dominated parts of West Asia for a time, then disappeared with almost breathtaking suddenness. Such an impression simply reflects the fact that for much of Hittite Anatolia we have only fragments of history. A few decades ago nothing was known even of the height of Hittite power; now we have at least filled part of the gap.[1] As yet most of the emphasis in Hittite study is on relations with regions east to the Euphrates and south to the Nile, the core area of early power politics. Actually, however, Hatti (the Hittite kingdom) had intense and important dealings with powers to the west, states of the Minoan and Mycenaean world. If Hittite aggression was not so intense in the west, it is almost certainly because Minoan and Greek neighbors controlled the seas; Hatti was always a land power.

One ethnic element of the Hittites may have been the Khirbet Kerak people who have already been discussed in Chapter IX. That particular group probably came originally from the Caucasus area to north Syria, and then drifted westward into west-central Anatolia, the area we now call Turkey. There is some archaeological evidence for such a migration, but the linguistic picture in the second millennium adds other complications, for some of the historic Hittites spoke an Indo-European language—indeed this was the official Hittite. We have already guessed that the Khirbet Kerak people were Hurrian-speaking and there may have been a Hurrian element in the Hittite kingdom. Certainly Hittite records tell of the various groups in Anatolia who were intermixed by historic times, and names that survive indicate that not all of them were Indo-European-speaking.

Actually Anatolia has a long history, with early agricultural communities appearing at about the same time as Jericho appeared on the Jordan. In the Konya plain of east-central Anatolia people lived on an advanced Neolithic level some eight thousand years ago. To the south, at the site of Mersin, near the Mediterranean coast, there is a long development from a Neolithic, beginning perhaps by 5000 B.C., through copper and bronze phases. In the west, Troy also began early (possibly 3000 B.C.) and there are other deeply stratified

## XI

*Hittites and Greeks*

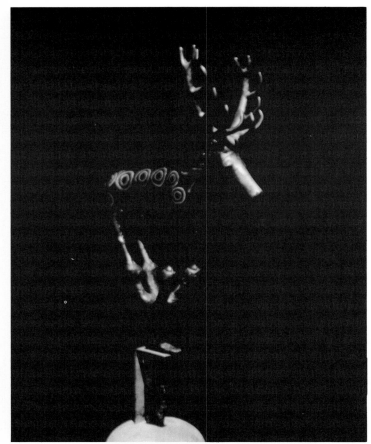

35
*Proto-Hittite bronze deer
with silver inlay, from Alaca
Hüyük near Boghazköy*

sites in central Anatolia. Eventually a detailed study may well establish Anatolia as one of the key areas of early civilization. At present we need much more data of the pre-Hittite period.

One curious interlude, even before the Hittites gained power, is given us from outsiders living in the area. For a century or more, on the outskirts of a city called Kanesh in east-central Anatolia, there lived a band of Mesopotamian merchants who wrote an early Assyrian dialect of Akkadian. The colony dates from about the end of the Third Dynasty of Ur (*c.* 1900 B.C.), for the name of King Ibi-Sin, last king of that Dynasty, is given in a document from this group. The colony was controlled by an organization known as the Karum, a sort of Chamber of Commerce, regulating trade and the relationships of the merchants with their Anatolian neighbors. They traded fabrics from Assyria

36
*Hittite pottery, Kanesh
(modern Kültepe)*

for copper, carnelian, amber, and a metal that may
have been iron.

The ancestry of the Hittites will undoubtedly be
clarified by future field work. What probably happened
is that small groups of Indo-European-speakers, of the
Hittite and related Luvian tongues, drifted into (or
were pushed into) Anatolia. They conquered and/or
intermixed with local tribes who themselves were not
culturally, linguistically, or racially homogeneous. The
newcomers managed to impose their speech on the
aboriginal inhabitants, though they doubtlessly absorbed a great many outside customs, especially in the
sphere of religion. The Hittites proper established
themselves at Hattusas near the present-day town of
Boghazköy not far from the Halys river.

By the seventeenth century B.C. the Hittite kings
were strong enough to launch imperialistic adventures

*Hittites and Greeks*

both east and west. In the west they pushed gradually toward the coast of Asia Minor where they encountered a number of small kingdoms (whose inhabitants spoke Luvian) and also, at this time, a Cretan-controlled Aegean. The push east and south, first against the state of Mitanni, was soon aimed at Egypt. At about the time of greatest Hittite power Egypt suffered a temporary decline. Under the rule of the reform-minded Pharaoh, Akhenaton, the Palestinian-Syrian Empire of Egypt was neglected. This coincided with a particularly aggressive Hittite king, Suppiluliumas, who began his rule about 1380 B.C. Suppiluliumas defeated the Mitanni and carried on a series of campaigns against Egypt. The fourteenth century was a trying one for the peoples of Palestine and Syria. Armies of the two great powers marched and countermarched up the coast, across the Esdraelon plain and inland to the upper Orontes. The key to control of the area was Kadesh on the Orontes river and here in 1286 B.C., a famous battle was fought between the army of Pharaoh Rameses II and that of the Hittite King Muwatallis. Modern writers disagree as to the outcome of this battle; assessments range from a smashing victory for the Egyptians to a terrible defeat in which Rameses was lucky to escape with his life. Actually it seems to have been somewhat of a draw; both royal armies were too far from home. The outcome was a peace treaty that essentially marked the end of Hittite-Egyptian rivalry. The Egyptians were becoming too impoverished to sustain a Syrian empire, and Hatti could not hold the Palestinian South. The treaty itself was a tacit admission of weakness on both sides and both countries now deterio-

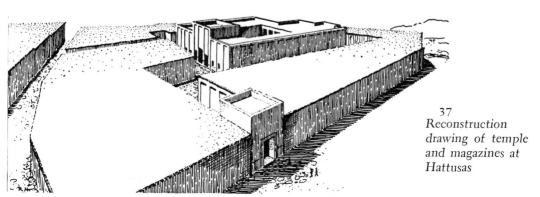

37
Reconstruction drawing of temple and magazines at Hattusas

Courtesy Oriental Institute, University of Chicago

38
*Goddess, post-Hittite or Phrygian period at Boghazköy, around 600 B.C.*

rated, the Hittites with explosive speed. Around 1200 B.C., the "Peoples of the Sea," or some other migrating group, destroyed Hattusas and put an end to Hittite power, though not, in fact, to the Hittites.[2]

The Hittite Empire disappeared and there was a general cultural decline in both the Anatolian and Aegean areas, nevertheless, local Hittite states continued to flourish in western Asia Minor and on the upper Euphrates from 1200 B.C. until the eighth century when such classic kingdoms as Lydia and the Greek Ionian cities took the stage. In the sixth century Persia overran Anatolia, as did Greeks and Romans in later centuries. The hinterland of Asia Minor was for a long period under Roman control, first ruled by Rome itself then by New Rome or Byzantium. Eventually, Turkic-speaking tribesmen moved into Asia Minor, giving it the modern name Turkey. Radiating from it they created an empire even more extensive than that of the Hittites.

What, then, did Hittites offer to early civilization? They were, like the Mycenaean Greeks, latecomers on the scene. Much of their culture was obviously borrowed from Mesopotamia or Syria. The Hittites learned to write using a cuneiform syllabary to render the Hittite language. The earliest period of this writing can be dated at about 1700 B.C. and is a variant form of Akkadian script. Actually there are a great number of records (some thousands of clay tablets from Boghazköy) mostly written in Akkado-Babylonian, not so surprising when one considers the fact that this was the diplomatic language of much of the ancient Near East, used, for example, in the Egyptian Amarna letters of Akhenaton. Additional data on the Hittites came to light when the philologist B. Hrozný deciphered the Hittite tablets, written in cuneiform, but in the Hittite language itself. A third type of writing was a hieroglyphic system that was used for carved inscriptions and for seals, and which was found throughout much of the

39
*Lion Gate at Hattusas*

Courtesy Turkish Tourism and Information Office, New York

40
*Relief figures of Hittite
deities, sanctuary at
Yazilikaya near Boghazköy*

Hittite land. The hieroglyphics vaguely suggest those of Egypt and those of Cretan pre-Linear A, although in both cases more in general spirit than in specificity. These were finally deciphered when a late example of them was found with a parallel Phoenician document. This example is actually from well after the end of Hittite power, dating from the reign of a king named Asitawandas (or Asitawatas) who ruled from Karatepe south of the Halys river. The date of Asitawandas is probably late eighth century B.C., thus bridging the gap between the Hittite glory of the Empire and the extensive realignments of power and peoples at the beginnings of the classic period.

Thanks to the texts and to the silent evidence of the ruined cities we know a considerable amount about Hittite life. At Hattusas vast military works are found; these include imposing walls decorated with giant figures of men and animals. Friezes of soldiers or of deities cut in relief along cliff faces are carved awkwardly, but do give a considerable feeling of power. The use of massive sculptured animals to flank gateways is reminiscent of the Mycenaean; Hattusas has its lion gate, as does Mycenae. As might be expected the decorative motifs often resemble those of Mesopotamia, especially in the use of balanced animal figures. Many of the reliefs, though distinctively Hittite, share certain features of the Ancient Near East; the stiffness of line, use of the full-face eye, and uncertainty of other perspectives, show that Hittite artists had learned their lessons from neighbors to the east and south. Temples in Hatti

*Hittites and Greeks*
111

never reached the size and impressiveness of those in Mesopotamia and Egypt. More time was spent on the citadels and palaces.

When we first find the Hittites (as Hittites) they are already an intensive agricultural and herding people and had domesticated the horse. One of the major reasons for Hittite success in war was the horse-drawn chariot, a mainstay of their armies. But they had no monopoly; this weapon had spread from India on the east to Greece on the west by about 1500 B.C. and was carried by the Hyksos as far south as Egypt. It is interesting that the oldest text on horse breeding was written in Hittite, though composed by a native of Mitanni. The Hittites were somewhat involved in one important contribution to civilization, the systematic smelting of iron. Actually the Hittites did not use any great amount of iron and possibly Mitanni was also instrumental in producing the metal. It was employed for weapons; an iron battle-axe dating about 1300 B.C., comes from Ugarit. Swords and daggers were occasionally used and the Hittites also seemed to have worked iron for jewelry.

It was in post-Hittite kingdom times that large scale iron-working appeared, perhaps spreading from Anatolia to Europe and the Mediterranean lands. It reached China later, around 500 B.C. The main value in iron lies in its cheapness, availability, and once advanced smelting and tempering techniques had been devised, its hardness. As a result, iron hoes, spades, axes, saws, tongs, and files became common, as well as purely military, tools. The Hittites were early and only partly successful in their use of iron; it was the first millennium B.C. that became the true Iron Age for civilization.[3]

Whereas the prehistoric sequences for the historic Hittites have not been well-worked out (giving the impression that Hatti arrived as a kind of Near Eastern *deus ex machina*), those of Greece are better known. We have already discussed the development of Cretan culture from Neolithic to the influential civilization of Middle and Late Minoan. The Cyclades north of Crete may in fact have received their first cultural impulses from Anatolia but they soon fell within the Cretan orbit.[4] Farther north along the coast of Greece there developed a series of cultures now known as the Helladic. Following the Trinitarian tendencies of Mediterranean archaeologists there is an Early, a Middle, and a Late Helladic, each segment divided again into three parts. These do not, in fact, correlate with their Minoan equivalents being, especially in the earlier period, a bit more recent.[5]

Early Helladic was preceded by the Sesklo and Dimini cultures, Neolithic with western Asiatic affiliations; and before Sesklo there is evidence of earlier contact perhaps from the Syrian or southern Anatolian coast.[6] The Early Helladic seems to represent a spread of influence from the Aegean or from the Anatolian coast. Certainly Cycladic elements were present, especially in a burnished dark-ware that seems to have western Asiatic affiliation and appears also in Sicily and perhaps even farther west. By the middle of Early Helladic times Cretan influence was beginning to infiltrate the mainland and near the end of the Early Helladic the Cretan dark-on-white wares began to appear.[7]

Middle Helladic was introduced by an invasion of peoples from outside the area, presumably from the north. These may have been Luvian-speakers, or the first Greeks, or possibly even some unknown third group. At any rate, the Middle Helladic begins around 1800 b.c. The newcomers were well-acquainted with the use of bronze weapons; they also introduced a type of cist burial which was ancestral to the later shaft tombs and probably to the still later tholoi. Middle Helladic ceramics are quite distinctive, especially a gray or yellow ware known locally as silver and gold Minyan.

Actually, though we are concentrating on Helladic, there were a number of parallel cultures in this part of the eastern Mediterranean. The Cycladic and Minoan have already been discussed; there were other local developments in the Troad and adjacent areas, in Thrace, and in Macedonia. None of these cultures were particularly advanced, their origins are obscure and they eventually fell, to greater or lesser degree, under the influence of Minoan and later Helladic cultures.

During the course of Middle Helladic there was a rise in size and influence of a number of towns, especially those on the Argive plain in the eastern Peloponnesus in Greece. The most important sites were Mycenae and

Tiryns, with the former probably the dominant power in the area.

At this time it seems reasonable that Minoan Crete was extending her influence over the Aegean and was perhaps beginning to interfere more and more in the internal affairs of the mainland cities. In this period there was some trade with the civilizations to the south and east, but also trade within the Aegean, and additionally there was contact with the barbarian north. There were several things that central and western Europe could offer the Aegean; perhaps the most crucial was tin for bronze-making (an alloy well-established by the Middle Helladic), though amber from the Baltic area was already ages old as a trade commodity. Probably even by early Helladic times slaves were trickling from the north to be scattered throughout the Mediterranean world. This was to continue for at least two thousand years, thus further complicating the complex racial makeup of Mediterranean peoples. A number of things seem to have been offered in return. Perfumed oil in stirrup-jars is indicated by later Linear B tablets and by archaeological finds. Wine was another export of Crete and the mainland alike, and other luxury goods including faience beads were also traded. It is the cutomary fare calculated to attract barbarians—flashy beads and alcohol.

The Helladic cities were never very large; the main citadel area of Mycenae, even in its heyday, was only some eleven acres. Actually, much of the population may have lived in villages surrounding the ceremonial and military centers; this is the pattern we will see in the Americas.

In the absence of written (or deciphered) records it is a bit risky to reconstruct too much; still it seems probable that Cretan artisans and specialists, such as potters, metal workers, architects and builders, metallurgists, and others, had spread over much of the Aegean world and were strongly affecting local crafts and local cultures. These artisans, like the nineteenth century (A.D.) European missionaries, may have been, willingly or not, the means of spreading Cretan power. The various craftsmen, however, regardless of their original point of origin, made interesting innovations. We have seen how Crete herself not only initiated a tradition of fine pottery—for unlike most of the civilized world the pottery did not decline stylistically with the introduction of the wheel—but also began excellent traditions in painting, stone carving, and in design. The elegant pottery, on which the mass production aspects of the fast wheel failed to have its usual vulgarizing effect on design, became rather a trademark in the Aegean world, and Athenian wine and oil vessels, a thousand years after the Helladic era, are so beautiful that we treasure them today.

The Late Helladic period, beginning around or a little after 1600 B.C., showed a continuation of the wealth and, indeed, the Minoanization of the mainland cities. This period is often called the Mycenaean, a tribute to the importance of that Argive city, and we will so call it here. The shaft tombs that characterize the early part of the period show something of the wealth of the times. These shafts are cut into the rock that closely underlies the surface soil at Mycenae. The largest chamber is about 13 by 20 feet, the deepest is something over 12 feet. They were probably burial chambers for important families, for they contain bronze weapons, gold and silver utensils and ornaments, including goblets, rings, bracelets, and earrings. Other luxury goods include amber, agate, and amethyst.

The later history of the Mycenaean period is one of increasing power and influence. Mycenae was only one of a series of successful centers. Another was probably the subject city of Tiryns, and others included Pylos, Corinth, and Eleusis and Athens in Attica. This latter site may have been of considerable importance; unfortunately, the Mycenaean settlement is now deeply buried under the modern city. In the Aegean Islands and in Asia Minor itself were other centers of power. By Mycenaean times these were Greek-speaking, or at least Greek was rapidly infiltrating the Aegean area.

About 1400 B.C. we can see, though only in a dim and distorted way, a major power shift in the eastern Mediterranean. The power of Minos was broken, probably by attack from the mainland. Actually, no one is sure that Mycenae was engaged in the revolt against the Cretans or that she emerged as the leader of the Greek world—remember that the Theseus story specifically singles out Athens as the leader against Crete. Homeric legend and the story told by the archaeologists, however, suggest the importance of Mycenae. At about this time massive walls gird the city which is entered through gates flanked with great stone lions. The richness of Mycenae, suggested by grave goods, indicates that part of the Mediterranean trade was passing into her hands. However, we cannot discount the importance of Athens and of cities of kingdoms farther east; it is unlikely that Mycenae was the center of an extensive kingdom.[8]

One interesting trend at Mycenae was the development of regular chamber-tombs and, finally, of the tholos (beehive shaped tomb), a chamber with a corbeled vaulted roof, the interior projecting stones being chiseled smooth to give the rounded beehive appearance. Like the earlier shaft graves, these seem to have been used by important families. An interesting facet of religion is shown in the grave goods of this period, especially in the use of terra-cotta figurines. One group of these, normally found with children, seems to be the familiar Mother Goddess in her most maternal aspect, protector and guardian of the tiny unfortunates in the tombs.

The Mycenaean period saw the use of Linear B script.[9] This seems to be an archaic form of Greek and hence readable,[10] though, to date, the inscriptions and clay tablets found (the latter at Pylos, Mycenae, and Knossos,[11] the former at a number of sites) have given relatively little information. Paradoxically, in some ways we know more about the eastern extension of Mycenaean culture. The Hittites' state archives at Hattusas contain mention of regions lying west of Hittite territory. The most important of these are the states of Ahhiyawa and Lazpa. Ahhiyawa is very probably the Homeric Achaea and Lazpa may have been the island of Lesbos. A city known to the Hittites as Millawanda seems to have been somewhere near the Maeander river in Asia Minor and is probably a forerunner of the historic Miletus.[12] It owed allegiance to Ahhiyawa, and the fact that the Hittites at the height of their power maintained a respectful attitude toward this mainland plum suggests that the home kingdom Ahhiyawa was on an island (or at least not in Anatolia) with sufficient

| | ANATOLIA | | CRETE | GREECE AND AEGEAN | SICILIAN AREA | |
|---|---|---|---|---|---|---|
| 1000BC | | Syro–Hittites | | Sub Minoan–Mycenaean | | Late Bronze |
| 1200 | | Troy VIIb | | | | |
| | Late Hittite | Troy VIIa | | Late Helladic (Mycenaean) | Thaspos / Milazzese | Middle Bronze |
| 1400 | Late Bronze | Troy VI | Late Minoan | | Capo Graziano | |
| | | (Late) | | | Castelluccio | |
| 1600 | Middle Bronze | | | | | Early Bronze |
| | Hittites | Troy VI | Middle | Middle Helladic – Minyan | | |
| 1800 | | Karum at Kanesh | (Early) Troy V | Minoan | (First Greek Speakers ?) | |
| | | | Troy IV | | | |
| 2000 | Bronze | | | | Local | Late Copper |
| 2200 | | Troy III | | Early | Traditions | Middle Copper |
| | | | Early | | | |
| 2400 | Early | Troy II | | Helladic | in | |
| 2600 | Cultures | | | | Sicily, | Early Copper |
| | | | Minoan | | Southern Italy, | |
| 2800 | | Troy I | | | the Aeolian | |
| 3000 | | | | | and Lipari | Painted Pottery |
| 3200 | | Mersin | | Dimini | Islands and | |
| 3400 | | | | | Malta | |
| | | and | Cretan | | | |
| 3600 | | | | | Ghar Dalam | |
| 3800 | Age | other | | | Stentinello | |
| 4000 | | | | | | |
| 4200 | Upper | local | Neolithic | Sesklo | | |
| 4400 | | traditions | | | | |
| 4600 | | | | | | |
| 4800 | | Neolithic | | Pre–Sesklo Neolithic | | |

41

*Comparative chronologies—Eastern and Central Mediterranean*

control of the seas to render her safe from Hittite ambitions. This kingdom probably was on the island of Rhodes,[13] though it may have been Mycenae or even Crete;[14] much spadework needs to be done in this area.

The Achaeans and Mycenaeans, in general, avoided the disaster that barbarian invasions visited on the Hittites around 1200 B.C. In fact they seem to have joined in the general wanderlust; in 1219 B.C. the Akkaiwash (that is, Ahhiyawa or Achaeans) made a major attack on Egypt. Another group, called Danaoi by Homer and

*Hittites and Greeks*

Danuna by the Egyptians, are known from the early fifteenth century and were one of the groups, collectively called "Peoples of the Sea," that struck Egypt around 1200. Both the Achaeans and the Danaoi were literate, for the better-known powers corresponded with them (the Hittite correspondence with Ahhiyawa extends over a considerable period of time and concerns a variety of things).

The Mycenaeans had inherited sea power from Minoans and were now rulers of the eastern Mediterranean, but their hegemony was quickly challenged. New groups of barbarian peoples began to filter into Thrace and into Greece proper in the twelfth century. Some of these were Greek-speaking, the iron-using Dorians. Around 1100 B.C. the flood of barbarians swept over the Peloponnesus carrying Dorian speech and rude manners and destroying the Mycenaean cities. The impetus carried these newcomers to Crete and Rhodes, both of which in classic times were largely Dorian-speaking. The Dorian wave faltered at Athens and it never reached the Ionic coast of Asia Minor. Still the damage was done, the balance of civilization was upset, and the Aegean entered on a dark age.[15]

By the beginning of the eighth century the Greeks were making a recovery on the Ionian coast, an area originally non-Greek but settled by refugees fleeing from the Dorians. Around 750 B.C. population pressure began to tell in Ionia and to some extent in Greece proper. The Greeks went adventuring again into the western Mediterranean, establishing very early colonies at Ischia (c. 750) and Cumae (possibly 740) in the Bay of Naples. Syracuse in Sicily was traditionally settled in 734 B.C., a date that seems to fit the archaeological facts. By 700 B.C. a number of Sicilian and south Italian settlements had been made and the Greeks were actively trading with the Etruscans. By 600 B.C. the Greeks had reached coastal France (Massalia), and northeastern Spain was settled, or would be in a short time. At this point the Greek colonists met the full force of Etruscan and Punic opposition and the centuries that followed were ones of retrenchment. Eventually Rome gobbled up Etruria, Carthage, and Greece-in-the-West.

No discussion of the early Greeks should ignore

*Lion Gate, Mycenae*

*Courtesy* **George E. Mylonas**

Homer! The historic Greeks had a series of epic poems relating to the glorious past; of these we now have the *Iliad* and the *Odyssey*, composed, so the ancient Greeks said, by a blind poet named Homer. The *Iliad* dealt with a great war against Troy in Asia, to recover a beautiful woman, and the later *Odyssey* describes the adventures of one of the Greek heros, Odysseus, when he tried to return from Troy to his native Ithaca on the west coast of Greece. In the *Iliad* the chief leaders are from Mycenae, the most important being Agamemnon, son of Atreus. A tholos at Mycenae, called from ancient times the Treasury of Atreus, may possibly be the tomb of Agamemnon's father—at least it dates from about 1250 B.C., while the Trojan war took place around 1200 B.C. (1184 is the traditional date for the fall of Troy).

The Ancients considered Homer to be history, but in more recent times there was a great tendency to discredit the entire story. However, Heinrich Schliemann, a German amateur archaeologist, discovered at Hissarlik on the Dardanelles a series of "Troys," one of which was presumably the city destroyed by the Achaean horde. The later discoveries of Schliemann at Mycenae and of Sir Arthur Evans at Knossos made it clear that the old stories must be re-evaluated.

For a time it was thought that Homer was describing the Mycenaean world but it now seems clear that this was not the case. Certainly, many of the stories and legends came down from that period, but the general makeup of the *Iliad* is ninth or eighth century B.C. which places it in the archaeological period known as the Geometric, so called because of the balanced designs on the wheel-made pottery. Gone is the sophistication of the Mycenaean world, with its written records and international commerce. The heroes of the *Iliad* did use bronze instead of iron, but this seems a deliberate archaism. They used chariots (a war weapon of Mycenaean times, discarded by the time of early Iron Age Greece) but seemed not to know what to do with them in warfare; they were simply used to carry the heroes to and from the battlefield. Another war device, the Mycenaean figure-eight shield, had completely disappeared. The Homeric Greeks cremated their dead, while the Mycenaeans buried theirs, as did later, classic Greeks. This cremation complex, incidentally, was part of a late Bronze Age and early Iron Age fashion that was practiced by Late Bronze Urnfield people in western and central Europe, by the early Early Iron Age Villanovans of Italy, and by some of the Etruscans. If this method was dominant in Greece, it was of very short duration. Such parts of the Mycenaean social structure as are revealed in the translations from Linear B are different from those of Homer's time. The politi-

43
*Defensive wall, Mycenae*

44
*Portal at Mycenae*

cal organization of the Homeric warriors was a loose
kind of feudalism, something like that of the early
Middle Ages of Europe, not what we would expect
from the bureaucratic trading states of Mycenaean
times. The gods of Homer are Olympian, with the
thunder god, Zeus, supreme; the Mother appears only
in her fractionized forms, that is, as Athena and
Aphrodite. Of really powerful chthonic goddesses there
is no hint; this surely cannot be Mycenaean.[16]

Who indeed was Homer? The controversy still goes
on, and though a final answer cannot be given, we will
make some suggestions here. The *Iliad* was probably
assembled by one man in the late nineth or early eighth
century B.C.[17] The poet likely came from the eastern
part of the Greek area, perhaps from the Ionian coast
itself. Since its author was a bard (a position very old
and widespread in Indo-European tradition), he
chanted or sang parts or all of the poem at public affairs

*Hittites and Greeks*

conducted or sponsored by the nobility. Some elements in the *Iliad* (for example the catalogue in Book II) are probably earlier than the historic Homer and may date from a Mycenaean legend.[18] Clearly there were a number of epic poems current during the dark ages of Greece; we know a little of the others from later quotations or summaries, but only the brilliant *Iliad* has come to us essentially intact. There has even been the suggestion that the *Iliad* in its structure is geometric, that is, balanced in its various parts, as an analogy to the skillfully designed geometric pottery of that period.[19]

Thus, we can say that the *Iliad* represented the work of a poet possibly of around 800 B.C. He surely incorporated earlier work and doubtlessly borrowed from or exchanged material with, his contemporaries. The poet sang his songs for the loosely organized nobility of the type that appear in the *Iliad* and, though set in the past, this epic reflected much of the social, political, and economic life of Homer's time. The theme is of a Greek attack on Ilios. The name Troy, incidentally, was used less in the *Iliad* than Ilios, some 50 as against 106 times. It is perhaps significant that a different set of descriptive adjectives, for example, broad, great, holy, steep, is used with each name—only "well-walled" is shared by both.[20] For this and other reasons some scholars feel that the word Troy had not been definitely identified with this area of the Dardanelles and may actually refer to something else, possibly even to the Etruscans. In fact, though the descriptions in the *Iliad* point to the Troad, there is no real assurance that a large segment of the Greek world ever attacked a Troy on the Dardanelles. Troy, after all, is a small site. It only covered six acres at its most expansive period and this earlier city was destroyed about 1350 B.C., long before the Trojan War. There are certain other possibilities. A late Byzantine summary of one of the lost epics tells of a Greek attack at Teuthrania on the Aeolic coast. This story parallels the Trojan one and perhaps a general "Trojan" motif was used to account for various raids. Even more important is the part played by Egypt. Later writers (especially Euripides) speak of Helen's journey to Egypt and suggest that the country had some connection with the Trojan war. In

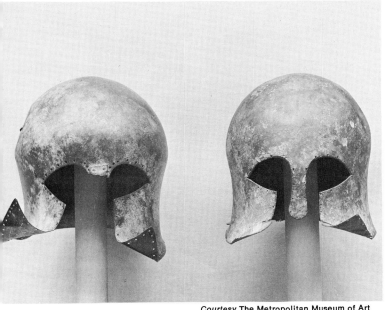

45
Greek bronze helmets—
Early Corinthian type, 7th
century B.C.

this respect we should remember that the kingdom of the Achaeans (assuming that Akkaiwash is Achaea) attacked Egypt in 1219 B.C., and a decade or so later a number of Greeks seem to have joined other "Peoples of the Sea" in their unsuccessful assault on Egypt. One wonders if the *Iliad* is not an interweaving of some local, possibly late, attack on Ilios with these grander traditions from an earlier time when the Mycenaeans could launch great naval adventures to more important parts of the world.[21]

The *Odyssey* is later and written by a different "Homer," though perhaps one following in the same tradition. It seems to fall into what is called the Orientalizing period, when the Greek world was shaking off its barbarian sleep and again receiving influences from the Near East. Dates for the *Odyssey* range from the late eighth to the late seventh century B.C., and there are quite cogent arguments for placing it at either end of this range.

In spite of attempts to trace the *Odyssey* it seems largely an adventure in some Mediterranean Land of Faery. Still and all, certain things can be made out. Odysseus seems to have touched at Egypt and Libya and to have ventured into the fringes of the western Mediterranean, guarded in the late eighth and seventh century by Etruscans in Italy and Carthaginians in North Africa. Already the Greeks were breaking into

*Hittites and Greeks*

123

46
*Tell of Hissarlik, Troy*

this charmed circle. They almost certainly had begun their settlement of southern Italy and Sicily when the *Odyssey* was composed, and the poem may not antedate by far the founding of Massalia in southern France. Actually, the composer of the *Odyssey* very likely sang his epic to a literate audience; the Greeks learned the alphabet from the Phoenicians and, before 700 B.C., had passed it on to the Etruscans. We are now on the edge of classic times. But let us remember that Greece was already a thousand years old.

SOME TWENTY to thirty thousand years ago, Paleo-lithic hunters and artists lived along the north shore of the Mediterranean sea. At that time vast amounts of water were locked up in the Würm glacier, sea levels were lowered and the western part of the Mediterranean may have been a lake. Paleolithic cultures of the European type existed not only in France and northern Spain but also in Italy and Sicily, though at a somewhat reduced cultural level.[1]

As the Würm ice shrank back from the Eurasian continent, the great Paleolithic florescence ended and the northern part of the area was left with a faint Mesolithic reflection of past glories. Meanwhile African cultures were impinging on Spain and France, thus making another pendulum swing in the age-old shifting relationship between Europe and Africa. The Neolithic in this area first appeared at about 4000 B.C. There seems a fairly good case to be made for a rather widespread movement of peoples from somewhere out of western Asia. These early groups brought with them the idea of agriculture, of animal husbandry, and of handmade pottery. They were already fairly skilled in the various crafts; obviously they had seaworthy boats or ships. We have already seen their traces in the Syro-Palestinian area and in the shell-impressed wares of the pre-Sesklo horizon in Greece.

At a guess, we can say that some of these peoples spread westward reaching Sicily, where they initiated the influential Stentinello culture. From the Stentinello area came the first settlers to the strategic islands of Malta, arriving around 3800 B.C.[2] These early Maltese were people who lived in the Ghar Dalam caves in the southern part of the main island. Here they used the impressed pottery in the shape of bowls, dishes (sometimes with annular bases), and jugs or ollas as their Stentinello forebears had done. Potters picked up handy cardium shells and pressed them on the wet clay in geometric patterns, or simply made the same patterns with a fingernail.

In the obsidian-rich Lipari Islands just to the north of Sicily, this same general pottery type is also found and can be traced westward and northward into Italy, southern France, east coastal Spain, and north Africa. Subsequent waves of influence brought painted pot-

## XII

## The Western Mediterranean

tery, the spiral decoration reminiscent of Dimini in Greece.

The earlier Neolithic peoples in the western Mediterranean introduced herds of sheep, goats, and cattle. The grains raised on their farms included emmer wheat and barley. There is some evidence that the olive tree, known to be early in the Syro-Palestinian area, spread also into the western Mediterranean during this fourth millennium B.C.

The diet of the Neolithic settlers was supplemented by hunting and fishing, for they left behind them the sling[3] and a considerable variety of fishing gear. The Neolithic peoples of the west do not, however, seem to have borrowed much from their Mesolithic predecessors. In some places, Malta for example, Neolithic man settled on virgin soil. In others, he presumably displaced or slowly absorbed small Mesolithic hunting-gathering groups.

About 3000 B.C. the idea of using metal began slowly to seep westward. The metal was copper. In spite of a number of rich tin deposits, no true bronze age appeared for several centuries. This first, limited, metallurgy made no drastic change in the lives of western Mediterranean peoples. The quickening that we saw in Crete, with the growth of the brilliant Minoan civilization, was not matched in the west.

Nevertheless, there were in general some spectacular events in the western Mediterranean and in western Europe. Out of early influences from the Cyclades, from Crete, and perhaps from Troy and the mainland of Greece, a religious cult of the Great Mother, or Earth Mother, was spreading. It seems possible that the original Neolithic settlers already had a form of this worship; if so, it was strengthened by continued contact with the Levant. Starting in the fourth millennium and continuing for some two thousand years, peoples in the Mediterranean Basin and adjacent areas fashioned large, communal tombs, using enormous, unworked, or very rudely dressed, stones. Elaborate spiral decorations, linked with the Mother Goddess, appear again and again in these great burial chambers. Their point of origin was probably the eastern Mediterranean or the Near East. The new fashion must have spread rapidly, however, for it swept the coastal areas of western Eu-

47
*Carved megalithic
stone, New Grange,
Ireland*

rope and penetrated deeply along river valleys, especially in France. Megalithic tombs in Brittany were
being built by 3500 B.C. A thousand years later these
sepulchres stood in Spain, Portugal, Great Britain,
Denmark, coastal Germany, and Ireland.[4]

A little after 3000 B.C. another type of megalithic
structure appeared in Malta. Here great stones, often
weighing many tons, were set up to form walls for
elaborately chambered temples containing cult statues
of the Mother Goddess. It may well be that the very
floor plans sometimes, or always, represented the
grossly fat figure of the goddess.

At some point between 2500 and 2000 B.C. the megalithic distributions were further complicated by the
rapid spread of people usually called the Beaker folk.
From some original homeland, perhaps in central Europe, small groups of these bronze-using people penetrated much of the old megalithic area. Sometimes they
continued the megalithic traditions, presumably marry-
ing into, or mixing with indigenous populations; at
other times they replaced them. The Beaker people
certainly helped to spread bronze technology and they
may actually have been itinerant bronzesmiths, merchants, or both. Their name derives from their habit of
burying drinking cups or beakers with their dead—an
indication that they were devotees of beer.[5]

The spread of megalith builders and Beaker folk had,
by 1500 B.C., linked the Mediterranean world and western Europe in a great lattice. From the eastern end of

this area the longboats of the Cretans, and then the Mycenaeans, carried traders and trade goods to the West. Mycenaean merchants settled in the Lipari Islands and Sicily and, at least indirectly, trade reached southern England where are found large numbers of faience beads from Egypt or the Aegean.[6] Both England and the Aegean saw the apogee of megalithic construction at this time, the former in the great calendrical circle of Stonehenge, the latter in the tholoi and the dressed cyclopean walls of Mycenae. Such cultures as the Milazzese and Capo Graziano in the Lipari Islands, the Castelluccio and Thapsos in Sicily, Los Millares and El Argar of southeast Spain, and, outside our area, the Wessex of southern England are near to urbanization.

Indigenous civilizations might well have appeared before the end of the Bronze Age but for the sweeping disturbances that began around 1200 B.C. in the eastern Mediterranean. At this time the Creto-Mycenaean and the Hittite kingdoms were wiped out and the Near Eastern heartland of civilization was seriously disrupted. Such far-flung outposts as those in Sicily and Spain withered, and when civilization did appear some centuries later it was largely imposed from the outside.

Several different peoples contributed to the rise of civilization in the western Mediterranean during the Early Iron Age (after 1000 B.C.). The Greeks we have already discussed. Slightly earlier were the Phoenicians, coming from the Syrian coast and settling large areas of the West. The Etruscans, a people of uncertain origins, controlled central Italy from the eighth century till the third. Living in a cluster of villages on or near the lower Tiber river were the Latins. At first they were dominated by neighboring Etruscans, but by the end of the second century B.C. had not only swallowed up Etruria but the whole of the western Mediterranean.

Phoenician merchants setting out from Tyre and Sidon began to explore the trade possibilities of the western Mediterranean even before 1000 B.C. After some cautious thrusts into the Aegean world, where they helped awaken the Greeks, Phoenicia concentrated on the West. One of the most obvious sites for early settlement was a port that could control the Straits of Gibraltar, thus opening up the Atlantic world. The Phoenicians founded Gades (modern Cádiz), on a long sandspit, near the mouth of the Guadalquivir river in Spain. Traditionally the city was founded in the twelfth century B.C., but that is probably a bit too early.[7] Utica, in modern Tunisia, was settled before 1000 B.C.; there were ninth-century settlements on the islands of Sardinia, and Malta was under some kind of Phoenician control by 800 B.C. Curiously enough, the rich island of Sicily was neglected by the Phoenicians till the 700's B.C., when Greek colonization forced Phoenicia to extend her sphere of influence northward.

The greatest of the Phoenician cities in the West, however, was Carthage—Kart-hadasht or New City— and with this settlement we can begin to talk of Punic (that is, Carthaginian) civilization in the West.[8] The traditional date for the founding of this Tyrian New City is 814 B.C. Such a date seems plausible both on archaeological and on historical grounds. The city, according to a story current in classic times, was settled by Elissa, or Dido, grandniece of Jezebel, queen of Israel.[9] After a stay in Cyprus, Elissa's colonizing group landed on the north Tunisian coast, not far from the modern city of Tunis. Here, probably at the spot of the modern village of Le Kram, the first settlement of Carthage was made.

Thanks in part to Phoenician contacts, something is known of the ethnic makeup in the western Mediterranean. In North Africa were people referred to as Libyans, a very general name for inhabitants of the southern Mediterranean coast. The Libyans of the Carthaginian area and westward were Berber-speaking —their language distantly related to Old Egyptian. In southern and eastern Spain lived Iberians, of unknown linguistic stock, presumably the descendants of Bronze Age Spaniards of El Argar and similar cultures. North of them, Celtic-speaking invaders began sifting into Spain and Portugal, perhaps as early as 1000 B.C., and eventually settled the northern and central highlands. Southern France was also coming under Celtic domination, as were parts of north Italy, though in the northwestern corner of Italy were the non-Indo-European-speaking Ligurians. On the Po river there were extensive villages, up to 18 acres, sometimes called

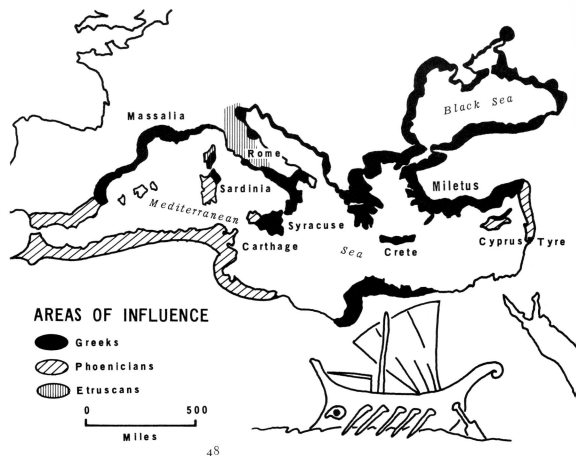

48

*The Mediterranean world 1000–400 B.C.*

terremare,[10] that continued through the dark ages virtually into historical times. Farther south about this time, villages appear whose people lived in flimsy, round huts and cremated their dead, burying them in large urns. A bit later, descendants of these villagers will make up one component of the Etruscans.

In Sicily the rich, peaceful period known technically as the Middle Bronze came to an end with a flurry of warfare and population movement. When the Greeks came to Sicily around 750 B.C., they found the island controlled by three major groups: the Sikels in the east, the Sikans in the center and west, and the Elymians in the very far west. These tribes all had migratory traditions, and the archaeological records for the end of the Bronze and beginning of the Iron Age suggest a time of wandering and general troubles.

In Malta, two late cultures, called respectively Borg-in-Nadur and Bahrija, existed until the Phoenician conquest of the Islands. Borg-in-Nadur tribesmen had invaded Malta around 1350 B.C. from Sicily, where their characteristic red-slipped pottery is also found. They were warlike and, from evidence of fortifications, must have divided the Maltese Islands into small, hostile, tribal communities. About 900 B.C. a group from the Early Iron Age culture of Campania, or perhaps from the toe of Italy, settled at Bahrija on the west coast of the main island of Malta. They, too, can be traced by their pottery, elaborately incised vessels with geometric decorations.

These village cultures flourished until Phoenician contact, about 800 B.C., then dwindled and disappeared. Unfortunately, we have no records whatsoever for Phoenician Malta. In fact, the Phoenicians, throughout their history, have left very few firsthand records; an ironical situation for the great disseminators of the alphabet.

Beginning 800 B.C., we can freely use the term Punic to refer to the western Phoenicians, and Carthage was soon the dominant Punic city. Founded on the seaside at modern Le Kram, Carthage gradually spread southward to what is now La Goulette and northward to Cape Carthage, while to the west it engulfed the isolated hills of St. Louis and Juno and part of the Odeon plateau. There the Carthaginians built their tightly packed houses of stone and mud brick and their temples to the Punic gods. These deities were carried westward from Phoenicia but became somewhat changed in the isolation of the West. In Carthage an important deity was the solar god, Baal Melqart, "Lord, Ruler of the city." The Greeks equated him with their oracular culture hero Herakles. We know relatively little about gods of other Punic cities, but Melqart was important in Gades where his temple may have been erected as early as 1000 B.C. At Carthage there was also the temple of the god of light and lightning, Resheph. Two other important deities were Baal Hammon, equated with the Greek Zeus, and the well-known fertility and Mother Goddess, Astarte (Babylonian Ishtar, Sumerian Inanna), in the West called Tanit. Few Punic temples have been excavated in detail, but one dramatic bit of religious evidence has been unearthed from Carthage itself, in the sacrificial precinct of Tanit, up-coast from Le Kram Bay. This precinct, or topheth, was used from the eighth century B.C. till the very end of Carthage (*c.* 150 B.C.). It contains literally thousands of cremated remains of children sacrificed to the goddess. The ages of these unlucky mites were mostly under two, but occasionally ranged up to twelve or more. This is clear evidence that Josiah had good reason when, in the words of the Old Testament (II Kings 23:10),

> he defiled Tophet, which *is* in the valley of the children of Hinnom, that no man might make his son or his daughter to pass through the fire to Molech.

Punic civilization was largely based on trade. The cities had been settled originally as trading stations and as they grew they established a network of trade relations with each other and with outsiders. Here again Carthage was the leader and, though she established no real empire until late in time, she had enormous influence over the other centers.

Soon after the initial settlement of the Punic peoples, two events greatly influenced the direction of foreign relations. One of these was the rise of Etruria beginning, perhaps, by 800 B.C. but not gaining much momentum until after Greek contact in the late eighth and the seventh century. The second was this very fact of Greek colonization that began in eastern Sicily and southern Italy about 750 B.C. In the seventh century central Italy was in the hands of a loosely organized group of Etruscan cities and the Greeks were ever-extending their trade contacts into the western Mediterranean. By 600 B.C. the Greeks had penetrated to southern France and were beginning to explore the Spanish coast. Alarmed, the Punic cities and the Etruscan federation united to deny the Mediterranean West and North to the Greeks. As part of the program, Carthage settled the south coast of Sicily and by 500 B.C. had barred the islands of Corsica and Sardinia, as well as the Straits of Gibraltar, to the Greeks. Massalia, at the mouth of the Rhone in France, was well-established, however, and the Greeks also clung to the port of Emporion in northeastern Spain.[11] The economic implication of the settlement of Massalia was considerable, for the Greeks now controlled the south

coast of France and therefore the vital overland trade routes to western Europe.

The fifth century saw a very considerable amount of Carthaginian exploration in the Atlantic. Two famous voyages are known—in 450 B.C. Himilco, following the earlier "Cornwall tin route," reached England and probably Ireland. In 425 B.C. Hanno, with a large fleet, sailed down the coast of Africa reaching at least to Sierra Leone and perhaps as far as the Cameroons or Gabon.[12] This was the period of very high development of Punic institutions. Carthage was now extremely powerful, the head of a loose federation of cities in North Africa, Spain, Sicily, and Sardinia. These cities were self-governing but drew on Carthage for military support. The Punic governmental organization was originally based on kingship, but by the fifth century— and probably earlier—power was in the hands of a monied aristocracy and the cities were nominally republics. As in Greece, Etruria, and Rome, the Punic statelets were ruled by a powerful "senate" of nobles and a more or less representative assembly of freemen. Supreme power, however, as in Rome and in certain Greek cities (for example, Sparta), and Etruria, was in the hands of two supreme magistrates. There was, in addition to nobles and freemen, a large slave class. Carthage also had an extensive hinterland where lived a large group of non-Punic, Berber-speaking, Libyans. As the centuries went by, more and more of the country folk became Punicized, and after the destruction of Carthage these agricultural and herding peoples kept up the traditions of Punic speech and religion, traditions that were still current in Saint Augustine's time, about A.D. 400.

We know all too little of the daily life of the Punic peoples. From excavations at Carthage and at places like Motya in Sicily it is clear that at least the upper classes readily accepted Greek fashions in architecture and in art—though in costume the Carthaginians retained the long Phoenician varicolored cloak.

In industry, the Punic people were excellent metallurgists, and skilled potters and weavers. They traded finished materials to their eastern Phoenician cousins and had a virtual monopoly on the dyeing industry. A rich purple dye was extracted from the putrified bodies of the shell fish, murex, and was used to color the excellent woolen and linen cloth that constituted such an important item in Punic trade. Success brought its own problems; the rotting murex has a powerful and all-permeating stench and dye workers normally were not accepted in the best Carthaginian circles.

The Punic cities, formed as trading stations, made trading a science. Punic seamen, mainly from Carthage but also from Gades and other sites, explored far and wide. Trade went to the continental interiors, both north and south. To western and central Europe the Carthaginians sent worked-metal, cloth, art objects, and, perhaps, wine and salt. In return they received tin, copper, gold, silver, amber, hides, and slaves. Trans-Saharan Africa produced gold and slaves in return for manufactured goods and salt. Some raw materials were used locally and some retraded to the rich cities of the eastern Mediterranean. Slaves were a specially favored commodity of the Punic traders, and captives from both northern Europe and Negro Africa were scattered throughout the Mediterranean world.

Punic hegemony in the western Mediterranean was seriously threatened, first by the Greeks and then by Rome. In the year 480 B.C. the Sicilian Greeks crushingly defeated a combined Punic and Etruscan force at Himera in northern Sicily. The fifth century, in general, saw the decline of both Carthaginian and Etruscan dominance in the Mediterranean. Around 450 B.C. Rome shook off Etruscan control and thereafter became a major force in Italy. A defeat inflicted upon her in 390 B.C. by the Celtic Gauls was actually a blessing in disguise, for the same barbarians virtually destroyed Etruria. Romans grew more internationally minded in the mid-fourth century, and they negotiated a treaty with Carthage, delineating spheres of influence. Carthage still considered western Greece its principal enemy and therefore allowed Rome to continue engulfing rivals, one by one. Having won Italy from the Greeks, Rome launched a war with Carthage in 264 B.C., and in 241 forced a ruthless peace treaty on her opponent. Carthage, having lost Sicily and, three years after the treaty, Sardinia, concentrated on Spain and revenge. In 218 B.C. she was led by the brilliant Hannibal to her last great military adventure, a dazzling invasion of Italy. Hannibal's victories establish him as one of the great military leaders of all times, but eventually the greater economic strength of Rome began to tell and finally in 204 B.C. her own great general, Scipio Africanus, invaded Africa. Two years later he defeated Hannibal near Carthage itself and enforced a harsh treaty on the city. That it was harsh and not annihilating was probably due to Scipio's humanity rather than Rome's policies. Magnanimity to fallen enemies was never one of Rome's weaknesses. After increasingly strident demands by such rabble-rousers as Cato the Censor,[13] Rome finally found an excuse to destroy her rival. In 146 B.C. a victorious Roman army burned the city and sold its inhabitants into slavery. In spite of Roman plans, Punic culture continued on in the countryside and when Julius Caesar refounded the city it became a center of Neo-Punic life. It was, however, now a minor part of the Roman Empire.

The northern allies of the Punic people, the Etruscans, are still somewhat mysterious.[14] In order to understand them we should turn back to the earlier periods in Italy.

During the Italian Bronze Age, there was a widespread Apenninic culture extending back into the third millennium B.C. The Apennine groups were skilled metallurgists who practiced the burial rites of inhumation, and were exposed to fitful influences from Minoan and Mycenaean culture to the east. In the extremely late Bronze Age and, especially, in the early Iron period (c. 1000–800 B.C.) groups of cremation-practicing villagers began to push into Italy, perhaps from the Urnfield culture of France. A complex mixing of new and old make the outlines of early Iron Age cultures in Italy somewhat obscure. In the period shortly after 1000 B.C. we can distinguish two major subareas in Italy and Sicily. In the north and west, roughly extending over the valleys of the Po, the Arno, and the Tiber, were peoples who practiced cremation, collecting the ashes of the dead in pottery urns. To the west and south cremations were rare, though isolated examples appeared in the Taranto area. Perhaps the best-known cremation culture was the Villanovan [15] and a variant sometimes called, or miscalled, the Latian culture. Villanovan was to provide at least one of the sources for the Etruscans, while Latian was the, or a, source of that sub-Etruscan culture of Rome.

The Villanovan peoples were iron-users, and at first practiced widespread cremation. They deposited ashes of their dead in biconical vessels of a crude pottery-ware called impasto, the vessel sometimes being covered with a small inverted cup. There were variations on this method. For example, in the region around or near to the later Rome, a ceramic model of a hut replaced the biconical pot. These "hut urns" are rounded, and are no doubt copies of real dwellings, probably of wattle and daub construction with a thatched conical roof. The burial urns and grave goods—iron weapons (sword, spear, dagger) for men, and ornately decorated metal fibulae, or safety pins, for women—were placed in small graves sometimes hollowed from rock. Designs on the pots were geometric and consisted of simple lines, dots, swastikas, and chevrons.

In the period c. 800–750 B.C. there is an increase in the number and richness of the tombs; bronze vessels are found in quantity and the human figure is sometimes molded on the outside of the urn. During this short period something has quickened the pace of Villanovan life. From c. 750 to 700 B.C. the changes in culture became still more drastic, in part due to increasing contact with the western Greeks. By 700 B.C. large, chambered tombs begin to appear with skilled stone-work utilizing the corbeled arch and dome. The simple geometric art of Villanova was enriched by the impact of the Greek Geometric style of pottery decoration. Around 700 B.C. also appears the first inscriptions of the Etruscan language, written with an early western Greek alphabet. Etruria now emerges into the full light of history.

A further approach to the Etruscan past comes from the evidence of linguistic distributions. Roughly speaking, in the ninth and eighth centuries B.C. there seem to have been three major groups of Indo-European languages in Italy. In the east, along the Adriatic, there were a number of related dialects including Venetic in the north, Picene in the Ancona area, and Iapygian in the Italian "heel." Down the center of the country, along the ridge of the Apennines, the languages were Umbrian, the Sabellic group, and Oscan; in the west Latin was spoken along the lower Tiber, and Latin was likely related to dialects in the Campania and those of Sikel in Sicily.

Another group of languages, quite separate but some of which were also probably related, had in common the fact that they were non-Indo-European and had in general a north and west distribution. These languages included Ligurian [16] and Raetic in the region of north Italy, extreme southern Switzerland, and extreme southeastern France. The Etruscan language itself was spoken from the Arno to the Tiber and was later to extend from the Po to the Bay of Naples. In western Sicily were non-Indo-European dialects, perhaps Sikan or Elymian. Sardinia and Corsica also had non-Indo-European languages, as did parts of Spain. In general, at least in Italy, Indo-European languages were spoken in areas where the rite of inhumation, or burial of the dead, was practiced; the non-Indo-European languages were in areas where cremation was practiced.

The group to which the Etruscan language belonged, the Raeto-Tyrrhenian, extended from the Alps to southern Italy, possibly with affinities to pre-Indo-European languages of the Aegean and Asia Minor. In addition, this speech family possibly had offshoots as far west as the Iberian Peninsula.

There are at present two major theories of Etruscan origins. One holds that this people was autochthonous, that is, they developed in the region that later became Etruria—or to put it another way, the Villanovans were early Etruscans. The second theory, widely believed in the ancient world, is that the Etruscans were immigrants from the East, perhaps from Lydia in western Anatolia. It is true that ancient Lydians had certain parallels and analogies to the Etruscans. For example, both peoples employed the matronymic (use of the mother's family name) and both accorded women a higher social position than did, say, the Greeks. Both groups were greatly interested in divination, especially by the examination of livers of sacrificial animals. More important, there are a number of parallels in the language especially in the root *tarch*, which in both areas was used in names for important persons.[17] In addition, the Greek name for Etruscans, Tyrrhenoi, is perhaps related to Lydian Tyrra.[18]

There are also ties to the Aegean world, as demonstrated by a funerary stele discovered in 1885 on the Aegean island of Lemnos. This stele, dated by its art style to the seventh century B.C., has an inscription in a Greek script which, though untranslated to date, is clearly related to Etruscan.

Perhaps it is unnecessary to decide between these two theoretical polar extremes. There is a good probability that the basic culture, language, and physical characteristics of the Etruscans came from the Villanovan peoples. Around 800 B.C. there began a series of contacts with the Oriental world—probably the same kind of conquests that were introducing the "Orientalizing" period into the Greek area. It may be that a certain number of actual migrants from Anatolia or Syria settled in Villanova country; if so, they seem to have been welcomed and may account for the rapid culture change that archaeology so plainly demonstrates. We do not know if the Villanovans were originally skilled in things maritime, but certainly in the eighth century B.C. these proto-Etruscans began to explore the possibilities of a seafaring life. During this time, if not before, they contacted the large island of Sardinia whose Bronze Age population lived in clustered round huts which encircled a truncated cone of

50
*Terracotta head of Apollo
from Veii, Etruscan, c. 500
B.C.*

dry masonry, the latter probably a chieftain's residence or a village stronghold. Such towers, or nuraghi,[19] must have been admired by proto-Etruscans who came to trade in the metal-rich island, for nuraghi soon began to appear on the Etruscan coast.

Sometime in the quarter century before 700 B.C. the first Greek settlers in Sicily and south Italy made contact with Etruscans. They found a people whose Villanovan villages were already growing into towns, whose political organization transcended the clan and the tribe, and whose art and technology already was specialized, complex, and elaborate. These were people who in a matter of two or three generations had passed from village to urban life and were receptive to more and faster change.[20]

*Western Mediterranean*

The Greek contact led to a cultural explosion. Shortly after 700 B.C. we find that the Etruscans had adapted the Greek alphabet, had wholeheartedly borrowed Greek ceramic techniques and art forms, and now had a cosmopolitan outlook. A league of Etruscan cities formed (if they had not already been in existence), naval power became a military and diplomatic

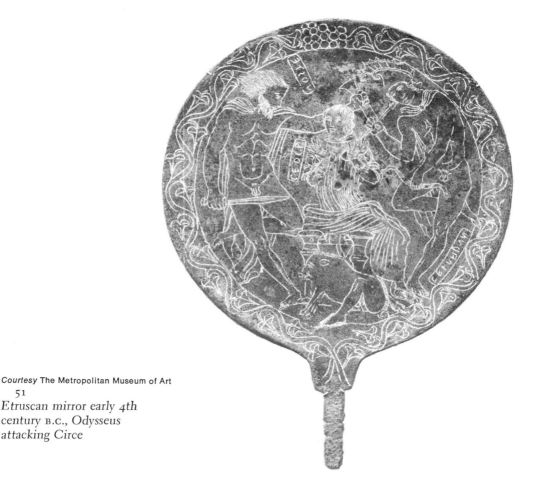

51
*Etruscan mirror early 4th century* B.C., *Odysseus attacking Circe*

mainstay, and the Etruscans started aggressively expanding to the north, south, and west.

The period of Etruscan greatness lasted from before 700 B.C. to approximately 450 B.C. The Etruscan federation clung to power for an additional two hundred years, though Celtic raids and Roman ambitions increasingly weakened the Etruscan city-states. Even after the loss of political autonomy the Etruscans continued a flourishing cultural life until the devastation of the Social Wars of the first century B.C. The Etruscans, then, were a great and powerful people for nearly half a millennium and their hegemony, political and cultural, extends for three-quarters of a millennium. They deserve to be better known.

After 700 B.C. we begin to see a federation of Etruscan cities emerging in the area between the Arno and the Tiber. From very early times there were a number of important cities: Tarquinii, Vulci, Veii, and Caere in or near the lower Tiber valley; Volsinii in the middle valley; Rusellae, Vetulonia, and Populonia across from the strategic island of Elba (the last named, the only large Etruscan city built directly on the seashore). Further inland were Clusium, Perusia, Cortona, Faesulae on the Arno, and Volaterrae.

The Etruscans expanded from this central area both to the north and south. In northern Etruria was Bononia (Bologna), captured toward the end of the sixth century from Villanovan country cousins. Further east, on or near the Adriatic, were Spina, Ariminum (Rimini), Caesena (Cesena), Mantua (Mantova), and others. In the sixth century the Etruscans also expanded southward to the Campania, settling Volturnum (Capua), Nola, Pompeii,[21] and Salernum (Salerno).

From the seaport cities of Tarquinii, Vulci, Caere, Populonia, and Vetulonia the Etruscans launched increasingly bold sea adventures. They rapidly gained control of the iron-rich island of Elba. Contact with Sardinia, already evidenced in the eighth century, became more direct and intense. Corsica was soon dominated by Etruscans, and the Etruscan ships sailed as far as southern France and Spain.

Contact with the Greek cities was frequent and it is clear that Greek craftsmen actually settled in the Etruscan cities. The pottery of the Etruscans copied that of the Greeks; first the Geometric and Corinthian wares, then in the sixth century, when the Athenians became artistic leaders, the Attic black-figure style. Etruria soon was producing her own version of these elegant Attic vases, cups, kraters, hydriae, oinochoai, pyxides, olpes, and amphorae.[22] Still later (fifth and fourth centuries), the Etruscan also adopted Attic red-figure ware. Etruscan potters experimented with the designs and shapes; for example, a gray to black ware called bucchero became popular, and soon beautifully made metallic-looking bucchero kantharoi were a favorite Etruscan trade item and, for the archaeologist, a sure indicator of Etruscan influence.

In spite of active commercial relationships with the Greeks, Etruria rightly regarded these southern neighbors as potentially dangerous to her own security. By the end of the eighth century B.C. Etruscan ships were raiding the Greek settlements, and as the Etruscan federation grew in power such raids became serious naval engagements. The major objective of the Etruscans was to bar the Greeks from central and north Italy, the Tyrrhenian sea, and especially the islands of Elba, Corsica, and Sardinia. It was not wholly a successful policy; for example, the Ionian city of Phocaea managed to settle Massalia and Emporion. The Greek colonies also held their own in the narrow confines of the Campania.

At this point Carthage took a hand, overrunning the western portion of Sicily and colonizing western and southern Sardinia. Though the Etruscans cannot have liked the idea of the Carthaginian Sardinia, Greek pressure was so great that an alliance with Carthage was deemed necessary. Around 535 B.C. the allies defeated the Phocaean colonies in a major sea battle off Corsica. The Punic hold on Sicily was secured and Etruria added Corsica to its overseas territory.[23] Greek France and Greek Italy were split, and for a half-century the Etruscans dominated the Tyrrhenian sea. During this period Etruscan trade flourished as never before. Etruscan ceramics and metal objects, vessels, weapons, and jewelry, were traded as far as the Danube valley, and Etruscan influence especially in art and metallurgy, appears in distant Ireland and Scandinavia. In order to open up these new trade horizons, and perhaps to deal with population pressure, Etruscans began, in the mid-sixth century, to spread to the Po valley. In the fifth century B.C., Spina at the mouth of the Po controlled much of the Adriatic trade, just as Venice was to do two thousand years later. From such centers as Bologna

on the flank of the Apennines, a wealth of Etruscan and transshipped Greek goods, vases, amphorae (sometimes filled with wine or oil), jewelry, art objects, and even coins, moved northward over the Alpine passes.[24] Etruria, in return, received tin, amber, hides, and slaves.

The Etruscans are in some ways quite well-known and in other ways still enigmatic. Thanks to their burial customs a great deal can be reconstructed; like the Egyptians, the Etruscans surrounded the dead with articles and pictures of everyday life.[25] From late Villanovan times, tombs had become more and more elaborate and after 700 B.C. they were dwellings underground, multiroomed rectangular houses presumably copies of real living quarters. As early as the eighth century the fashion of inhumation began to spread, though it never completely replaced cremation. In Etruria's Golden Age, the dead were housed in the eleborate tombs whose walls were bright with paintings of everyday life, feasting, games, hunting, or scenes from mythology. We see husbands and wives seated together in dignified calm while servants bring food, and dancers and musicians perform. Surrounding the body in its coffin or urn are fine painted pots, metal implements and exquisite

52
*Wall painting from Etruscan tomb, Tarquinii, 4th or 3rd century* B.C.

*Western Mediterranean*

53
*Etruscan tumulus, Caere 4th century* B.C.

jewelry, often of gold. The walls and supporting pillars of the tomb have modeled or painted representations of household objects and of domesticated animals.

Only later, when the Etruscan state was in decline, does another leitmotiv appear. Gaiety vanishes and on the tomb walls appear scenes of somber demons and other half-glimpsed horrors. The Etruscans have failed in life and are now afraid to die.

We know a little of political and social life during the great period. Originally the cities of Etruria had kings, but in the sixth and early fifth centuries the idea of kingship was fading, as it was in the Greek and Phoenician cities. By 500 B.C., kings had been largely replaced by magistrates throughout Tuscany, though in some backwater areas (for example, Rome) they may have continued for a bit longer. The Etruscans had a large number of clans, or gens, possibly separated into patrician and plebeian groups, as they were in early Rome. At any rate, the struggle between noble and commoner was as sharp in Etruria as it was in Rome, especially in the declining period of Etruscan power.

Several of the Etruscan cities—according to legend, twelve—formed a loosely structured league; the exact cities are not known at present but they certainly in-

*Origins of Civilization*
144

cluded such major sites as Tarquinii, Vulci, Caere, and
Volsinii—the latter a national religious center. The Po
cities may have had their own league. The actual mechanism of power in the leagues is not clear, but certainly
the Etruscans, operating jointly, were able to maintain
powerful naval forces to hold colonies against Greek
pressure in southern Italy, and to negotiate with foreign
powers.

In later classic times, the Etruscans were famous for
their intense religious feeling. The Etruscan idea of the
universe, now seen only dimly, was one in which
human beings were essentially passive and helpless.
The future could seldom be controlled, but often it
could be foretold by such methods as interpreting the
pattern of lightning, flights of birds, or by examining
the liver of sacrificed animals. There were a large number of deities, some—like the powerful Dii Superiores—
now hardly more than names. Other gods and goddesses were borrowed from Greece, or in some cases a
native deity was identified with one from Greece. Some
of these passed into the Roman pantheon. For example, the Etruscans identified their Menerva (Latin Mi-
nerva) with Athena, Maris (Latin Mars) with Ares.
The name of the Etruscan god, Turms, is probably
specifically borrowed from Hermes and became Mercury in Latin. Aphrodite became identified with Turan,
probably an ancient Mother Goddess, and this goddess
in Latin became Venus. The Greek Herakles became
Hercle in Etruscan and Hercules in Rome.

Certain traits set off the Etruscans from their Greek
neighbors. Women were given a great deal of freedom,
banqueting with men and taking part in public affairs.
This scandalized the Greeks and seems to have been
the basis for most of the stories concerning Etruscan
immorality. Another, darker, side of Etruscan life was
that of the funeral games, where combatants fought to
the death in honor of the dead. These games were later
taken over by Rome and developed into elaborate glad-
iatorial combats.

The general picture of life in Etruria during the
seventh and sixth centuries is one of high culture.
Large, thriving cities, united in formal alliances, controlled much of Italy. In the homeland of central Italy
and on adjacent islands the Etruscans controlled the

largest iron mines in the Mediterranean. Their technological achievements were very great; Etruscan bronze-
and gold-casting is recognized today as technically and
artistically very fine. Etruscan engineers were engaged
in huge projects of marsh drainage, especially in the Po
and the Campania. The stone-hewn tombs show something of Etruscan constructional skill—at first using the
corbeled vault, they soon moved to the true arch and
vault, and probably initiated the Romans into these
skills. Roman aqueducts may in fact have been borrowed from Etruscan ones. In warfare the Etruscans
graduated from chariotry to cavalry by the sixth century
and their infantry formations, though not well known,
probably were prototypes of the more famous Roman
infantry.

Rome, then, forms a bridge between the Etruscan
past and western civilization. The city dates from the
middle Bronze period of *c.* 1600–1500 B.C.[26] On this
foundation, perhaps after a period of depopulation
(the archaeological evidence is not very clear), there
appeared Villanovanlike settlements on the Palatine,
the Oppius, the Quirinal, and the Esquiline hills. The
people in these villages varied somewhat in terms of
culture; there were minor differences in pottery and
some villages practiced inhumation, some cremation,
and some both. This preurban Rome already had certain of the traits that we think of as "Roman"; certain
ceremonies of the later period surely had their origin in
the preurban Iron Age, or even earlier, villages. Most
important and probably oldest of these was the Lupercalia, a purification and fertility ceremony involving the
sacrifice of goats.[27]

About 575 B.C. there was a sudden and explosive
expansion of Rome, from a series of villages, huddled
on hilltops, to a unified city with monumental architecture, planned streets, a market and harbor area, and
well-built houses—these often found directly above the
leveled remains of the old huts. Rome had been drawn
suddenly and dramatically into the Etruscan orbit and
had benefited by Etruscan urbanization. The reason for
the rapidity of development was the strikingly strategic
position of Rome. Built on the lowest area of the Tiber
that could be easily bridged and, because of the hills,
easily defended, Rome in effect dominated the natural

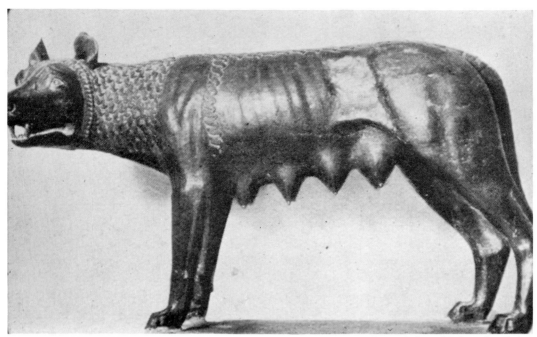

route from Etruria to the Campania. It was essential for the Etruscans to hold the site of Rome. The later independence of the city was one of the factors that spelled ruin for Etruria. We have seen the sixth and early fifth century B.C. as a time when both Etruscan and Punic peoples were following the Greek example and throwing off the rule of kings. These kings in Rome were mostly drawn from Etruscan families, and in later centuries eviction of the kings was explained as a struggle between the Roman people and their Etruscan overlords. According to the legend, the Etruscans were finally expelled in the year 510 or 509 B.C. and their place was taken by dual magistrates, later to be called consuls. It is fairly clear, however, that Etruscan domination lasted until the early or perhaps middle fifth century, but when Rome did become independent, control of the lower Tiber made her the coming power of central Italy.

Nevertheless, the period from *c*. 450 to 250 B.C. was one of decline, not only for Etruria, but initially for Rome herself. The Rome of the early Republic was not the sophisticated Greek-influenced city of earlier Etruscan times. In this context the anti-Greek attitudes, as exemplified by Cato the Censor as late as the second

54
*Etrusco-Roman she-wolf in bronze, c. 500 B.C.*

century B.C., reflect the provincial attitudes of the some-day imperial city.

It would seem that Rome of the Republic was drawn out of isolationism more by accident than by design. Forced to protect her ever-expanding frontiers by bigger and bigger defensive wars, Rome quickly learned to balance her military budget with loot and tribute. This expansionist road led late Republican Rome back into the larger world of the Mediterranean, but as a conqueror and mainly on her own terms.

THE PREHISTORY of China is all too little-known. This is not due to the fact that archaeological data on this Oriental area are particularly inscrutable. The point is that the Far Eastern complex is vast, taking in an area larger than Europe and, except for certain favored places, has seen very little archaeological work. From what we do know it seems that traditional Chinese culture developed in the Hwang Ho, or Yellow river area, though coastal China, central and south China, and possibly even Southeast Asia may have contributed strongly. On the other hand, Japan and Korea derived their own high cultures, at least in part, from an already historic China. Because of our general lack of knowledge it should be stressed that this outline, or any outline for that matter, of the origin of civilization in the Far East will eventually be revised, perhaps drastically revised. But then the archaeologist, like any other scientist, deals mainly in probabilities.

Man is early in China. From limestone caves near Choukoutien, a few miles south of Peking, remains of a mid-Pleistocene man were found in the 1920's and 1930's. This type was originally named *Sinanthropus pekinensis* (Peking China man) but now is generally considered to be a species of the genus *Homo*. Pekinensis (using the species name to avoid the taxonomic issue) was a somewhat smaller-brained specimen of humanity than modern man, but he already had certain vices that seem strikingly modern; he was an unembarrassed cannibal and this trait led to his discovery in modern times. What is found in the north China caves are remnants of cannibal feasts and stone implements of a type known as chopper-chopping tools, products of a crude industry that flourished throughout the Far East a quarter of a million years ago. From our point of view, Pekinensis is interesting because in certain physical traits he resembles modern Mongoloids, the physical type that includes most East Asiatics. One of his more noticeable traits is what is called the "shovel-shaped" incisors, or front teeth. Shovel-shaped means that these teeth are somewhat indented or hollowed out on the inside. It may be that historic and modern populations in the Far East are direct descendants of this ancient type of man. It has also been suggested, however, that many of the classic Mongoloid physical

## XIII

*The Birth of China*

traits, jutting cheek bones, inset nose, rounded body, scanty face hair, and the epicanthic eye fold are the result of rapid evolution under conditions of extreme dry cold. This evolution is presumed to have taken place during the last glacier period, perhaps within the last ten or twenty thousand years. Whatever their origin, it is reasonably clear that Mongoloid peoples had penetrated eastern Asia in prehistoric times and were the originators of Chinese civilization.

We know little of the Chinese Upper Paleolithic and even less of a Mesolithic, though the latter is represented by microlithic cultures, a part of a group of cultures that extended across north Asia. The Neolithic in the Far East is also somewhat shadowy, though some rather general details can be made out. These appear, first of all, as a culture marked by gray and cord-marked ceramic wares that has been very imperfectly described. This was widespread in the Yellow river region and adjacent areas of northern China. The bearers of this culture had the bow and so presumably enriched their diet with wild game. They domesticated the dog and the pig, both for food, and they raised millet, kaoliang, and possibly wheat. The growing of millet set a pattern that has continued in north China to the present day.

The origins of the early Neolithic is obscure and its distribution in China is not completely known. The culture does occur as far west as Kansu State and as far east as Shantung. It is tempting to see this culture as an extension of the pervasive "Gray Ware" cultures of Iran and Pakistan, but a great deal more work needs to be done before such an idea can be stated even as a probability. There are certain points that should be made, however. Both the cultivated grain and the domesticated animals of early China are almost certainly from the West. The idea of pottery making (aside from any connections with specific wares) and of the bow and arrow is also probably Western. It is almost beyond question that agriculture and animal husbandry, spreading from Mesopotamia to Iran and Turkistan by slow stages of diffusion, eventually reached western China. From there, via the Yellow river, they gradually infiltrated to the coastal plain. It is not clear why millet should have been the popular cereal grain unless, as suggested earlier, it had gradually replaced

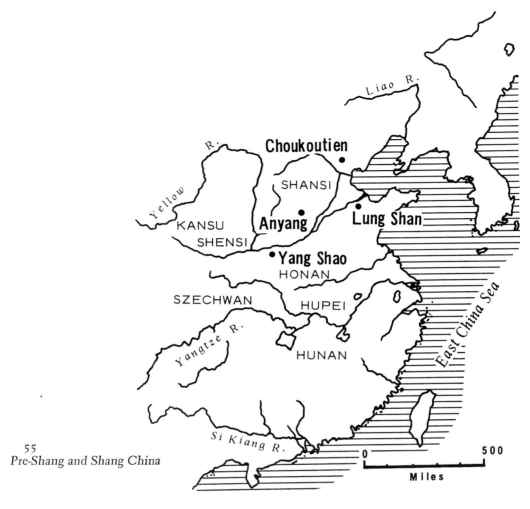

55
*Pre-Shang and Shang China*

the less adaptable wheat on the long slow journey
across Central Asia. Another trait of this early culture,
the pit house, suggests that early Chinese populations
may also have been influenced by a circumpolar Mesolithic culture.

From the early Neolithic appeared the famous li
tripod, a pot with curious thickened, in some cases
almost mammiform, hollow legs, possibly invented as
an improvement on an original practice of balancing
three pointed-bottom pots over a fire. A developed form
of this tripod, the hsien steamer, consisted of a li tripod
topped by a second vessel, the latter with a perforated
bottom. Water or soup could be put in the lower pot
and grain or meat in the top. When the water boiled,
steam would rise and cook the food in the upper part of
the vessel.

It is quite possible that some of the impetus toward

*Birth of China*
151

high culture in China came not from the west but from the south. At least in early historic times we find many southern elements in the Yellow river valley and one important domesticated crop, rice (*Oryza* sp.), probably was developed south of the Yellow river.[1] The wheres and whens of this domestication are still unknown, and also unknown is the date of the Chinese early Neolithic. Tentatively we can suggest the fourth millennium B.C., but this is only a guess; eventually, Carbon-14 dates should resolve the question.

The early period was replaced by what is often called the Painted Pottery culture (more technically the Yang Shao culture, after the type site in the state of Honan). There is some reason to believe that the Painted Pottery culture—so called for a series of brilliantly colored wares—spread from the west, at least it seems to have had its greatest time-depth in China in the west, in Kansu State.[2] That this is an important culture is quite clear, but unfortunately all too little is known about it. In Painted Pottery times, new items were presumably added to enrich Chinese life and many of these came from the west. In fact, it now seems that the Painted Pottery culture was very much in the mainstream of Chinese civilization.

Later than the Painted Pottery culture, at least in its eastern Chinese homeland, was the Black Pottery, or Lung Shan culture. This is perhaps best-known from the type site in Shantung, the site of Ch'eng Tzu Yai. Here was actually found a large city surrounded by a pounded earth wall some 30 feet wide at the base and a mile in length. The Lung Shan people had an excellent thin black ware, made on the wheel, and also, by the end of the period, they had produced a white porcelain ware. They continued such exotic forms as the li tripod and, in addition to a millet (and possibly rice) agriculture, domesticated the pig, cow, and horse. Actually these people seem to be an early stage in the urbanization that a little later was to produce Shang. Their cultural origins are not surely known but, in part, they must have derived from the Yang Shao.

In the traditional Chinese histories there is, after a succession of purely mythological rulers, a dynasty known as Hsia. It seems to represent a civilized China, and it was the precursor to the dynasty known in the historical sources as Shang, which is traditionally dated at 1765–1123 B.C. Until a few decades ago there was a tendency to disregard the traditional sources, but now the Shang is firmly established, and there seems a good chance that the Hsia represented some early dynasty or at least some early Chinese state. It is very tempting to equate the Hsia with some subregion of the archaeological Lung Shan culture which is Neolithic only in the sense that no metal has been found with it. We need to know a great deal more about pre-Shang life in China.

The Shang culture draws extensively from the Lung Shan culture which it overlies in some sites. The two share a number of food crops and domesticated animals, certain pottery forms and materials, a fondness for jade,[3] the use of pounded earth to build walls and other structures, and the idea of divination (very important to Shang). To this the Shang cultures added elaborate stone carving, monumental structures—temples, palaces, and the like—probably absent in earlier times, an elaborate technique of bronze-casting, large chamber burials sometimes associated with human sacrifice, the use of the chariot in warfare, and a system of writing. Shang, then, may be an outgrowth of the earlier culture but is far richer and more developed.

Probably the sequence of events that produced early Chinese civilization went something like the following. In the third millennium B.C., certain peoples of northern China had attained that surplus necessary for large concentrations of populations and elaborate political organization. They may have been warlike, at any rate the great walls at Lung Shan sites were almost certainly for defense. There were by this time probably heavy populations along the Yellow river and its tributaries, the peasants growing millet and perhaps rice, and very likely using some form of irrigation. This is a rich region covered with yellow, windblown, glacial soil called loess, and throughout historic times it has supported very heavy populations. From the considerable size of the sites and from the ambitious nature of communal enterprises, we can assume a power elite who, probably in the form of a royalty and nobility, dominated the political scene. Of priesthoods and religion nothing is known, but the importance attached to ancestors that we find in the Shang may have already

a

56, a-d

*Li tripods, Shantung
area*

b

been present in the earlier period. It is likely, also, that the beginning steps in writing were taken at this time, though presumably on some perishable material. Even most of the Shang writing has disappeared—only that carved on oracle bones remains, though it is reasonably certain that books of bamboo strips and perhaps also of cloth were present in Shang times, and it is not inconceivable that they predated Shang. One of the states or statelets of the Lung Shan culture could have been that of the Hsia. It is unlikely that there was any large-scale power controlling great parts of north China; the situation was more like that of early Mesopotamia or predynastic Egypt.

Around, or a little before, 1500 B.C. certain cultural impulses from the West began to stir this early civilization. A hint of what may have been happening comes from the appearance of chariots in China. At about this same time the chariot was being introduced to India by the Vedic peoples and there are indications that in the period 2000–1500 B.C. chariot-using barbarians were astir, moving from some Asiatic homeland. These people, however, certainly did not bring other of the Shang traits, such as writing or the elaborate carving in stone, though they might conceivably have introduced bronze. It is true that certain specific Western elements appear in Shang art, for example, the motif of animals with interlocking necks, and jars with counter-sunk handles, often phallic-shaped, both originally Mesopotamian.[4] Nevertheless, Shang art, except for isolated motifs and some pottery forms, was not Western. Certain practices, including the carving of one animal figure on top of another in a totem pole technique and the tendency to split an animal along the long axis of the body and carve the sides two-dimensionally, may be part of an old "Circum-Pacific" tradition. These techniques appear on the Northwest Coast of North America in recent times and in more diffuse forms in Polynesia. One cannot be certain; three thousand years and many thousands of miles separate Shang from the Northwest Coast Indians, and the art forms may have risen independently.[5]

Wherever the influences, by about 1500 B.C. new ideas were in the process of elaborate reworking and the result was the Shang culture.[6] Shang, or Yin as it is sometimes called, seems to refer to a state in the middle Yellow river region, with a capital (at least in the latter portion of the period) near the present city of Anyang.[7] The Shang is fairly typical as an early, exuberant, yet barbaric stage of civilization, comparable, in some ways, to Mesopotamia or Egypt of 3000 B.C. For example, one of the most dramatic series of finds in the Anyang area are the great chamber tombs of kings and queens, in which are also buried large numbers of slaves and retainers, slain to accompany their master or mistress to the other world. In general, this type of mass human sacrifice for funeral purposes comes at an early stage in civilization, while later on substitutes for real people (figurines, paintings, and so forth) are devised as a practical measure. It is, in a sense, not properly a part of the civilized ethos at all, but a carry-over from an advanced barbarism (examples of it come from such diverse barbarian areas as pre-Columbian Panama and pre-Christian Scandinavia). Civilized communities normally put a high value on the human being as a producer and are understandably reluctant to send a skilled craftsman or beautiful dancing girl to attend a dead king. The practice essentially died out at the end of the Shang time in China, as it had earlier in Egypt and Mesopotamia.

c

d

The Shang peoples, at least in the Anyang area, preferred to live on the rich loess plains, though at Anyang they were only some twenty miles east of a mountain spur which supplied game, wood, and, probably, summer vacation resorts for the upper classes. In the flatlands there were scattered villages of peasant farmers. Anyang itself was a fortified site, the defenses formed by a bend of the Huan river to the north and east and by great pounded-earth walls to the south. This structural technique which we found in pre-Shang times has continued in China to the present day. It is based on the fact that loess soils tend to stand in vertical walls and perhaps this was first noticed by early peoples who tunneled into loess cliffs. To make a sturdy house wall, a form is first constructed and then wet soil is poured into it. This is trampled or pounded until it is quite solid and then new earth is added and pounded until the required height is reached. The forms are then removed leaving a free-standing mud wall. By Shang

*Birth of China*

155

times houses, palaces, and temples were normally built on platforms of pounded earth, some of these so hard and dense that they have resisted the weathering of three thousand years. The Shang houses were gabled and had massive roofs carried by great wooden pillars. The roofs were probably thatched and were in no way supported by the walls.

Stone carving appears in highly developed form in the Shang period. The figures, usually of marble, include animals (sometimes life-size), mythological beasts, and the always popular dragon.[8] Even more impressive are the magnificent bronze vessels, vast numbers of which have been found in Shang tombs. These were probably cast, using the lost-wax method, and they represent a development of metal work unequaled in ancient times. The designs on these vessels are often of incredible intricacy, and the shapes, particularly of such forms as the annular based drinking vessel, the Ku, are extremely graceful and elegant. Shang bronzes are collectors' items today and command fabulous prices.

The Shang people of the Anyang area had extensive agriculture and animal husbandry. They raised more than one kind of millet, as well as rice, wheat, and a number of root and leaf crops. Like earlier peoples of China, they domesticated the dog, growing a special breed for food. Besides cattle, pigs, sheep, and horses, the water buffalo (probably imported from South China) was also domesticated, and the elephant was possibly tamed. It now seems likely that silkworms were grown and silk was spun in Shang times; in fact it is quite possible that silk culture was originated in Yang Shao days. One curious aspect of animal domestication is that the Chinese never seem to have made any use of cow's milk. Indeed, milk is not drunk in East Asiatic countries even today. Since the cow must have come to China from the West where milk and milk products have been important from early times, it is most puzzling why such foods never caught on in China. The fact remains that they never did.

The Shang culture must have had considerable contact with the east and south of China. Not only were such things as rice and water buffalos imported, but several other items, for example cowrie shells, came from south (or central) coastal China. These were

57
Archaic Chinese writing on
tortoise plastron

highly valued and probably formed a species of cur-
rency. Another item important to the Shang people
and which probably came from outside the area was
tortoise shell, used in divination. The idea of divination
(foretelling the future by magical means) was known
as early as Lung Shan times, with both animal bones
and shells being used. The surface of the shell or bone
was carefully scraped off, then heat was applied. The
pattern of cracks that appeared on the surface could be

*Birth of China*

read by a professional magician; it normally indicated the yes or no answer to a specific question.

It is from the oracle shells and bones that we get much of our information about the Shang people. Most of the bones in Shang, like all those of the earlier culture, contain simply the prepared surface and the cracks from the heating process. A certain number, however, perhaps 10 per cent of the total, were inscribed with the question to be divined and, occasionally, with the answer. Questions relate to a number of things: success in war, in the hunt, in diplomatic relations; some are quite trivial, asking the state of the weather on a given day. Through the oracle questions we can see something of the political and military makeup of the Shang state. War was carried on with, at most, a few thousand men, and war chariots were still somewhat of a rarity. The power of the king was great, but already a feudal nobility seemed to be forming. The Shang people were passionately fond of hunting and often listed the animals they killed. There was considerable development of a political bureaucracy, and it is likely that there were formal diplomatic relations between various states. Archival records would seem to be a necessity, but these were probably written in books of bamboo or silk, and none have survived.

The writing itself is a remarkable achievement.[9] Though crude in form it is unquestionably ancestral to the modern Chinese script and has been deciphered by modern experts on early Chinese writing. The origin of this script is not at all clear. Superficially it resembles Sumerian-Akkadian cuneiform in the complex formation of the symbols, usually a series of lines branching off from one another. In function, however, Chinese is quite different from cuneiform, being more closely related to Egyptian hieroglyphics, sharing with the latter the concept of ideographs and determinatives. Like Egyptian, the Chinese script has many elements of picture writing, and both systems demand large numbers of symbols or symbol combinations. Specifically, however, Chinese writing resembles no other known early script. It seems that again the idea of writing came in from the West and that this idea was developed by the Chinese in a highly original and elaborate way. Though our first evidence is from Shang times, it seems likely that the origins of writing took place in the more distant past, perhaps in the third millennium B.C.

The oracle bones gave some hint as to the religious organization of Shang. Divination questions were often put to ancestors, thus suggesting that ancestor worship was already underway. Such worship has continued to the present day in China; briefly it involves the concept of the family extending indefinitely into the past and the future. When a family head dies he simply attains another and higher status and has a more powerful voice in family affairs. It is necessary to sacrifice to him; to do otherwise would be to risk grave vengeance at the hands of an angry ghost. The ancestors of the Shang kings, real or mythical, may have served as nationwide deities, but on this point the short inscriptions from Shang times do not give enough information. It is reasonably certain that other gods and goddesses (aside from divine ancestors) existed; some of them may have been nature deities such as sun, moon, and earth. One important deity was referred to simply as Heaven.

The end of the Shang dynasty came around 1000 B.C. with the conquest of Anyang by armies from peoples on the Yellow river further west in the present-day state of Shensi. The new dynasty, known as the Chou, ushered in full historic times, with highly elaborate feudal states and many written records. There was also the beginnings of certain very typically Chinese things, including the keen respect for scholarship that later was to lead to regularized examinations for a civil service. Probably in this period there also appeared the concept of yang and yin, the two counterpoised principles that dominate the world, one male, bright and hard, the other female, soft and dark.

About 500 B.C., toward the end of the Chou, China obtained iron and technologically caught up completely with the Western world. At about the same time there appeared the series of brilliant philosophical ideas that put China, along with Greece of the same period, in the forefront of the world of ideas. To this late Chou period belong Confucius, Mencius, and a host of lesser thinkers, the like of which the world had not seen before. It is interesting that in this period, around 500 B.C., there was considerable intellectual activity not only in China, but also in Greece, in India,

| | | |
|---|---|---|
| 亻 | 人 | MAN |
| ⍦ | 牛 | AN OX |
| 𦍌 | 羊 | A GOAT |
| 龜 | 龜 | A TORTOISE |
| 虎 | 虎 | A TIGER |
| ☽ | 月 | MOON |
| △ | 土 | EARTH |
| 夨 | 天 | HEAVEN |
| 木 | 木 | TREE |
| 巛 | 水 | WATER |
| 立 | 立 | TO STAND |
| 祝 | 祝 | TO PRAY |

58
*Shang writing with modern Chinese and English equivalents*

and in western Asia. Much of the activity seems the result of independent, parallel development that reached culmination in various parts of the world at roughly the same time. Though the life-span of Confucius and Buddha probably overlapped, it seems doubtful that they ever heard of each other. Neither, as far as we can tell, knew of Thales nor of Anaxagoras.

WE LEFT the New World after a brief glance at Paleo-Indian and the cultures of the Mesolithic. These latter peoples, adapting themselves to a variety of climates and discovering the usability of a great range of foods, probably spread over much of North and South America. From them, quite early, though probably not so early as in the Old World, came the discovery of agriculture.

The early agriculture of the New World presents us with some puzzling problems. There is no doubt that the cereal grain, maize, eventually became the dominant food crop over much of the New World, changing from a wild ancestor (still unknown) consisting of small husk-covered grains arranged on a small core. As maize was domesticated these podded grains changed —the result of some mutation—the individual seed cover disappeared, and a husk enclosed the whole. The steps involved in this complex evolution are unknown. Probably more than one cereal-type plant goes into maize ancestry; a likely one is teocintle, a grass that, today, grows wild in Mesoamerica, and is itself a hybrid of domesticated maize and a wild relative.

Maize appeared early, probably by 5000 B.C.[1] It was likely first domesticated by some Middle American group, but peoples in various parts of Middle and North America may have joined in the experiments and observations that produced the various grain corns of today. Certainly if our radio carbon dates are correct, corn had spread to the Tamaulipas area by 3000 or possibly even 4000 B.C., and to New Mexico by four thousand years ago. In the first millennium B.C., it reached the eastern United States producing Neolithic cultures there. Maize is found in South America around 2000 B.C., and in that continent maize had considerable competition from other domesticated crops.[2]

Actually, on the face of it, there seems to have been two major centers of domestication in the New World, one in Mesoamerica and the other somewhere in western South America. This second agriculture was a root agriculture consisting of the "Irish" potato, a New World bean, and perhaps sweet manioc, the yam, and the sweet potato.

We know all too little of these early cultures, especially in South America, and it is impossible to say

## XIV

*The American Way*

if the South American agriculture was influenced by that to the North (or vice versa), by what is termed idea-diffusion. There is also the possibility that early Africans or Europeans were the instigators of South American root agriculture [3]—at least, they are more likely candidates than are the Asians, though in the present state of knowledge any Old World contact at this time level seems a rather remote possibility. We need to know a great deal more of the earliest agriculture in South America; especially the when and where. It is even possible that an early jungle group in the Amazon or Orinoco drainage invented, completely independently, the techniques of planting tubers in prepared soil (not a really drastic idea after all). If so, South America represents a third focus for the independent invention of agricultural techniques.[4] The main jungle crop today is bitter manioc, a root that contains prussic acid, but when squeezed dry of juice, a very good food.

At any rate, there are fairly elaborate cultures appearing in South and Middle America before 2000 B.C., in both areas based on agriculture. The earliest, to date, seem to be those of Puerto Hormiga in Colombia, excavated by G. Reichel-Dolmatoff, and Valdivia in Ecuador, reported by Betty J. Meggers, Clifford Evans, and Emilio Estrada.[5] At these sites, possibly as early as five thousand years ago, a people are found making pottery and apparently cultivating some crop or crops; good candidates are sweet manioc and beans. A little later, on the north Peruvian coast, beans and maize definitely appear as agricultural crops.

It would seem that the South American continent has been inhabited at least ten thousand years. We can guess—without really knowing—that the very earliest people sifted down the west coastal plains, probably sending offshoots into the Andean Cordillera, until some of them reached Tierra del Fuego. At the same time, other groups may have followed the eastern seaboard or perhaps penetrated some of the river valleys. It is tempting to believe that the massive jungles of the Amazon and Orinoco were settled rather late and owe their settlement to techniques first worked out at the jungle edges. As the present writer can testify from field experience, jungle life is specialized and exacting, and it seems probable that the jungles were still virginally free of man until population pressure forced people into them. The original inhabitants of the jungle probably had a Mesolithic economy, but they were supplanted by groups with agriculture, first of manioc and yams, then those plants plus maize. The earlier Mesolithic groups were forced upstream to refuge areas in the tributaries of the great rivers. In such refuge areas are also found descendents of certain early Neolithic groups. The time of these great migrations is not certain but they may have begun as early as 3000 B.C. Some of the early lowland settlers probably came from the Andean area, or more likely the Montaña. Some may have entered the river valleys via the east coast, thus working their way upstream. Agriculture is relatively early in the east; by the beginning of Christian times, if not before, the elaborate cultures, Ronquín and Barancas, flourished along the middle and lower Orinoco. The Amazon drainage had cultures as early or earlier, but the situation on the La Plata, southernmost of South America's great east-draining river systems, is less clear. The most evolved agricultural cultures found there at Conquest time seem to have shallow roots. However, the archaeology of the area is in its infancy.

Jungle adaptations in the Orinoco-Amazon area include use of bitter manioc rendered by pressing finely ground manioc in an elongated fiber bag (the "manioc squeezer") till the juice is removed. Other typical traits are the large communal house that shelters an entire extended family; the blowgun, a highly specialized hunting implement for jungle environment; and a scantiness of clothing, necessitated by the hot, wet climate. In South America none of these jungle groups developed civilization. They were still expanding when Spaniard and Portuguese invaded their domain, taking up new land and sending surplus population upstream or downstream as the case might be. Given a few more centuries (or millennia), a native lowland civilization, paralleling that of the Maya lowlands of Mesoamerica, might well have appeared. We will never know.

Maize agriculture spread both north and south from its Middle American homeland. As near as we can tell, it had begun its spread into the southern continent by 2000 B.C. If the possible connections between Mexico and Peru, to be suggested in the next chapter, prove to be true, it may be that maize was part of an early complex diffused intercontinentally, though for the moment this must remain one of several hypotheses. Nevertheless, maize spread over much of the old root crop area and by historic times was utilized up and down the Andes from Colombia to Chile and over much of the Amazon, Orinoco, and La Plata valleys. It was a matter of addition rather than supplantation—in fact, bitter manioc is widely used today, not only by Indian, but also by mestizo groups.

In Middle and North America not only was maize early, but there were plants in the present archaeological record still earlier, particularly squash and gourds. Many varieties of the pigweed were also grown quite early, though we are not sure when their cultivation began. Maize never completely replaced these plants, in fact, it combined forces with squash and, later, the bean to form what is called the New World trinity of plants. The bean was very important, for it supplied much-needed protein among populations that were expanding beyond their supply of animal proteins. Nor were the pigweeds replaced; amaranth (*Amaranthus* sp.) remained popular till Conquest times and was the center of many religious ceremonies that suggest great antiquity. But the precursors to civilization, going back perhaps four thousand years in Guatemala, were maize-using and all New World civilizations were based, at least in part, on it. When Europeans arrived, maize was still spreading, though slowly, and they gave it added impetus—in fact carried it around the world. In such diverse areas as south Russia and parts of Africa it is today an important part of the economy.

The New World was quite deficient in domestication of animals. We have seen how, in Afrasia, such useful beasts as the sheep, goat, and cow were very early domesticated. They supplied wool (or hair), labor, milk, meat, and hides. Later additions fell into these functional niches and, with the exception of eggs from chickens, no new uses for domesticated animals were discovered—thus pigs became the great source of meat for Europe and East Asia, the ass and horse took over part of the ox's function as a beast of burden (the horse also being milked), while the camel, still later, supplied hair, meat, milk, and labor. These were the primary domesticated animals in the Old World and the most adaptable and important of them, cattle, sheep, horses, spread throughout much of its area. Southeast Asia probably domesticated the chicken, while peoples of the Asiatic or European circumpolar area adapted the reindeer to diverse purposes; it was used for pulling sleighs and for riding; it was also milked and was slaughtered for food.

Interestingly, the New World peoples, though they domesticated dozens of plant foods, never became intensely involved in the domestication of animals. There were probably several reasons for this. First of all, certain animals were unavailable—the American horse, for example, seems to have died out in Late Pleistocene or Early Recent times. Perhaps the caribou could have been domesticated, as was the reindeer, but a factor of diffusion enters here. The reindeer almost certainly was domesticated by peoples who had received the idea of animal domestication from centers further south. The New World peoples of the far north were never exposed to such ideas. In the North American Great Plains and Mississippi valley bison herds roamed and in the latter area there had been agricultural communities settled for at least fifteen hundred years before European contact. As far as we know, however, none of these people attempted to tame the bison. It may simply be that the American buffalo (*Bison bison*) does not lend itself to domestication.

The New World civilizations therefore grew up without any animal that would pull a plough or a wheel and so, of course, neither of these devices (except for toy wheels!) was invented in the New World. In fact, only the Eskimo and Plains Indians managed to use an animal to pull a contrivance; the Eskimo had the dog-sled and the Plains peoples the dog travois. One of the two great civilized areas, the Middle American, was amazingly lacking in domesticated animals, having only the dog, turkey, bee and a variety of duck. The other great focus of civilization, the Central Andean region was more blessed. It had, for one thing, several species of native camel. One at least—the llama—was large enough to serve as a pack animal. Both the llama and alpaca had hair that could be made into cloth and both were used as food. On the other hand, neither was ridden and neither was large enough or tractable enough to be hitched to a plow or a wheel, even if such items had been known. Milk and milk foods from domesticated animals, so important in many parts of the Old World, were unknown in the New. The Central Andean peoples did have a small food animal, the guinea pig, and of course they owned the dog, though generally they did not eat it. The richer and more affluent New World cultures set considerable store on owning human beings—in this they were at one with their Old World neighbors. Human chattels were used for work, or for prestige purposes—in neither area were they commonly eaten, at least by civilized man, although the Aztecs were a partial exception for ceremonial reasons. Indeed, gastronomic cannibalism does not seem to have been practiced by any civilized people, probably because the human animal breeds too slowly to make the effort worthwhile. Slaves were used as pack animals, but no wheeled cart was ever developed for them. The high cultures did make use of litters, but they were mainly for ceremony or show and hardly affected the economy.

The important point to make concerning the Americas is that by about 2000 B.C. certain favored areas in western South America and in Middle America had reached a reasonably advanced Neolithic. In the next thousand years the earliest civilization would appear, partly as a result of wide, perhaps intercontinental, contacts. It must be noted that all this is quite late in terms of events of the Old World; the time gap is on the order of two thousand to three thousand years. Yet this does not mean that civilization was exported wholesale from one hemisphere to the other. East Asia, the most favored jumping-off point of diffusionists, was late in developing civilization and in any case shows only generic relationships to the New World civilizations in early times. Certain specific resemblances of later date (structural features of pyramids, the "water lily" motif, specific items such as the loom, blowgun, panpipes, and tie-dyeing) can best be explained otherwise. Even if there were contacts they would seem to be of a peripheral nature, with little effect on the rise of autonomous American civilization. Thus the suggestions made in an earlier chapter concerning the essential parallelism of civilizations—that they are similar because of certain internal factors—would seem to be borne out by data from the Americas.[6]

In summary, we can say with fair probability that man entering the New World via the Bering Straits, in a series of waves over many thousands of years, brought certain culture items, and signally failed to bring others. Introduced from Asia were items that pertained to an Upper Paleolithic level of existence plus certain later elements such as the bow and arrow and, still later, pottery. The Old World pottery, if indeed it is Old World, probably spread into the eastern United States at a time when ceramics had already been indigenously invented in Middle and South America.

Independently invented or discovered were agriculture, animal domestication (except for the dog which was brought from Asia), cloth-weaving techniques, the major pottery traditions, elaborate structures (temples, pyramids, palaces), political and religious hierarchies, advanced art (especially sculpture), metallurgy, writing, and urban life. There is a possibility of late influences from some Asian or African homeland, but even if these can be demonstrated they do not affect the essential autonomy of American civilization. A somewhat stronger possibility is of Polynesian contacts with the coast of South America, but these would have been of minor importance. There is also a chance that South Americans sailed, possibly on balsa rafts, to eastern Polynesia, thus making up one element in the ancient population of Easter Island. Such contact, if it actually happened, made no significant contribution to Polynesian society and none to that of the Andean peoples. Though remote, these remain our best possibilities of ancient interoceanic contacts to date. There are wilder theories; continents like Atlantis or Mu, now submerged, which provided stepping stones between the hemispheres; invasion by Alexander's fleet; and blue-eyed blondes, perhaps from Scandinavia, bringing the blessings of civilization to feckless Indians. In very recent years flying saucers have become popular as carriers of civilization to the New World and the Old. Usually the saucers originate on Mars or Venus. Perhaps man has too much imagination.

# MESOAMERICA

| Vera Cruz–Tabasco | Oaxaca | Valley of Mexico | Maya Area |

# H I S T O R I C   P E R I O D

| Date | Vera Cruz–Tabasco | Oaxaca | Valley of Mexico | Maya Area |
|---|---|---|---|---|
| 1500 | Aztec Influence — Post Classic — Local Post–Olmec Cultures | Mitla / Monte Albán V | Aztec II–V | |
| 1200 | | | | Mexican Period in Yucatan — Maya |
| 900 | | Monte Albán IV | Aztec I / Tula Toltecs | Abandonment of Peten — South Lowland Maya |
| 600 | Classic | | | Tepeu / Tzakol — Yucatecan |
| 300 | Upper Tres Zapotes | Monte Albán III | Teotihuacán III | |
| A.D. 0 | Late — Formative | | Teotihuacán II | |
| B.C. | | | | |
| 300 | Middle Tres Zapotes | Monte Albán II | Teotihuacán I | Formative Maya |
| 600 | Middle — Formative | Monte Albán I | Tlatilco | |
| 900 | Lower Tres Zapotes — Ceremonial La Venta | | | |
| 1200 | Early — Formative | | | |
| 1500 | | | | |
| 1800 | Pre–Ceremonial La Venta | | | |
| 2100 | | | | |

# A R C H A I C

59

*Comparative chronologies—Mesoamerica*

MESOAMERICA, ONE of the two great nuclear areas of the New World civilization, includes much of the modern countries of Mexico and Guatemala plus bits of Honduras, British Honduras, and El Salvador.[1] This is a region of great geographical contrast. In the north of Mexico two massive ranges, the Sierra Madre Occidental (west) and Oriental (east), stiffen the narrowing waist of the New World. Beginning just south of the present United States border, these two mountain chains run roughly parallel, one near the Pacific coast the other near the Atlantic. Between them is a high, dry plateau with arid remnants of Pleistocene lakes extending for hundreds of miles across the north of Mexico. This area has been a frontier of civilization for twenty centuries.

At about the 20th parallel, a great chain of volcanic mountains cuts across the peninsula of Mexico—directly east and west. The mountains contain a series of basins—the most famous being the interior-draining basin of Mexico, a key area for the development of civilization in the past two thousand years. South and east of this are the basins and ranges of Oaxaca and Chiapas, Mexico; the limestone peninsula of Yucatan sticking like some great mayoid thumb into the Gulf of Mexico; and, still further south and east, the mountain ridges of Guatemala. In this region the first intensive agriculture of the New World was produced and, if our assumptions of north-south movements are correct, the earliest civilization as well.

At some point around 1500 B.C., certain groups in Mesoamerica managed to improve on species of maize that had been grown for thousands of years and also, because of conditions about which we now know very little, to achieve the stability that is necessary for more intensive agriculture. During five or six hundred years these Early Formative groups gradually spread over southern and central Mexico and adjacent areas. Population increased and with it a number of technological skills that were eventually to produce civilization. The Early Formative peoples lived in small villages of wattle and daub houses, cultivating maize and a variety of other plants, including squash and the cereal amaranth (pigweed). The bean, so important to agricultural peoples because of its high protein content, was slowly

## XV

*Mesoamerica*

pervading the area. The pigweed was of great importance—it grows readily in disturbed soil and has a considerable yield.

Little is known of the social organization of the
Early Formative groups. They were, in all probability,
organized in small family bands, as had been their
ancestors. Political leadership was poorly developed, as
it always is on this technological level, and religion
must have been essentially of the shaman variety, with
the religious practitioners acting as guardians of traditional wisdom, curers, and perhaps group leaders all at
the same time. Technology was advancing: good pottery was already being produced, and in all probability
the art of weaving was invented by this time. In fact
weaving may have been earlier, for evidence from the
early site of Tehuacán in Puebla, Mexico, shows that
cotton had been domesticated in that area by about
5800 B.C.[2] There is a good chance that the earliest
cotton was grown for its oil-rich seeds, but cotton fiber
was soon used to make string, thread, and then cloth.

An important harbinger of the future was the appearance of the fired-clay figurines that have been found in
village sites and in graves. These are almost always of
women; usually nude, sometimes with breasts and geni-
tal organs carefully (even exaggeratedly) molded. They
are probably fertility figures used in some rite connected with the agricultural round—such figures were
common also in the early agricultural cultures of the
Old World. It has been suggested that they indicate a
strong female orientation of society, but this seems
unlikely, for in the occasional multiple burials, men
occupy the place of honor in the grave.

The Early Formative is found in much of southern
Mesoamerica, a good example being the site of Chiapa
de Corzo in Chiapas, Mexico. By the beginning of the
first millennium B.C., the ideas of the Formative had
spread somewhat more widely and were beginning to
bear the fruits of increased complexity. The Valley of
Mexico, hitherto very scantily populated, began its slow
rise to the premier position it would occupy in another
thousand years. At Tlatilco, west of modern Mexico
City, a modestly successful town grew up, a quarter of a
square mile in size. There the richer life of Middle
Formative incipient civilization appears. Burials show a

considerable wealth and the development of an upper class. Attractive figurines of nude maidens still appear, but molded figures of men are now found, some with the elaborate dress of a developing priesthood. At the site of Tlatilco there are also stirrup-spouted vessels, the technique of rocker stamping on pottery, and certain artistic conventions that are reminiscent of Chavín, the earliest high culture, far to the south, in Peru. It is doubtful if either the Valley of Mexico or the Central Andes was the origin point of these traits. We must look further afield.

From present evidence it would seem that the first New World civilization grew up in the lowlands of eastern Mexico. In coastal Vera Cruz and Tabasco, in an area of swampy rain-sodden lowlands, there appeared shortly after 1000 B.C., one of the most colorful and yet most enigmatic of societies. At the time of Spanish conquest this lowland area was called the Olmeca (land of the rubber people) and the name has become associated with the brilliant Middle Formative civilization. The only clue to what these people were called comes from Aztec legend which refers to a land called Tamoanchán, a word which, interestingly, is not Nahuatl, the language of the Aztecs, but rather Maya. In Mayan it means "land of mist," an excellent description of east coastal Mexico. The linguistic hint may be significant; in historical times Mayan was spoken in Guatemala and Yucatan to the south and east, but also in an isolated area, the Huasteca, along the northern end of Mexico's gulf coast. It seems quite possible that three thousand years ago a solid wedge of villages inhabited by Mayan-speaking Indians extended along the eastern coastlands of Mexico. If so, it might help to explain the generalized but real Olmecoid flavor of the later classic Maya civilization.

In the early part of the first millennium B.C., great centers such as La Venta in Tabasco dominated the lowlands of eastern Mexico. La Venta was a ceremonial establishment built on an island in the mosquito-ridden coastal swamps. Its main building is a earthen pyramid some 240 by 420 feet at the base and rising to a height of over a hundred feet. Originally it had, presumably, a temple on top, but such structure has entirely disappeared. The pyramid overlooks a complex of plazas,

60
*Olmec giant head*

mounds, walls, and stone columns.[3] In the La Venta site are found impressive stone sculptures, including giant heads carved in the round from basalt, eight or more feet in height. These represent round-faced heavy-lipped individuals with helmetlike headgear.

At La Venta, as at other sites of the Olmec, there appears, again and again, representations of the jaguar, often exquisitely carved in jade. Carved masks or figures may have a merger of feline and human, so that the jaguar figure becomes a human baby with the mouth pouting in catlike fashion.[4] The feline and human world were very near, for depictions of jaguars mating with women are known. It seems fairly certain that the Olmec jaguar became, in later times, the omnipresent Mesoamerican god of rain. Along with the jaguar appears the serpent, also representing a deity.

The Olmec climax, at such sites as La Venta, was Middle Formative. The ordinary pottery and the figures belong to that period, and the items already described from Tlatilco (rocker stamping, stirrup-spouted vessels) that relate to Chavín in Peru may have actually originated in this coastal area. It was a peaceful period and one of very strong religious orientation. Presumably, priestly rulers directed scattered villagers in the building of magnificent ceremonial centers, just as their South American counterparts were doing at Chavín de Huántar at approximately the same time. We can only dimly see the great ceremonies and festi-

61
La Venta, jaguar throne

vals, the ardent worship of jaguar and serpent, that
went on at La Venta and echoed across Mexico reaching Tlatilco in the isolated central basin. We do not
even know the economic base for such an elegant and
sophisticated society. A food surplus must have existed,
as well as large populations, in order to make possible
the building of the great pyramids and immense ceremonial enclosures. To organize, direct, and feed such
numbers of people implies a high level of political
control, but we know little or nothing of it. It is tempting to see the beginning of irrigation agriculture bringing, as it did in the Old World, a sharp rise in
population and in technological skills. There is, in fact,
firm evidence for irrigation in Middle Formative times,[5]
though not from the Olmec area itself.

Some kind of warfare that ravished the heartland of
the Olmec brought to a close the Middle Formative in
that area. About 400 B.C. unknown enemies razed the
great center of La Venta. The legend of this sacred and
mysterious place remained alive, however, and religious
offerings would still be made in the La Venta swamps
for two thousand years.

During the Middle Formative, Olmecoid influences
traveled not only to the Valley of Mexico but also

62 and 63
*Danzante figure, Monte
Albán*

*Mesoamerica*

173

southward and eastward as far as El Salvador. In fact, it may have been from some such area on the Pacific coast that these influences spread still farther, eventually reaching Peru. In Mexico, more than one region that would later become a focus of civilization felt the impact of the Olmecs' way of life, and we find it at this time in the beautiful Valley of Oaxaca, south and west of Vera Cruz. At the huge site of Monte Albán, overlooking present-day Oaxaca City, there still remain structures and statuary from this early date. Series of figures in low-relief, carved on stone slabs, some nearly life-sized, are incorporated in later construction. They are of nude men, sometimes depicted mutilated or decapitated. Their purpose is unknown and they relate most nearly to another series of relief carvings in stone found at Cerro Sechín in coastal Peru—carvings that are probably Chavín in date.

In the Late Formative the center of civilization shifted from the lowland forests of Vera Cruz to such intermontane basins as the Valleys of Mexico and of Oaxaca. Some sites in the lowlands, especially that of Tres Zapotes, remained important. In the Middle Formative period there had already appeared glyphs or ideograms in the Mayan style, another suggestion that the Olmec people may have been Mayan-speaking. On stelae from Late Formative times, at Chiapa de Corzo in Chiapas and at Tres Zapotes in Vera Cruz, appear the two earliest calendar dates in the New World, 36 and 31 B.C. They are in the Long Count, a count of days since the creation of the earth, the creation having taken place in the year 3113 B.C.[6] The count is based on a vigesimal (20 number) system, the numbers running from 0 to 19. The Long Count is best known from the Maya where it had its highest development. In the Maya system the day, *kin*, is listed; then a 20-day week, *uinal*; an 18-week "year," *tun*; and two longer periods, a 20-year *katun* and a 20-katun *bactun*, the latter of 144,000 days or approximately 394 solar years. The Long Count numbers were written as complicated glyphs, or more simply as a bar and dot numeration, a dot representing one and a bar five. The Long Count represented on the stone slab or stela at Tres Zapotes is

(7:16:6:16:18 or 31 B.C.).

From Formative times on, the peoples of Mexico and Guatemala were obsessed with the problems of time. Evidence from Oaxaca shows that another calendar was developing—actually an intermeshing of two calendars, one a permutation of 20 named days with 13-day numbers for an almanac year and another 20-day, 18-month solar calendar plus five additional "year-end" days. When these two systems, one of 260 days the other of 365, are used together, a given day and number in the almanac year will appear with a given day and month of the solar year once every 52 years. This Calendar Round was later used throughout Mesoamerica, and in the non-Mayan areas it measured the longest period that could be calculated.

In Late Formative times this developing Mesoamerican culture spread northward to the remote mountains and barren basins of north-central Mexico. A little later, in Classic times, civilization was to establish itself in a long, irregular frontier pressed against the wild tribes of the north, the Chichimecs of later tradition. To some degree the history of Mesoamerica in the last two thousand years has been tied up with this frontier and its fluctuations. Even today, after the leveling and distorting effects of alien European culture, this line of demarcation can still be traced.

With the Classic period (beginning around A.D. 300) came the culmination of trends that were hundreds of years old. Out of an Olmec background two majestic centers of civilization grew up, one in the Valley of Mexico and the other in northern Guatemala and adjacent regions. Other secondary but still impressive centers continued in Oaxaca, along the east coast of Mexico, in Yucatan, and now also in the west and north.

In the Valley of Mexico rose the great city of Teotihuacán, set in a small valley in the northeast part of the Valley near the shores of the lake. The settlement was founded in Late Formative times; Teotihuacán I dates from about 200 B.C. Teotihuacán II, expanded during a period of extensive building operation, appeared in the early Christian centuries; then, about A.D. 300, came the full Classic splendor of Teotihuacán III. This city was dominated by mighty structures, especially the four-sided pyramids of the Sun and Moon. The larger pyramid, that of the Sun, is on the eastern side of the great artery

64
*Aerial view of Teotihuacán*

street of Teotihuacán, now called the "Avenue of the Dead." It rose in four steps to a commanding height of over 200 feet and was probably crowned with a temple. At one end of the avenue is the somewhat smaller, but still impressive, Pyramid of the Moon. South of the great pyramids lies a complex which includes courts, platforms, rooms, and a smaller pyramid ornately decorated with carvings of Tlaloc, the rain god, and of the culture hero Quetzalcoatl (bird serpent). This collection of buildings may have been the headquarters for the temple priests or it may have been a royal palace. That there was an aristocracy is demonstrated by other elegant residences, designed with spacious rooms built around courtyards, of stone and adobe brick or of wattle and daub construction. The rooms had plastered interiors, often with large mural paintings, including one famous scene of the paradise of the rain god. Other murals show animal paintings or geometric figures.[7]

*Origins of Civilization*
176

Not only are upper-class houses known but also those of the artisans or peasants who provided the working force for the city. East of the main ceremonial area there has been excavated a tangle of small houses of adobe and wattle and daub, grouped around courtyards and intersected by lanes and small streets. Some of these structures contain several rooms and have tiny interior courts of their own. The impression they give is one of considerable wealth shared not only by a priesthood and aristocracy, but to some degree by the general population.

Technological skill was quite high. Teotihuacán artisans hand-molded elegant pottery, including tripod vessels. An especially delicate pottery called thin orange was traded far and wide. Figurines were still important, but were now moldmade. Teotihuacán architects could construct massive and showy buildings but, as elsewhere in Mesoamerica, these were rather uncomplicated works of engineering. The architects depended on the spectacular use of solid mass, especially delighting in pyramids that rise in great terraces to the sky. Such buildings are really architectually simple, somewhat like a child's structure of blocks; the large blocks below, the smaller ones above.[8] Even so, with the aid of skilled sculptors who, at least in one case, lined the faces of a pyramid with grotesque figures of the Tlalocs, the rain gods, and of the mighty feathered serpent, Quetzalcoatl, the structures of Teotihuacán were awe-inspiring to their builders as, indeed, they are to us.

Unlike the Andean civilization to the south the Classic world of Mesoamerica hardly knew metallurgy.

65
Detail, Temple of Quetzalcoatl, Teotihuacán

Even at the period of Spanish conquest, a thousand years later, the working of metals was an alien art, of little real economic importance. Just as the Andean region produced a civilization without writing, so did Mesoamerica evolve civilization without metallurgy. A written script, however, they did have. The glyphs that already have appeared in the Olmec region and in Oaxaca now are found (but in tantalizingly scarce supply) in Teotihuacán. These are complex ideograms that contain rebus elements and conventionalized picture drawings. Too few glyphs have survived from Teotihuacán for any possibility of interpretation, for the native paper on which the Classic peoples wrote numerical calculations, and possibly legends and histories, is long lost.

In Teotihuacán times stone-chipping reached dazzling heights of virtuosity. Obsidian was shaped in a bewildering variety of forms and jade, the jewel stone of the Olmecs, was much valued and widely used.

The Teotihuacán economy was primarily based on agriculture. There was some hunting of small animals, especially with a blowgun using clay pellets. The great basic food, however, was maize supplemented with beans, squash, chile, and amaranth. We have little direct evidence for any sort of irrigation techniques in Teotihuacán.[9] The city itself had a large population; estimates range from ten thousand to a hundred thousand. Even if we assume a figure near the lower end of this range there were many mouths to feed, many non-food-producing artisans and aristocrats to support. In this first great city of the New World and in other contemporary towns scattered over the valley there must have been techniques of intensive food production. A good guess, though as yet unproven, is that the construction of floating gardens, or chinampas, had begun. This involved building a reed and twig raft which was anchored in the shallow, still waters of the lake and plastered with mud from the lake bottom. Crops were then planted in this rich bed of soil, and as time went on long-rooted water plants gradually anchored the chinampa to the lake bottom. At a still later stage the chinampa became solid land. Then another adjacent floating garden was built and the process was repeated. Thus man gradually transformed the lake, a

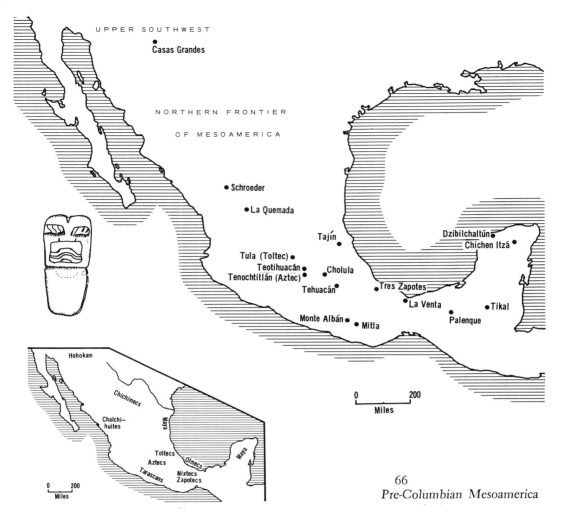

66
Pre-Columbian Mesoamerica

transformation that may well have begun by Teotihuacán times.

Whatever its basis, the culture thrived. By peaceful, perhaps religious, penetration the Teotihuacán styles and practices spread to the valley of Puebla and produced the mighty pyramid of Cholula, a structure that sprawled over twenty-five acres and was the largest man-made building in premodern Mesoamerica. Further east, Teotihuacán peoples influenced those of Tajín (and perhaps were influenced by them) and gave an indelible stamp to the venerable cultures of Vera Cruz, Tabasco, and Oaxaca. What may have been actual settlers from the Valley of Mexico migrated ever further, and some six hundred miles to the south and east built a miniature Teotihuacán at Kaminaljuyu near modern Guatemala City. There the dead autocrats

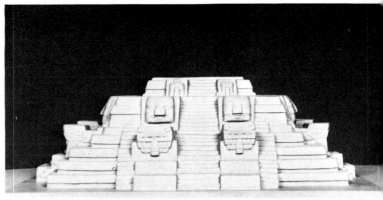

67
Model of early Maya pyramid (E-VII-Sub Uaxactún, near Tikal)

still lie entombed with their treasures of jade and fine orange pottery, some of it actually made in the parent city.

Teotihuacán influences also spread west and north. Man of Classic times here inched beyond the boundaries set by his Formative forefathers. At such remote places as La Quemada, Alta Vista, and Montehuma in Zacatecas, and Schroeder in Durango, pottery reflects the motifs of the Classic world. At these sites a people influenced from the south built pyramids, and surrounded them with ceremonial towns supported by a rich, perhaps an irrigation, agriculture. The omnipresent bird-snake appears in pottery motifs along with the star snake of the milky way (or of rain) and other graphic examples of Classic cosmology.[10]

If the culture world of Teotihuacán dominated much of Mexico, another world, that of the Maya, was rising in northern Guatemala and Yucatan. Its roots were set in the Olmec past, as were those of Teotihuacán, but the Mayan debt to Olmec was at once more direct and more pervasive than was that of Mexico. Again we must remember the possibility that a great isthmus of Mayan-speakers once extended up the east coast of Mexico. Though the formal features of Teotihuacán and Maya are similar, the spirit is quite different, a difference that survived the leveling effect of the later invasions and wars and, indeed, continued into historic times.

The key area of the Classic Maya was in the flat jungle country of the Petén of Guatemala. Here appeared such enormous sites as Tikal stretching for miles, a vast complex of temples, pyramids, courts, and other structures, some of forgotten use. Builders

*Origins of Civilization*
180

worked largely in stone, and in temple and hall they utilized the clumsy corbeled arch and corbeled vault. Maya architecture differs from that of Mexico in that the temples and pyramids soar; height, rather than massive strength, is the key. Temples were often topped with a façade of stone grillwork giving an aery quality to the structures.

Technologically, the Maya of Classic times were on a par with the Mexicans. Metallurgy was virtually unknown; this was offset by skillful stonework, and by virtuosity in such crafts as pottery, weaving, architecture, sculpture, and in the production of written records, and elaborate and highly accurate calendrical and astronomical calculations. The latter had little or nothing to do with any budding science of astronomy. Rather, the Maya were obsessed with the idea of lucky or unlucky days. As they had several calendars operating, the almanac calendar, the solar calendar, a lunar calendar, and perhaps a Venus calendar, plus the Long Count of days since creation, a vast number of permutations were possible. Individual days were sacred to particular gods, good or evil, so that a given day would be seen as a focus for a large number of forces. Occasionally, a day of darkness and death in one calendar would coincide with an evil day in one or more of the other calendars. It was the computation of such days so as to guard against their evil influence that played such an important part in Maya calendrical lore. Another very important use of the Long Count was to obtain genealogical data on individual rulers and even to record important events of their reigns.

Like the Teotihuacán people, the Maya were intensive farmers basing their agriculture firmly on maize and its New World plant satellites. In this area irrigation techniques are not necessary to support large populations. The Maya lowlands were so rich and the weather so mild that ordinary husbandry would produce sufficient surplus. The Mayan sites were perhaps not cities in the Teotihuacán sense of the word. Such large centers as Tikal and Uaxactún in the Petén, Copan in Honduras, Palenque in the Usumacinta valley of Chiapas, and Dzibilchaltún of Yucatan were great ceremonial clusters with groups of villages scattered around them and milpas, or cornfields, inter-

*Courtesy* Andor Braun

68
*Corbeled vault, Uxmal*

69
Maya Temple,
Palenque

spersed between the villages. The great centers were
probably also used for markets and were the residences
of both the religious and political elite. Excellent roads
radiated out from the centers, connecting the village
and ceremonial area, and we can envision, on important days, crowds of colorfully costumed Maya flocking
to trade, participate in or observe ceremonies to the
chacs, the rain gods, or to one or the other of the many
deities. One of the ceremonies that was performed, as
in Mexico, was a ritual ball game played in a great
prepared court. In this game only the head or body
could be used to strike the heavy, native rubber ball—
not the arms. More than a game, it was an important
religious event—some later accounts say that the losing
team was sacrificed. But in the Classic period, both in

70
*Temple I, Tikal*

*Courtesy* Lisa Ferree

the Maya area and in Mexico proper, human sacrifice was probably uncommon.

From paintings and burials, and from archaeology we know something of the home life of the Maya. As in Teotihuacán, men and women wore cloaks of cotton and the women also wore a loose dress of the same material. The common people lived in small wattle and daub houses, often on raised platforms. Inside were the simple furnishings, a few pots for water and cooking, a flat tortilla stone, a chile grater in the form of an interior-roughened bowl, and the ever-present metate and mano. Platforms were used for storage and the family slept on mats on the floor. In many places the cooking may have been done in a separate house, as it often is today in this area. The pellet blowgun was used to hunt

71
*Ball court, Chichen
Itzá*

small game, but man's work, and often that of woman
and child, was in the maize field, planting, weeding,
guarding against animal or insect marauders, and har-
vesting. Some of the crop went to supply the priests in
the great temple complexes that had sprung up on
every side. It was a peaceful life and perhaps a satisfy-
ing one.

Nevertheless, in the period after A.D. 600, throughout
both the Mexican and Mayan areas, there came a series
of drastic and far-reaching changes that altered the
cultural face of Mesoamerica. We would know more of
the reasons for, and the direction of, this change if we
had a better idea of the actual structure of Classic
society in Mesoamerica. In spite of the powerful position of Teotihuacán it does not seem to have been the
center of an empire. Strong regional centers in Oaxaca
and elsewhere were obviously influenced, but it was
stimulus influence—in some areas very direct and
strong, but in the north and west of Mexico actually
rather more derived and secondhand (for example, the
bird snake or feathered snake in Durango and Zacatecas
becomes a combination of two animals, a road runner
and a snake). Even at Kaminaljuyu there seems more a
pattern of migration than conquest. The same is true in
the Maya area, for no one city or region can be demonstrated to be a dominant political power. Probably the

*Origins of Civilization*
184

72
*Pyramid of the
Niches, Tajín*

*Courtesy* Dr. and Mrs. J. Charles Kelley

Mexicans and Maya were both organized in a series of city-states or statelets, though such giants as Teotihuacán, Monte Albán, Tajín, and Tikal may have controlled larger areas. If the evidence of tombs, frescoes and other paintings, and the persistent legends of a later time are correct, the priesthoods were very important in the political as well as the religious sphere. There was, however, considerable warfare, something usually associated with secular rule.

Probably a number of languages were spoken in Classic times, thus encouraging the diversity of political organization. The Mayan people, indeed, spoke Mayan; their continuity with historical people has been established and the language may well have included the Olmec of the Formative period. It is not sure what was the linguistic situation in Teotihuacán. Nahuatl, the language of later Aztecs is a good possibility but Otomí, in early historic times spoken in the basin area north of the Valley of Mexico, is also a possibility. The people of Oaxaca were very likely Zapotecan-speaking and likely had been so from the early period at Monte Albán. Other languages, Totonac on the east (forming a wedge in historic times between the wings of Maya-speakers), and Tarascan on the west, may have had roughly their historic distribution by the end of Classic times.

The collapse of the Classic civilization in Mexico and in the Maya area seems to have been for somewhat different reasons. In central Mexico there was a shift of population, with tribes, later to be called Chichimecs ("dog people"), sifting in from the arid and inhospitable regions of northern Mexico. These new groups, perhaps aided by peasant unrest at home, moved into the old civilized areas, burning Teotihuacán and looting other centers.[11] Warfare now comes into its own and the war leader becomes a dominant figure. In the Maya area a fifty-year break in ceremonial construction (the last half of the sixth century) may reflect troubles further north. Then there was a recovery, and Long Count dates are recorded until A.D. 889. After that, however, the impressive stelae, with Long Count numeration and other glyphic information, and the majestic buildings were no longer constructed. The lights of the great centers winked out, leaving the broken cities to be reclaimed by the jungle. The reason is not clear. Perhaps, as the Mayanist J. Eric Thompson has suggested, it was a revolt of a peasantry against the exactions of the priestly overlords. Whatever the reason, only Yucatan survived the changes, and even here with a lessened vitality. In the troubled days such long-lived and sacred institutions as the Long Count were lost. In Postclassic Maya a simplified "Count of Katuns" only, remained.

The impression from archaeology is that in the eighth and ninth centuries there was turmoil in Mesoamerica and new ideologies and institutions were being born. In the Puebla area, groups of (presumably)

73
*Tula, Toltec period frieze*

Mixtec-speaking peoples sifted into the region, vying with Indians of the older Classic strata and producing the vigorous Mixteca-Puebla art styles and culture. North of the Valley of Mexico, in Hidalgo, the tenth century, saw the expansion of Tula, home and ruling city of the Toltecs. These people were, at the time of the Spanish conquest, legends in their own right; the Toltec period was seen as a great golden age for Mexico, and the kings and heroes of the Toltecs were demigods in the eyes of the Indian Mexico of a later day.

With the Toltecs we clearly see a change to a strong military orientation of society. The god Quetzalcoatl competed with blood-hungry war gods who demanded mass murder of war victims. Tezcatlipoca and other deities of this period are dark and cruel and even Quetzalcoatl, where he manages to hold his own, takes on a new ferocity.[12]

The Toltec capital of Tula is largely unexcavated but it obviously continued many patterns of life from earlier Classic cultures. Names of kings and heroes that have come down to us from later traditional histories suggest that the Toltecs were Nahuatl-speaking, as the Teotihuacán people may also have been. Nevertheless, Tula is no slavish copy of Teotihuacán. There is a new formalism shown in stiffness of line, in massive block-shaped human figures formed into columns, in depictions of clan totems, jaguars and eagles, and in scenes of human sacrifice.

Tula may well have been the center of an empire, for sites showing Toltec influence are spread widely throughout west and central Mexico. There is also a strong and curious link with the Yucatan area. Among the Toltec "histories" related by later Aztecs, one had to do with the semidivine King Quetzalcoatl who, after losing a long struggle with the cruel new gods, turned eastward to the sea and set sail on a large serpent-raft with his devoted followers. The Yucatan Maya have legends, recorded by early Spaniards, that tell of a great hero called Kukulkán (feathered snake) who comes from the west and conquers the great Maya city of Chichen Itzá. In the tenth century (about the time of the traditional Quetzalcoatl voyage) there was indeed a burst of Mexican influence in the Maya area and Chichen Itzá was rebuilt as a copy of Tula. This

Courtesy Andor Braun

74
Atlantean figure, Tula

75
*Detail, Temple of Warriors,*
*Chichen Itzá*

*Courtesy* Andor Braun

Mexican influence remained strong in the Maya land
and there were still reflections of it at the time of the
Spanish conquest.

The Valleys of Puebla and Oaxaca managed to escape the full flood of the Toltec and the Tajín area also
kept a nominal independence. In Oaxaca the Zapotecs
clung to at least a semblance of priestly rule. At the site
of Mitla, a few miles from Monte Albán, there is a vast
complex of rooms, courts, and temple structures decorated with intricate geometric designs. Mitla is still,
today, an awe-inspiring place. It might be well at this

76
*Chacmool, Tula (perhaps a
sacrifical basin in form of
reclining man)*

point to quote the words of the nineteenth-century
archaeologist Adolph Bandelier.

A stillness as of the grave rules in the well cleaned
courtyard, which encloses the short, narrow halls. Not a
bird sings, no cricket chirps in the "Ruins of Mitla."
Lizards rustle over the stones, on the walls sits the carrion
vulture and watches the body of the incomer with a cold,
inquiring look.

In the low broad gates horror really dwells, while in
the narrow passages the footsteps resound like a dull roar
out of the depths. But in whatever direction the eye may
turn, it is not encountered by ugly faces or horridly
twisted snake-like bodies, but by simple geometric figures
which, to be sure, reveal the stiffness of death, but, too, a
striving for symmetric harmony. This was all so completely different that what I had thought; not larger or
more imposing, but purer, more noble that I had imag-
ined.

77
*Pyramid, Chichen Itzá, with
chacmool in foreground*

78
An interior courtyard,
Mitla, Mexico

With the Postclassic period came the first real metallurgy to Mexico, copper and gold cast by the lost-wax technique. This traffic in metallurgical ideas presumably represented trade, or at least some kind of contact with South America, either directly or through some, as yet unknown, intermediary. In the north and west of Mexico, Toltec-influenced cultures flourished in the Chalchihuites area of Durango and the Cañatillo area of Zacatecas. Even earlier, in Classic times, ideas of the civilized south had seeped into present-day United States and influenced the large-scale irrigation culture of Hohokam in southern Arizona and the Pueblos of Anasazi of New Mexico. In the tenth and eleventh centuries, Hohokam would reach its fruition with large villages along or near great irrigation ditches that tapped the waters of the Salt and Gila rivers and carried them for miles to turn desert into farmland. This is also the period of the compact thousand-room towns in Chaco Canyon, New Mexico, with their enormous kivas, or underground ceremonial rooms, some of the latter scores of feet across with lofty roofs held up by great shafts of spruce or fir. And even further north in caves of the Mesa Verde and elsewhere, the first of the large cliff dwellings were being built. At about the same time Mesoamerican individuals or bands were trekking into the eastern United States to produce the near-civilization of the Mississippian culture.

Though such far-off peripheries might flourish, the heartland was in trouble. In the late eleventh century more marauding bands of Chichimecs broke into the Toltec world. Mighty Tula was sacked and abandoned and the wild tribes, some of them Nahuatl-speaking kinsmen of the Toltecs, others speaking Otomí and other languages, filtered through central Mexico.[13] Farther south and east, Mixtecs began to expand, pushing into the remotest corners of the Valley of Oaxaca. In Yucatan the old culture of the Maya slowly reasserted itself, though now indelibly stamped by Mexican ways.

One of the wild Nahuatl tribes was called the Tenochca or Colhua Mexica. Since the Tenochca people claimed to come from the mythical northern land of Aztlán they later became known as the Aztecs and this name will be used here. Moving into the relatively cultured region of the Valley of Mexico these upstart barbarians soon acquired a fake Toltec genealogy and a thoroughly bad name in the eyes of their civilized neighbors. It was deserved! Their tribal god Huitzilopochtli (Humming bird-on-the-left) was a demonic deity who thirsted daily for the still-quivering hearts torn from the chests of captives and slaves. Even in the period of warriors and bloodthirsty war gods the Aztecs stood out for dark and cruel ways. They were also lacking in tact; when the king of Colhuacán, Coxcox, gave their chief his daughter as a bride, the Aztecs

79
*Shell gorget, Mississippian culture, Kentucky*

80
*Shell gorget, Mississippian culture, Illinois*

*Courtesy* Jon D. Muller

*Courtesy* Jon D. Muller

promptly sacrificed this unfortunate maiden. As a result of this escapade they were driven to take refuge in flat, unhealthy islands in the southern part of Lake Texcoco.

This forced move proved a blessing in disguise because from their island city of Tenochtitlán the Aztecs gradually gained power throughout central Mexico. They quickly made an alliance with the flourishing city of Texcoco on the eastern side of the lake. Under such skillful leaders as Itzcoatl (1428–40), and Montezuma I (1440–69) the Aztecs soon acquired a plunder empire. Though checked by the Tarascans in the west, they gradually infiltrated the eastern highlands and finally reached the Vera Cruz coast. It was there that Aztec officials of the vacillating mystic, Montezuma II, first saw the ships of Cortez.

CENTRAL ANDEAN civilization was profoundly shaped by the peculiarities of regional geography. The dominating feature is the majestic ridge of the Andes rising some 20,000 feet above sea level. This is paralleled by an offshore trough approximately as deep as the mountains are high. The area, then, has one of the greatest altitude ranges in the world—40,000 feet from sea bottom to mountain top.

Along the coast from southern Ecuador to northern Chile stretches a dry, yet fertile coastal plain. The dryness is caused by the cold Humboldt current, running north along the Peruvian coast. The warm ocean air passing over this current is cooled, and as it moves over the coastline it produces fogs but little rain. Beyond the narrow coastal plain the land rises rapidly to the first line of the Andes. Air moving inland is forced upward to the cold heights and loses much of its moisture content. The result is a series of short, rapid streams rushing across the desert foothills and coastal plains to discharge into the Pacific. Along the courses of these miniature Niles the first South American civilizations were built.

The Andes proper run in a series of narrow chains throughout present-day Peru finally widening to form a mid-continental mountain knot in Bolivia. The upper reaches of the mountains are far too high for human habitation, but interspersed between the main ridges are a series of high valleys, ranging from a pleasant and subtropical 8,000 feet to a cold, bleak terrain 12,000 feet or more in altitude. These basins were centers of early settlement of man and contributed greatly to Andean civilization.

East of the mountains is the rain forest of the Montaña. Here the Andean people failed to penetrate; their economy and their technology were too alien to adapt to jungle conditions. Indians of the rain forests never reached a status of civilization and remained fringe groups, trading and raiding, but benefiting very little from Andean civilization.

On an early agricultural base (probably not including maize) there appeared by 1500 B.C., or before, a monumental architecture both on the coast and in the highlands of Peru.[1] Into this precocious ferment, a little after 1000 B.C., ideas were introduced, religious and

# XVI

*The*

*Central*

*Andes*

CENTRAL ANDES

| | North Coast Peru | South Coast Peru | Highlands North Peru | Highlands South Peru and Bolivia |
|---|---|---|---|---|
| | l | n | c | a |

1500
1200 — Chimu
— Coast — Tiahuanaco — — Late Tiahuanaco
900 — — A — Tiahuanaco–Influenced Cultures —
600 — Mochica / Gallinazo / Salinar — NASCA — — Classic Tiahuanaco
300
A.D. 0 — — classic Paracas — Necropolis — White on Red — Tiahuanaco
B.C. — — — Cavernas — —
300 — — Coastal Chavin — Early Paracas (Cerrillos) — —
600 — Cupisnique — — — Early
900
1200
1500 — **E a r l y    F a r m e r s**
1800
2100

81

Comparative chronologies—Central Andes

otherwise, that spread over much of the central Andes, but especially the north coast of Peru and the adjacent Andean highlands. Maize joined the other agricultural crops, and farming villages began to be organized by political and religious leaders who used the new surpluses of men and food to construct temples and shrines. The period of this increased activity, called Chavín, is a most interesting one for several reasons. Religious architecture becomes extraordinarily sophisticated, and a cat (probably jaguar) figure, and other art motifs resembling those of the Olmec rather suddenly appear. The general picture of Chavín is really quite reminiscent of Olmec of the Middle Formative of Mexico. People (surely living in small scattered villages) were mobilized for large religious works, some of which are extremely ambitious and impressive. Though we know nothing of the political organization, the necessities of controlling, feeding, and rotating labor gangs, of establishing quotas, and bringing people long distances to work on the temples would demand a strong central control, and strong motivation too; surely motivation of a religious nature.

Little is known of the villages themselves. They were small sites; people lived in mud brick or stone houses in the coastal areas, and perhaps wattle and daub structures in the highlands. They manufactured simple but technically good incised pottery, wool, and cotton, and cultivated their small fields, using stone and bone agricultural implements. There were certainly class distinctions; we have evidence for them in the burials of the period, the sites of which sometimes contain fine polished black pots occasionally decorated with the feline design. One pottery type that has a long history in the Central Andes is the stirrup-spout pot. The spout opens from the top of a curved tube that is attached to either side of the upper surface of the vessel. Also from the graves come a few gold, mixed gold and silver, or gold, silver and copper ornaments. These are hammered, but were heated for annealing. The mixing of metals was probably accidental, but already sophisticated techniques are used including welding, champlevé, and incising.

The best-known temple is at the type site of Chavín de Huántar in a small valley in the northern highlands. Here villagers, many of them surely coming from a distance, built under priestly control and direction a vast complex of religious buildings. There are plazas, courts, platforms, and other structures oriented, generally, in an east-west direction. Most impressive is the Castillo, a three-storey structure of dry stone masonry, the walls of which still stand in places to a height of 45 feet. The building (roughly 245 by 235 feet) has massive rubble-filled walls faced with dressed stone. In its interior there is a regular maze of rooms, stairs, ventilating and drainage shafts, alcoves, and galleries. The ventilating shafts were needed, for there are no external windows and only a main entrance door. This structure was certainly not used as a living quarters, but its exact function—probably religious—is not now known. Nev-

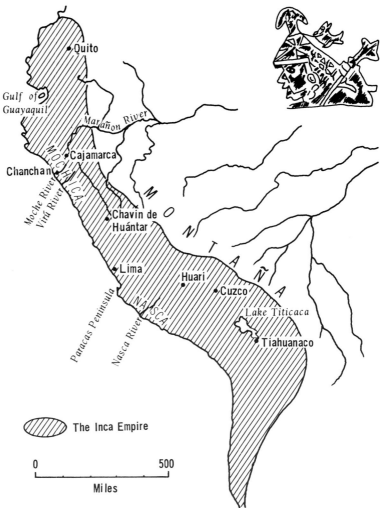

82
Central Andes to A.D. 1500

ertheless, it indicates a real architectural skill on the
part of those who planned and directed the work.

The cult of serpent and jaguar was very likely practiced at Chavín de Huántar. In addition, there may
have been a trophy-head cult. At the site there are
carved stone heads set in vertical walls, heads which
have the sunken features of the elderly—or of dried
trophies.[2] The art forms of Chavín in general are dominated by fanged felines, and serpents in intricately balanced designs.[3] A. L. Kroeber has described Chavín art
as monstrous, and indeed it is sometimes nightmarish.[4]

The Chavín seems to be, basically, a widespread religious cult linking various local cultures. The late Peruvian archaeologist Rafael Larco Hoyle, many years ago

suggested that the Cupisnique area of the coast may have given rise to more widespread Chavín manifestation.[5] This cannot be demonstrated one way or the other at present, but it might be said that the north coast of Peru, homeland of Cupisnique, is the kind of region in which one would expect to find the kind of elaborate organization that would lead to civilization. Here, fast-flowing rivers drop rapidly from the mountains and spread across an almost rainless coastal desert. Because of the rapid flow of the rivers, large-scale irrigation is relatively easy. Water can be tapped in the middle valleys and brought to the lower valley by simple ditches that run parallel to the rivers. The actual engineering is simple, but a considerable amount of upkeep is needed, for the ditches must cross rough terrain including dry arroyos. It is this kind of cooperative, directed labor that would give the surplus food needed for such cultural extras as temple building. It also would give a developing elite class the experience in planning large-scale operations and directing large numbers of laborers. It might also encourage certain kinds of engineering skills that could be utilized for construction of the temples.[6]

Such a situation once well-started might be expected to develop very rapidly, perhaps in only a few generations, and the archaeological evidence from the north coast suggests this. From a relatively simple culture of the Guañape type there is rapid superposition of the elaborate ceramics, metalwork, and highly developed technical skills in such things as weaving. Jewelry from the period becomes technically advanced; the Cupisnique people used pyrite, jet, turquoise, quartz, bone, wood, and shell for beads, rings, necklaces, and other articles. It is generally thought that the period was peaceful, but some of the implements do suggest warfare and certainly the north coast, at a later period, was devoted to war.

The extent of contact between Olmec and Chavín is quite unknown. There seems a good possibility of a generic relation between the feline-snake cults of the two areas, and certain art motifs do seem related. It is not even certain that such influences came from north to south, though if the introduction of maize to the north coast of Peru can be related to the beginnings of

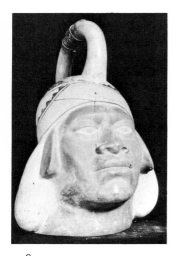

83
*Mochica portrait vessel,*
*Peru*

84
*Mochica portrait vessel,*
*Peru*

*Origins of Civilization*
198

Chavín-Cupisnique it would strongly suggest such a north-south movement. At any rate metallurgy was not derived from Mexico; this craft seems to have spread the other way at a much later date. It is hard to escape the conclusion that the origin of Peruvian civilization was largely the matter of internal growth.

A beginning date, at least for Cupisnique, of somewhere between 1000 and 800 B.C. seems reasonable. At the end of the period there is, from the evidence at hand, a lessening of importance of the feline-serpent cult. What actually happened we do not know. Perhaps there was a revolt against exactions of the priesthood, or possibly new fashions more local in character gradually replaced the more widespread religion. If Chavín does have a historical reality, and was spread by evangelical enthusiasts who established contacts over much of Peru and Bolivia, this kind of collapse might be expected. Later Peruvian history certainly is one of alternative unifying waves, religious and political, followed by periods of intense regionalism. The regionalism is not surprising in a land containing as it does two such different zones; rather it is the remarkable drive for unification that should puzzle us. But unification there was, on occasion, and the reasons are still unknown.

The end of Chavín (probably before 300 B.C.) can be traced in detail on the north coast of Peru and from this area there is also extensive evidence for the later cultures. The central and south coasts were now beginning to be well-populated. First, a series of white-on-red pottery styles, then negative-painted wares link parts of the north coast, central coast, and highlands.[7] One of the better described cultures is that of Salinar on the north coast; it is uninspired, but does give a foundation for the flamboyant Mochica or Moche period that followed.[8] From Salinar there is evidence for the continuation of irrigation agriculture; some new plants may have been introduced at this time, one that grows at high altitudes is quinoa (*Chenopodium quinoa*). The llama, or American camel, was domesticated well before Salinar times.[9]

Jutting out from the central Peruvian coast is the barren peninsula of Paracas where many years ago extensive burial areas were found. These are of two main types called respectively, Paracas Cavernas and Paracas Necropolis. The Cavernas group is earlier—it has a gay polychrome pottery that has suggested links with both Chavín and the later Nasca (or Nazca) of the south coast, and may actually date in this transitional post-Chavín period. The Necropolis is later and is probably contemporary with (or even a part of) Nasca culture. These latter burials (often mummified by the dry air) have wrappings of superbly woven cotton textiles, showing a great variety of techniques. A dramatically high standard of weaving, producing great works of textile art, is characteristic of Peru and the craft had already reached a high plateau of excellence by Necropolis times, two thousand years ago.

At some point between *c.* 300 B.C. and the beginning of the Christian era, the period began which is known to some archaeologists as the Florescent era, to others as the period of Master Craftsmen. Here on the base of Salinar, and the other White-on-Red cultures, appeared one of the most spectacular developments in Peruvian prehistory. On the north coast there appeared the Gallinazo, and a little later the vigorous Mochica (Moche) culture,[10] and on the south coast the Nasca. We know much less about the highland areas, but in the southern highlands, perhaps in the Titicaca Basin, the formative stages of Tiahuanaco were developing. Tiahuanaco, a little later, was to represent the second great Pan-Peruvian horizon.

Of the Florescent cultures Mochica is very well known—in fact, it is the best-known nonliterate culture in the world on this formative stage of civilization. The reason for this is simply that the Mochicans were devoted to graphic representation on the walls of pots. This took the form of painting on the pot surface or of modeling the clay. The scenes (and there are many thousands) include ceremonial or religious processions, warfare, political activities, hunting, fishing, trading, and agriculture, and various vignettes of everyday life including an awe-inspiring variety of sexual practices.

From the evidence of the representational art and from other archaeological data we have a good idea of Mochica life. The north Peruvian valleys were densely settled and valley-wide irrigation systems were in operation. The people lived in fairly large towns and wor-

85
*Mochica stirrup-pot, Peru*

86
*Huaca del Sol,*
*Mochica culture, Peru*

shiped their gods on large, stepped pyramids of sun-dried and baked clay—good examples are the "Huaca del Sol" and the "Huaca de la Luna," the former 750 by 450 feet on the sides and 60 feet high. The military and religious leaders were carried in litters and lived in multi-roomed houses of stone and clay. These leaders, during the Mochica period, gradually increased their power and as time went on the archaeological record suggests that some sort of Mochica empire or confeder-ation spread through valley after valley on the northern coast of Peru.[11]

Meanwhile, on the same time level the dynamic Nasca culture—developing out of an earlier Paracas level—held the southern coast of Peru. The Nasca peo-ple also lived in towns of adobe houses though the evi-dence is much less clear than in the north. This area is very dry, so that some sort of irrigation was a necessity.

Nasca has an exceedingly rich and developed pottery, the polychrome ceramic vessels found mainly in tombs. An individual piece may have six or more colors, and the vessels are decorated with stylized designs, mainly birds or animals, and mythological monsters. The latter group includes a feline, perhaps the ancient jaguar god in still another form.

As might be expected from a culture closely con-nected with Paracas, the textiles, many well-preserved in the dry soil, were of high quality. Both wool (llama and alpaca) and cotton were used and the Nasca peo-ple were skilled at a variety of techniques including tapestry and brocade making. Like the pottery, woven stuff was often multicolored; the Nasca craftsmen or craftswomen had a strong feeling for color.

While the people of coastal Peru were elaborating their strong regional traditions, a new way of life was being developed by other Andean Indians in the highlands of southern Peru and Bolivia. The men and women who originated and spread Tiahuanaco culture were certainly influenced by Nasca or Nascoid cultures of the south coast. They added ideas and techniques from the highlands and, sometime before A.D. 1000, began a dynamic spread across Peru. It is still not known whether this expansion was the result of a vibrant new religion or was simply a military adventure. The evidence from the north coast suggests that the latter was one element, at least, in the success of the Pan-Peruvian Tiahuanaco culture. In the north, the Mochica kingdoms, as traced by pottery styles and other archaeologically recorded traits, were aggressively expanding, and military adventures are recorded over and over again on pot walls. Then suddenly—very suddenly—these dynamic societies are blotted out and in their stead is Tiahuanaco—attested by very new and different pottery styles and different settlement patterns. The great pyramids fall into disrepair and people gather together in large enclosed sites. There may have been an actual population decline—at least in the northern valleys. A new, warlike people, carrying new religious and political ideas, have overrun much of Peru. They may even have built a political empire—at least the later Inca duplicated the Tiahuanaco feat and the Inca wave was undeniably political in nature.[12]

87
*Mochica zoomorphic stirrup-pot, Peru*

Tiahuanaco actually brought little cultural enrichment to the central Andes. The majestic site of Tiahuanaco (a political or religious capital) on the shores of Lake Titicaca shows certain new skills in stoneworking—walls are made of massive smoothed stones with the individual blocks often held together by metal clamps.[13] This technical addition to large-stone construction would be continued in the later highlands, though the coast remained dedicated to adobe structures. Tiahuanaco pottery and weaving continue the excellent Andean tradition—they are different, but not better, than the earlier work. There may have been some advance in metallurgy, but metallurgical techniques were already quite sophisticated. Possibly the Tiahuanaco people foreshadowed the Inca in their political organization but this we do not really know.

After A.D. 1000 local cultural patterns, seen archaeologically in pottery styles, reappeared both on the coast and in the interior. In southern Peru the Inca were slowly differentiating themselves from a dozen other small intervalley groups. On the north coast of Peru the old Mochica population obviously had a resurgence—the culture of this area is called Chimu or Late Chimu. It combined traits from the brilliant Mochica with those (especially in city building) of Tiahuanaco. The greatest of the Chimu cities, Chanchan in the Moche valley, is an enormous site. A series of great walled enclosures, covering some eight square miles are filled with a dazzling array of adobe brick buildings including houses, pyramids, temples, and palaces. These are surrounded by large, mud brick walls; some, even today, stand 30 feet high and were once considerably higher. The walls are sometimes ornately decorated with conventionalized designs of animals and with purely geometric figures done in arabesque—many of them quite reminiscent of designs on fabric. Within the enclosures there were streets with a regular grid layout. The meaning of the separate, perhaps partly self-sufficient, enclosures or compounds is not now certain but it may reflect the organization of the Chimu people into the ayllu, a social organization basic to the slightly later Inca.

88
*Mochica bird stirrup-pot, Peru*

These latter people started in a rather small way. When Chanchan was in its heyday the Inca groups were struggling to keep a part of the intermontane basin of Cuzco in southern Peru. For some centuries they operated from a tiny base and their wars, raids, and political maneuvers were all held within a few miles of Cuzco. Finally around A.D. 1430, with the coming to power of the "Emperor" Pachacuti, the Inca began a rapid military expansion. Within approximately one-half century Pachacuti and his son, Topa Inca, had extended Inca control and influence over some 350,000 square miles in a great elongated area stretching 3000 miles from modern Ecuador to modern Chile.[14]

This empire was, in fact, rather strictly limited by

ecological and environmental factors. In the series of intermontane basins in Peru, Bolivia, and Ecuador, where lived peoples of similar culture, conquest was easy and rapid, and the same held for the heavily populated coastal valleys. Eastward, however, the great rain forest of the Montaña effectively halted Inca conquest. Inca imperialism met almost no challenge in the areas of central Andean high culture; even the highly organized Chimu state fell virtually without a struggle.

The empire reached its greatest expanse in the reign of Huayna Capac (1493–1525) who filled in a few corners of the Inca domain and spent much of his reign in the northern city of Quito (now capital of modern Ecuador). Apparently the empire was becoming too vast to rule from one center and so was rapidly developing sectional centers—this in spite of the excellent road system that stretched from northern Ecuador to central Chile and from the high Andes of Bolivia to the Peruvian coast.

89
Mochica battle scene
stirrup-pot, Peru

The centrifugal tendency seen under Huayna Capac reached a climax after his death. The emperor left two sons in command, a favorite, Atahuallpa, in Quito with the better part of the army, and the legal sovereign, Huáscar, in Cuzco. That these two should clash was probably inevitable—the important historical accident was the appearance of Pizarro and his Spanish army, 1532, just after the climax of the fighting.

The Inca are mainly interesting to us because they seem to reflect conditions that Old World areas passed through at the very beginning of civilization. Peru of A.D. 1500 is really very like Egypt of 3000 B.C., not, of course, in specifics, but in the general outline of events. What we have with the Inca (and Aztec) is, in part, a "fossilized" early civilization. It may be tempting to go farther and equate the volatile Mochica statelets with the nomes of Gerzean Egypt or the predynastic Sumerian states. However, it is dangerous to press these parallels too far, because we must realize that the similarities are of a very broad evolutionary nature and the differences are striking and important.

For example, neither the Inca nor their predecessors had a writing system. The Inca kept records with a mnemonic device: a series of different colored knotted strings on a stick called a quipu. This could be used for tax and other records that were essentially numerical in nature. The mnemonic aspect was involved because verbal messages and even religious procedures and traditions were memorized and recited by specialists who, as they spoke, ticked off points on the quipu.

90
The quipu,
from a drawing by the early
chronicler Poma de Ayala

Though deficient in the matter of writing the Inca were the inheritors of a long metallurgical tradition and made bronze tools and weapons (something unknown in Egypt of 3000 B.C.), cast gold, silver, copper, as well as bronze and other alloys, using the lost-wax process. Inca craftsmen also used mercury and lead, knew how to anneal, solder, and gild, and made inlays of gold and silver in wood, metal, stone, and bone.

Several other crafts had been raised to superb heights long before the Inca period. Weaving of cotton, and of llama and alpaca wool was, from early times, on a master craft level, and continued so into the Inca period. On the other hand, the Inca pottery though well-made lacked the flair of the earlier Mochica or Nasca pots; mass production, here, went hand in hand with reduced quality. Nevertheless, some Inca forms are pleasant, especially the pointed-bottom aryballi, some of which are covered with geometric decorations, and have a freakish resemblance to Greek Geometric Period pots. Inca pottery was never wheel-made—the wheel was simply not used in pre-Columbian America.

The Inca social system was based on the ayllu, a kind of territorial clan that probably was old in the Andean area. The Inca rulers themselves were drawn from a "royal ayllu," and each emperor was supposed to have started his own royal clan. According to early historical accounts, the population of the Inca Empire was divided, for tax and labor purposes, into decimal units: basic groups of ten members, ten of which groups composed a larger organization of 100; ten of the latter an organization of 1000, and so forth. It is very doubtful, however, that such an elaborate and highly mechanical system was ever used by the Inca, though the germs of it may have been present.

The ordinary Andean Indian of the period around A.D. 1500 was a peasant living in a small village and, with other members of his ayllu, cooperatively tilling the fields. The Inca state took a part of his produce as presumably had earlier organizations such as the Chimu state. For most people, being part of the empire probably meant little change. The villagers paid taxes not only in agricultural produce (maize, potatoes, quinoa, sweet potatoes, and a number of other plants) but also in manpower for royal works on the roads, on military or political structures, and for service in the army. There were a number of specialists who worked for the state. Skilled engineers built the impressive fortresses and palaces of gigantic worked stones while other specialists fashioned metal tools and weapons, made pottery, and served in the bureaucracy. Pretty girls were drawn from all over the empire, trained to weave, and then were apportioned out to the harems of high officials and the ruling Inca.

Higher posts in the government service were filled by children of the ruling Inca, by descendants of past rulers, or by those of nonroyal nobility (in many cases

91
*Nasca vessel,*
*south coastal Peru*

chieftains or rulers of non-Inca states who collaborated with the conquerors and so kept their important positions). There is even evidence at the time of Pachacuti and Topa Inca of some social mobility, especially in the army, so that bright peasant children might attain high office. The Inca political organization resembled that of ancient Egypt more than any other early civilization of which we have adequate knowledge. To some degree Pachacuti may be equated with Menes as the organizer not only of an empire but of a point of view.

The Inca rulers considered themselves divine descendants of the sun-god, Inti. This was a reason for brother-sister marriage, as it was in Egypt, though in both areas an original descent through the female line may have been involved—to marry one's sister was simply to validate a claim to the throne. There were a number of other deities; the earth goddess Pacamama, the sea goddess Mamacocha, and the moon goddess Mamaquilla (mama, meaning lady in Quechua, the

92
*Nasca vessel,*
*south coastal Peru*

Inca language). A thunder god, Illapa, was of considerable importance as might be expected in this highly
developed agricultural society. Another and very interesting deity was named Viracocha, a kind of supreme
god and creator god. Actually Viracocha was only a
title; possibly his name was so sacred that it could only
be uttered by the priesthood. This god was a culture
hero and may have resembled the Mexican culture
hero, Quetzalcoatl. At least legend had it that both
deities were white-skinned, a concept that may have
helped Pizarro as it clearly did Cortez in Mexico.

Into this highly organized, yet brittle society came
Pizarro and the Spaniards in 1532. The war between
Atahuallpa and Huáscar had just been won by the
former and Atahuallpa, in fact, was on his way to
Cuzco when intercepted by Pizarro. The last emperor
was captured by an exercise of cold-blooded treachery
on the part of Pizarro. Holding the person of the emperor, and with complete control of the coastline, the

Spaniards moved quickly to overrun the Inca empire. An uprising in 1536 threatened Spanish control of Cuzco for a few weeks, but it was no more than an incident in the Spanish struggle for South America. The great Inca structure fell almost as quickly as it had risen.

IN THE preceding chapters we have dealt primarily with two kinds of civilized areas and we have treated them in different ways. There was first of all the regions such as Egypt, Mesopotamia, India, China, and the nuclear civilizations of the New World where the emphasis has been essentially one of process. For such areas the question was asked, "How did civilization come about?" We saw the dynamic factors of geography (river valleys in warm lands) which allowed man to produce a surplus and we then saw the triggering effect of that surplus under these peculiar geographical conditions. Surplus meant a rise in population, thus an increase in the available labor supply which could be used to produce new surpluses. Cooperative labor was essential, for the wealth of the Nile and Tigris-Euphrates valleys could be tapped only by elaborate measures of water control. Once a population depended on irrigation agriculture it was essentially on a one-way track. In order to support a large and growing population, efficient cooperative work was necessary and this, in turn, demanded elaborate political control. Under these conditions the rest of the civilized complex seems to have grown automatically.[1] Whenever invasion, or breakdown in authority, weakened or destroyed the governmental structure there was collapse of the civilization, often with catastrophic results.

The second kind of area is the secondary center of civilization, which includes much of the Mediterranean region discussed in this book. In such places, diffusion was more important than the evolutionary development of complexes per se, and the amount of civilization depended on the strength and frequency of contacts with older civilized nuclear areas. The western Mediterranean provides only one of a number of examples of this process. From the Egyptian-Mesopotamian nuclear area, civilized concepts spread to the Syro-Palestinian region, to sub-Saharan Africa, and to Anatolia. The Indian subcontinent influenced Southeast Asia while influences from north China reached secondary centers in south China, Korea, Japan, and again Southeast Asia. The New World Mexican nucleus was to influence north Mexico and to promote incipient civilizations in the American Southwest and Southeast. From the central Andes, influences spread to the Co-

## XVII

*From the Past the Future*

lombian Andes, to coastal Venezuela, and more dif-
fusely to Central America.

In some cases there were natural barriers to the
spread of civilization. East of the Andes was the lush
Montaña, a great, gloomy, rain forest. The particular
ecological adjustments of the Andean peoples were val-
ueless in this rain forest and so civilization never
reached the area. The harsh desert of north Mexico also
acted as a barrier for civilization, and a long frontier
across the north of Mexico fluctuated through the
centuries; vigorous influences from Mexican civilized
communities alternating with back-movements of wild
and nomadic tribes. North of this frontier, in a more
satisfactory environment, the Southwestern Indians received and reworked Mexican influences but never produced the surplus necessary to reach a real degree of
civilization. The Southeast United States in late prehistoric times received influences from somewhere in
Mesoamerica, powerful enough to stimulate temple-
pyramid complexes and the beginnings of an elaborate
socio-political structure. These impulses from the south
were not constant nor particularly strong and it is prob-
lematic if the Mississippian culture could have actually
achieved a civilization.

All in all, certain generalizations can be made about
the diffusion of civilization to peripheral areas. Obviously ease of contact is important, and perhaps
scarcely less so, is similarity of environment. In the
Nile-Mesopotamian-Indus axis there was a great deal of
diffusion going from the Mesopotamian center both
east and west, with a significant back-flow. Here people
were on the same evolutionary "train" and lived in very
similar environments, and many traits adapted to one
area fitted nicely into the others. A good example of
this is the flat-roofed adobe house; many others, technological and otherwise, can be found. The subsequent
rise of civilization on the Hwang Ho in China followed
the same pattern and certainly was somewhat influenced from the West even if the specific influences are
hard to trace.

When there is a spread from a nuclear area to another environment, more serious problems appear and
the uptake rate is slower. As just mentioned, the Andean people never managed to export their civilization

to the rain forest to the east. That they might eventually have done so is indicated by the situation in Southeast Asia where great forest-land civilized centers eventually appeared. Another, less well-known, example is Negro Africa. Impulses from Egypt led to the development of a flourishing high culture in Nubia on the upper Nile by about 1000 B.C. From that point the uses of civilization slowly penetrated to both west and central Africa, finally culminating in the elaborate kingdoms of West Africa; kingdoms of great cultural sophistication. In Africa, a later massive deculturation caused by the slave trade in early modern times has tended to hide the fact of native African high culture. The disruptive effect of slave trading should be kept in mind for we shall see it in other areas.

The north shore of the Mediterranean remained for many thousands of years a frontier between the barbarians of its own continental hinterland and civilized communities further east and south. Agriculture spread to Europe before 4000 B.C. and most of the continent was metal-using by 2000 B.C. Nevertheless, except for Crete and the Aegean, Europe was slow in producing civilization. Even Crete and the mainland of Greece were basically unstable areas with high culture institutions and traditions of such fragility that they could be crushingly disrupted for centuries. Further west, along the Mediterranean Coast, civilization was imposed late in time (post-1000 B.C.) by outside powers (Phoenicians, later Greeks) whose lines of communications were secure.

It was in fact largely pressures from the European hinterland that made the position of civilized communities on the coasts so precarious. A vast amount of tribal displacement throughout the centuries certainly occurred; it can be documented archaeologically and we have excellent historical records for later times. As late as the fifth and fourth centuries, for example, marauding Celtic tribes posed a serious threat to the stability of north and central Italy.

The motives for this tribal wanderlust are surely varied. One obvious reason is that Europe is a cul-de-sac, open to the east, so that the upsetting effects of large tribal migrations were felt over thousands of miles. Another factor, and one that is ignored by most students of the area, was that slaving was an important European occupation for thousands of years. Slaves were probably obtained by Near Eastern dealers very much as the African slaves later were procured for European depots, that is, by purchase from particular tribes. This situation set one tribe against another and actively promoted slave raiding. It encouraged an unstable situation by making warfare on this cultural level much more profitable than it would ordinarily have been. Conditions such as these profoundly disrupted ordinary human relationships over large regions, and for long periods of time.[2]

Diffusion of such cultural complexes as related to civilization, then, depend on the well-known factors of ease of access and sufficient similarity of environment, the latter because traits that work out well in one area will fit ecologically into another. The general level of culture is also important; though the upper Nile is similar to the lower Nile environmentally, it took thousands of years to spread Egyptian civilization southward, except as an alien and rootless transplant. The way of life of Nubian peoples had to be drastically altered in order to permit them to function in an adaptation of Egyptian civilization. Even in the same environment there may be more than one set of economic and social adaptations, and the participants in one may not easily adjust to the other. A good example of this is in the American Southwest. The Pueblo Indians easily accepted Mexican traits and reworked them to fit their incipient urban and intensive agricultural society. Neighbors of the Pueblos, the nomadic Navajo and Apache Indians, were much less responsive to such influences, which do not fit a hunting-gathering way of life. Eventually, certain highly modified Mexican traits, especially in ceremonialism, reached the Apachean peoples through a Pueblo Indian screen.

It is clear that no significant amount of the native American civilization came from the Old World. Proponents of schemes that have American Indians dependent on the Old World for their complex societies simply ignore the implications of time, space, and common sense. It is possible that a few items, pottery types, certain art motifs, one or two food plants, were so transported, but there is, as yet, no definite proof for any one of these. It is then reasonable to believe that in the Old World and the New very similar civilizations grew up independently. This, as we said earlier, is no more than an indication of the basic unity of the human species and of the mechanistic and channeled nature of the steps that lead to civilization.

We have surely not touched on all the factors that led man to civilization. One idea that had great popularity in the past and even has some followers today can probably be ruled out: that is the belief that race differences are significant in explaining levels of culture. At present it seems pointless to invoke racial factors to explain the rise of civilization. First of all, it can be demonstrated that every major racial group has had a role both as innovator and participant in civilization.[3] We cannot evaluate such participation, however, for the mental and emotional abilities and attitudes of the different racial groups are simply not known. The groups themselves can be defined differently by using different criteria; problems of intermediate or hybrid groups have yet to be worked out; the amount of genetic versus environmental influence on human-learned behavior is unknown, and no really usable definition of intelligence has yet been made.[4] It is not so much that we lack the answers to the problem of race and intelligence; it is that we are not yet able to frame the questions. Under the circumstances, the only useful course is to consider race as a constant, and examine other factors in the development of civilization.

Whatever the forces involved in its origins, civilization has radically changed the relationship of man to his planet. Because it fosters a high degree of technology, civilization gives us all a decided advantage in the continuing competition of life-forms for a place in the scheme of things. Living enemies whose body organization is complex like ours (other mammals for example) had actually ceased to be serious competitors long before man became civilized. Technology has put into our hands weapons against microorganism pests and we are now ready to challenge the viruses, those "half-life" blobs of nucleoprotein. Yet man remains his own worst enemy. Not only have we yet to prove an ability to handle the terrible war machines of modern times, but we seem unable even to meet the new and novel problem of surplus, especially the overproduction of human beings. It would be well to remind ourselves that we are vulnerable; the Egyptians and Mesopotamians with their first canal systems not only ended their self-sufficiency, but also ended ours. With every increase in the complexity of living, it becomes more necessary that the economic system should always work. When the canals failed, ancient Egypt was faced with disruption and starvation. How much worse if there were a collapse of the normal services that allow New York, London, Moscow, or Tokyo to operate. In attaining civilization, man reached for and achieved a vastly richer life, but he paid the price with a certain loss in individuality. His own welfare is occasionally sacrificed for that of the larger organization and often his personal aims and ideals will conflict with his society as a whole. No less than the richer life, this depersonalization is a legacy from Mesopotamia and Egypt. It may well become the overriding problem in our future as civilized man.

## I  The Meaning of Civilization

1. One of the most amazing things about language is the great similarity in basic sounds around the world. Men only use a few hundred of the thousands of phonetic possibilities and these tend to be duplicated in remote areas of the globe. The more aberrant phonetic elements, the clicks of South Africa and the coarticulated stops of West Africa and Oceania, are not actually of a great order of difference. I am personally tempted to believe that most or all modern languages derive from some mother tongue, perhaps no older than thirty to fifty thousand years.

## II  In the Beginning

1. This is simplifying a rather complex situation. Many physical anthropologists consider *Zinjanthropus* to be a variant form of *Paranthropus* and L. S. B. Leakey, the discoverer of *Zinjanthropus*, who first opposed this view now agrees. He feels that the crude pebble tools found on this level were produced by *Homo habilis* who is on a different branch from both *Paranthropus* and *Australopithecus*. Other specialists believe that *Homo habilis* is nothing more than *Australopithecus*. W. E. Le Gros Clark, *Man-Apes or Ape-Men?* (New York, 1967), pp. 30–31, feels that *Paranthropus* and *Australopithecus* can perhaps be subsumed under the genus *Australopithecus* and are possibly only varieties of the same species. Professor J. T. Robinson, "The Genera and Species of the Australopithecinae," *American Journal of Physical Anthropology*, Vol. 12, No. 2 (1954), 181–200, however, sees *Paranthropus* as a quite separate, herbivore, form.

The question of absolute dates also enters in here. The *Australopithecus* group (in Le Gros Clark's sense of the term) has been dated by the potassium-argon system (one of the new methods that measure the rate of radioactive decay) much earlier than was expected, in fact, about 1,850,000 years ago. The whole question of Pleistocene time is now somewhat confused. Assuming the

93
*Chimpanzee—Gorilla—Man*

potassium-argon dates to be correct it looks as if the Villafranchian (early Pleistocene) was a very long period indeed and extensive glaciation climaxed rather than initiated the Pleistocene as a whole.

2. Gordon Hewes has suggested that the upright stance in man is in part an evolutionary result of food-carrying. See "Hominid Bipedalism," *Science*, Vol. 146 (1964), 416–18.

3. Recent comparative studies of primate serum proteins suggest that man is closer morphologically to the African apes than we suspected. It may well be that man differentiated very late in time from an ancestral stock that also included the chimpanzee and gorilla. Morris Goodman, "Man's Place in the Phylogeny of the Primates as Reflected in Serum Proteins," *Classification and Human Evolution*, ed. S. L. Washburn (London, 1964), pp. 204–34, feels that the African apes should be included, with *Homo* in the family *Hominidae*, while Frank Livingston, "Reconstructing Man's Pongid Ancestor," *American Anthropologist*, Vol. 64 (1962), 301–5, suggests, on the basis of present-day dis-

tribution and ecological adaptation, that gorilla is our nearest nonhuman (or perhaps non-Homo) relative in the animal kingdom.

For a more recent study that tends to verify Goodman's work, see Vincent M. Sarich and Allan C. Wilson, "Immunological Time Scale for Hominid Evolution," *Science*, Vol. 158 (1967), 1200–1203. Sarich and Wilson suggest (p. 1201) that man, gorilla, and chimpanzee split off a common line about five million years ago.

4. I place the invention of language on the Australopithicine level. This is by no means universally accepted. For comments on the matter, see MacDonald Critchley, "The Evolution of Man's Capacity for Language," in Sol Tax ed., *Evolution After Darwin*, Vol. II, *The Evolution of Man* (Chicago, 1960), pp. 289–308.

## III Enter *Homo Sapiens*

1. I certainly make no claim to the last word on this extremely complex subject; in fact, generalizations about the origin of *Homo sapiens* are apt to be quite misleading. For a recent airing of the problem, see C. Loring Brace, "The Fate of the 'Classic' Neanderthals: A Consideration of Hominid Catastrophism," *Current Anthropology*, Vol. 5, No. 1 (1964), 3–43. This includes critical comment by some seventeen scholars.

2. But we can speculate. See Christian Zervos, *L'art de l'époque du Renne en France* (Paris, 1959), pp. 35–38 ff.

## IV Setting the Stage, Old World and New

1. Howard D. Winters, "The Archaic Period," *Illinois Archaeological Survey*, Bulletin No. 1 (1959), pp. 9–16.
2. H. M. Wormington, *Ancient Man in North America*, Denver Museum of

Natural History, Popular Series, No. 4, Fourth ed. (rev., 1957), pp. 169–73.

## V The First Farmers of the Old World

1. Of course I cannot do justice to such a complicated subject as the origin of agriculture (and animal husbandry) in this general summary. Problems include the nature of genetical experiments, conscious or unconscious, to produce acceptable cultigens, the spread of such cultigens from environments that are optimum for the origin of agriculture to those optimum for high yield agriculture, and the questions of man's utilization of different ecological zones for different agricultural purposes. For a concise discussion of these matters, see Kent V. Flannery, "The Ecology of Early Food Production in Mesopotamia," *Science*, Vol. 147 (1965), 1247–56.
2. Kathleen M. Kenyon, *Archaeology in the Holy Land* (New York, 1960), pp. 43–45. Kenyon feels that Natufian settlers at Jericho on the Jordan made the transition to agriculture and became the Jericho "Pre-Pottery Neolithic A" culture.
3. *Panicum miliaceum*, broomcorn millet, has been found in early contexts in Mesopotamia. The early millet agriculture of China involved *Panicum, Setaria italica*, and "grand millet" or kaoliang, *Andropogon sorghum*. In early agricultural Europe both *P. miliaceum* and *S. italica* were domesticated.
4. Radiocarbon data from the early Neolithic (or proto-Neolithic) site at Zawi Chemi Shanidar in Iraq indicates that sheep (or goats) were domesticated by approximately 8900 B.C. Dexter Perkins, Jr., "Prehistoric Fauna from Shanidar, Iraq," *Science*, Vol. 144 (1964), 1565–66.
5. Difficult, but not impossible if the horn-core remains. Teeth are not diagnostic.

6. For a cautionary note on uncritical assignment of domesticated animals to early cultures, see Charles A. Reed, "A Review of the Archaeological Evidence on Animal Domestication in the Prehistoric Near East," in *Prehistoric Investigations in Iraqi Kurdistan*, eds. Robert J. Braidwood and Bruce Howe, Oriental Institute "Studies in Ancient Oriental Civilizations," No. 31 (Chicago, 1960), pp. 119–45.

7. As we will be giving a series of absolute dates throughout this book it might be well to say a word about the method by which many of them are derived. The Carbon 14 (C-14) system of dating was developed by Dr. W. F. Libby and his associates in the immediate post-World War II years. It is based on the knowledge that ordinary carbon, the basic element in organic materials, has mixed in minute proportions (perhaps a million to one) with a radioactive isotope called C-14. This isotope is formed by bombardment of nitrogen atoms in the atmosphere with subatomic particles that rain in on earth from outer space. The nitrogen nucleus is affected, changing the nitrogen atom to one of carbon but with a different atomic weight from ordinary carbon. The rate of production of Carbon-14 is presumably constant (of course only a miniscule fraction of nitrogen atoms are affected). Also constant is the absorption of the isotope (as radioactive carbon dioxide) by living matter through the ordinary processes of metabolism. Thus a tree, while living, will have a calculable amount of C-14 in the body; an amount that changes very little from day to day, or year to year ( a gram of carbon from a living or recently dead organism will have radioactive decay at the average rate of 15.3 disintegrations per minute). With the death of the organism, metabolism ceases and the carbon content remains stable. The tiny portion of C-14 then gradually dissipates by radioactive decay. C-14 has a fairly long half-life, some 5730 years; that is, in 5730 years half the original amount of C-14 will have disappeared, in another 5730 years half of the remainder, and so on. Since the radioactivity of fresh carbon is known and does not vary significantly from one sample to another, the amount of radioactivity in an archaeological sample is a direct index to its age. Main complications of the system are the difficulties in preventing contamination of the sample and, more especially, difficulties in accurately measuring such a small amount of radioactivity as is found in Carbon-14.

8. I feel that growth of complex centers such as Jericho can be best explained as having resulted from cooperative agriculture based on irrigation. This seems to be Kenyon's explanation for the rise of urban Jericho, but Emmanuel Anati, *Palestine before the Hebrews* (New York, 1963), pp. 246–50, disagrees. Scorning (p. 246) ". . . the old theory according to which 'the need for irrigation has called into being the social organization of which defenses are evidence . . . ,'" Anati suggests that control of local sources of salt, bitumen, and sulfur was the key factor. Trade of these presumably much-desired materials to neighboring peoples brought the surplus that led to large populations and elaborate political control at Jericho.

9. James Mellaart, *Çatal Hüyük a Neolithic Town in Anatolia* (London, 1967).

10. E. J. Baumgartel, *The Cultures of Prehistoric Egypt* (London, 1955) pp. 20–23, challenges the validity of the Tasian period. Tasian is, in fact, based on typological rather than stratigraphic evidence. For further discussion, see G. Brunton, *Mostagedda and the Tasian Culture* (London, 1937).

11. For a technical discussion of early metallurgy, see H. H. Coghlan, *Notes on the Prehistoric Metallurgy of Copper and Bronze in the Old World*, Pitt Rivers Museum, Occasional Papers on Technology, 4 (Oxford, 1951), pp. 74–98.

12. E. O. James, *The Cult of the Mother-Goddess* (London, 1959), p. 37.

13. In any case the final result was the "typical" Egyptian who was, in the felicitous phrasing of John A. Wilson, *The Culture of Ancient Egypt* (Chicago, 1957), p. 23, "short, slight, long-headed, and dark, a mongrel of Africa, Asia, and the Mediterranean."

14. Robert J. Braidwood and Linda Braidwood, "Jarmo: A Village of Early Farmers in Iraq," *Antiquity*, Vol. 24, No. 96 (1950), 189–95. Also Robert J. Braidwood and Bruce Howe, "Southwestern Asia," in *Courses Toward Urban Life*, eds. Robert J. Braidwood and Gordon R. Willey (Chicago, 1962), pp. 132–46.

15. Henri Frankfort, *The Birth of Civilization in the Near East* (New York, 1956), pp. 48, 51. But indeed, were they? Samuel N. Kramer, *The Sumerians* (Chicago, 1963), pp. 40–41, drawing on the linguistic researches of Benno Landsberger, suggests that the Ubaid people were "Proto-Euphratean" speaking. This language is as yet largely unanalysed and, in fact, is known only from non-Sumerian words in later Sumerian documents. These include the "Sumerian" names for both the Tigris (idiglat) and the Euphrates (buranun), names of many of the Sumerian cities, and such basic words as farmer (engar), herdsman (udul), metalworker (tibira), weaver (ishbar), and a number of others. The place-names are especially indicative for it is here that displaced languages often maintain themselves over very long periods of time. On the other hand, Woolley (Jacquetta Hawkes and Sir Leonard Woolley) *Prehistory and the Beginnings of Civilization*, UNESCO, *History of Mankind Series*, Vol. 1 (New York, 1963) 369, suggests on archaeological grounds, that the Uruk people were originally non-Sumerian-speakers but by the time writing originated they had taken over Sumerian from the indigenous Al Ubaid population.

# VI The River Lands: Egypt

1. Henri Frankfort, *Kingship and the Gods* (Chicago, 1948), pp. 19–23, suggests that the "two lands" concept was actually an abstraction representing the Egyptian concept of totality as an equilibrium of opposites. Frankfort points out that there seems to have been no prejudice toward northerners in the early dynasties (of course our records are very incomplete). John A. Wilson, *The Culture of Ancient Egypt* (Chicago, 1957), p. 15, however, seems to feel that the "two lands" idea was based primarily on geographical differences between Upper and Lower Egypt. It is quite possible that both these points of view are correct and, in fact, that geographical distinction reinforced the dualistic point of view. Another obvious dualism in Egypt is, of course, that of desert and sown.

2. In a brief but helpful appendix, Henri Frankfort, *The Birth of Civilization in the Near East* (New York, 1956), pp. 122–38, discusses the Mesopotamian influence on late predynastic Egypt (Gerzean). The Asiatic influences possibly were the result of a migration of outside peoples. E. J. Baumgartel, *The Cultures of Prehistoric Egypt* (London, 1955), pp. 50–51, feels that the Gerzeans may have penetrated the upper Nile valley via the Wady el-Hammamat and then spread northward, conquering and absorbing the Amratians. According to Baumgartel the Gerzeans spoke a dialect of West-Semitic which eventually merged with the Hamitic language of the Amratians.

A word about terminology is necessary here. Baumgartel used the older terms Nakada (Naqada) I for Amratian and Nakada II for Gerzean. These various names can also be related to the relative dating system devised by Sir Flinders Petrie more than a half-century ago. Made on the basis of changes in the forms of wavy-handled pots, Petrie's "Sequence Dating" involved the assigning of a number to each stage in the evolution of these ceramic vessels. In modern terms the Amratian covers the period S.D. 30–39, and the Gerzean S.D. 40–62.

3. See Julian H. Steward, "Cultural Causality and Law: A Trial Formulation of the Development of Early Civilization," *American Anthropologist*, Vol. 51 (1949), 1–25; Steward *et al.*, *Irrigation Civilizations: A Comparative Study*, Pan American Union (Washington, 1955); and Karl A. Wittfogel, *Oriental Despotism* (New Haven, 1957). For supporting opinions, cf. Wilson, *Culture*, p. 11, V. Gordon Childe, *New Light on the Most Ancient East* (New York, 1957), pp. 77–78 ff. and, especially, William T. Sanders, *The Cultural Ecology of the Teotihuacán Valley* (University Park, Penn., 1965), pp. 199–200. I am well aware that the "hydraulic determinism" of Wittfogel and some aspects of Steward's "evolutionism" have been vigorously challenged, particularly by Robert M. Adams, see, for example, *Land Behind Baghdad* (Chicago, 1965), pp. 41 ff., and *The Evolution of Urban Society* (Chicago, 1966), pp. 14–15, 66–68 ff. I feel, however, that critics of Wittfogel, and neo-evolutionary explanations in general, rely too much on negative evidence and have failed to put forward any really systematic and coherent alternative explanation for the rise of high cultures. A discussion of various aspects of this problem can be found in the symposium volume *City Invincible*, eds. Carl H. Kraeling and Robert M. Adams (Chicago, 1960).

4. Emery believes that the First Dynasty kings were actually buried at Saqqara near the apex of the Nile delta, not far from the great pyramids of the Third and Fourth Dynasty. A series of tombs found at Abydos in the south are actually cenotaphs. As the tomb of Narmer has not been found in the Saqqara area it may be that in his day the unification of Egypt had not extended so far north. Walter B. Emery, *Great Tombs of the First Dynasty*, III, Egypt Exploration Society (London, 1958), pp. 3–4.

5. For a contrary view, see Henri Frankfort, *Ancient Egyptian Religion* (New York, 1961), pp. 8–9.

6. James H. Breasted, *Development of Religion and Thought in Ancient Egypt* (New York, 1959), pp. 17–43, 142–64. The reader must be cautioned that the Old Kingdom and predynastic dates in Breasted (whose volume was first published in 1912) are several hundred years too early. For a warning against reading too much into the Osiris popularization theory, see Frankfort (*Birth*), p. 18. Walter B. Emery, *Archaic Egypt* (Baltimore, 1961), has an excellent summary of the First and Second Egyptian Dynasties. Emery's "Dynastic Race" idea, however, seems doubtful to the present writer.

7. The Egyptian king was, in fact, not deified but was already a god. In other words his godhood in no way depended on the actions or the attitudes of his subjects. See Frankfort, *Kingship*, p. 5.

8. I have, here, been influenced by Wilson's ideas concerning the evolution of divine kingship, *Culture*, pp. 46–47. Wilson suggests that in the first two Dynasties the concept of a god-king was actively promoted by the dynasts and their practical-minded advisors, essentially as a political device. The king (his divinity constantly and vigorously expressed) was gradually identified, by the Egyptian people, with the far reaches of the sky rather than with any particular geographical part of Egypt. This placed the ruler above regional jealousies and made him a powerful symbol of the unity of the country.

# VII The River Lands: Mesopotamia

1. At least this is the generally accepted view. For a contrary opinion, see

G. M. Lees and N. L. Falcon, "The Geographical History of the Mesopotamian Plain," *Geographical Journal*, CXVIII (1947), 24–39.

2. However, Sir Leonard Woolley in a publication shortly before his death, *The Art of the Middle East* (New York, 1961), pp. 22, suggests that the Uruk element represented an infiltration of mountaineers from the east who overran Sumerian Ubaid. At the end of the period the Sumerian component of the population reasserted itself.

3. The sexagesimal, or sixty-based system of counting, may have come from the habit of allotting one or two daily measures of grain to workers and calculating this in terms of a thirty-day month. See H. Lewy, "Origin and Development of the Sexagesimal System of Numeration," *Journal of the American Oriental Society*, Vol. 69 (1949), 1–11.

4. And the ass and ox were probably ridden. James F. Downs, "The Origin and Spread of Riding in the Near East and Central Asia," *American Anthropologist*, Vol. 63, No. 6 (1961), 1193–1203.

5. The Sumerian language can be read with some ease, its words can be more or less pronounced, and its morphology and syntax can be analyzed. It is an agglutinative tongue, that is, it builds ideas by attaching together word or morpheme complexes. There is some feeling that Sumerian may be distantly related to the modern Finno-Ugric family but this is far from certain and various other linguistic associations have, at one time or another, been suggested. In the uncertainty of its associations Sumerian differs from certain other ancient Near Eastern languages. Egyptian was part of the Hamitic family which has a number of modern representatives. Akkadian, and its later dialects (Babylonian, Assyrian, Neo-Babylonian), is a Semitic language, member of a widespread present-day family. The Hittites and other Near Easterners plus many of the later Mediterranean peoples spoke languages of the Indo-European stock.

6. Agade is the Sumerian and Akkad the Semitic form of the same word.

7. The Mesopotamian concept of the king is best indicated by the literal meaning of the Sumerian word lugal, great man. Henri Frankfort, *Kingship and the Gods* (Chicago, 1948), p. 6.

8. For a discussion of the Sumerian flood myth and a comparison of this myth in Sumerian, Babylonian, and Hebrew folklore, see S. H. Hooke, *Middle Eastern Mythology* (London, 1963), pp. 46–49, 133–36.

9. An extremely readable English version of the epic of Gilgamesh has recently been published by N. K. Sandars (London, 1960). Sandar's long introduction is especially helpful.

10. A book of uncertain date, but probably composed between 500 and 300 B.C. The Book of Job, then, was written at a time when the Neo-Babylonian Empire was a fading memory and few people could read the cuneiform tablets. Nevertheless, the Mesopotamian flavor of the books seems clear enough. A recently translated Sumerian poem contains most of the essential elements of Job, Samuel N. Kramer, *The Sumerians* (Chicago, 1963), p. 296, and it is quite possible that there were also Akkadian versions of the story. The basic plot or story-line may have been known to the Hebrews centuries before the formal composition of our Biblical Book of Job.

There is another possibility. Bishop Theodore of Mopsuestia (in Cilicia), writing about A.D. 400, suggested that Job was done in imitation of a Greek drama. This idea does not seem to have taken hold in ancient times, but a recent Hebraic scholar, Horace M. Kallen, has advanced the ingenious theory that Job was not only modeled on Hellenic drama but specifically on Euripidean tragedy. See *The Book of Job as a Greek Tragedy* (New York, 1918).

11. These examples are adapted from

*Notes*

Samuel N. Kramer, *History Begins at Sumer* (New York, 1959), Fig. 1.

12. Edith Porada, "The Relative Chronology of Mesopotamia. Part I," in Robert W. Ehrich, *Chronologies in Old World Archaeology* (Chicago, 1965), pp. 133–200.

13. Several documents composed for Urukagina (fl. *c.* 2350 B.C.) have survived. Here are some passages that I have freely paraphrased from Kramer (*Sumerians*), p. 319.

> When a good donkey is born to a common man and his supervisor wishes to buy it the commoner may say "Pay me as much as I think fair." [If this request is refused] and the commoner then refuses to sell he must not then be coerced.
>
> If a commoner has a house next to the house of a noble and the noble wants to buy it the commoner may say "Pay me as much as I think fair." [If this request is refused] and the commoner refuses to sell he must not then be coerced.
>
> Urukagina amnestied the citizens of Lagash who were imprisoned because of debts, or because of claims of barley made on them by the palace, or because of theft or murder and set them free.
>
> Urukagina made a covenant with [the god] Ningursu that a man of power must not commit an injustice against an orphan or widow.

This and a large amount of similar legislation suggests that such abuses were widespread in the Lagash of Urukagina's time.

14. Actually the Amorites formed an important element in the Babylonian dynasties that followed the final collapse of Sumer.

# VIII Civilization Spreads to the Indus

1. In late years more and more early Neolithic sites in the Near and Middle East are being discovered. Louis Du-

pree, "Prehistoric Archaeological Surveys," *Science*, Vol. 146 (1964), 638–40, reports possible agriculture in an Afghanistan site (p. 640), that is dated by C-14 to *c.* 6500 B.C. and thinks it possible for the ". . . northern slopes of the Hindu Kush to be *one* of the centers of early agriculture."

2. See the comments of Walter A. Fairservis, Jr., *Archaeological Surveys in West Pakistan*, AP-AMNH, Vol. 47, pt. 2 (New York, 1959), 289. Actually Rana Ghundai is in the Loralai valley south of the Zhob river.

3. E. O. James, *The Cult of the Mother-Goddess* (London, 1959), p. 32, also Stuart Piggott, *Prehistoric India* (London, 1952), p. 127. Much of the basic material in this chapter is drawn from Piggott.

4. On the basis of cross ties with C-14 dated sites in the Quetta Valley, Fairservis suggests that "the beginnings of the Harappan civilization (as such) are probably nearer 2200 B.C. than 2500 B.C." He also suggests that the Indus valley civilization may have survived to *c.* 1300 B.C. Walter A. Fairservis, Jr., *Excavations in the Quetta Valley, West Pakistan*, AP-AMNH, Vol. 45, pt. 2 (New York, 1956), 356–57.

5. Nevertheless, this conservatism does seem extreme in view of our experience with other cultures. Robert L. Raikes, "The End of the Ancient Cities of the Indus," *American Anthropologist*, Vol. 66 (1964), 284–99, has recently suggested that the generally accepted terminal date for the Harappa culture may be too low; that, in fact, the Aryans had nothing to do with destruction of the Indus cities. Raikes sees the possibility that drastic tectonic activity around 2300 B.C. caused the desertion of the city of Mohenjo-Daro and possibly resulted in shifting the capital of the Indus to Harappa. At a later date Harappa itself might have been deserted in favor of still another site. The picture of an unchanging empire, of vast extent in both space and time then is modified to

that of a culture spreading rather rapidly to a favored hinterland area as catastrophe struck its nuclear area.

See also Walter A. Fairservis, Jr., *The Origin, Character, and Decline of an Early Civilization*, American Museum of Natural History, Novitates, No. 2302 (October 1967). Fairservis (p. 42) discounts ". . . the civilization as representing a vast empire with twin administrative capitals, a fully developed riverine commerce, and a flourishing sea and overland international trade as some authorities suggest." He feels that Harappan political organization was too primitive and unspecialized to direct the building and maintenance of large irrigation systems. Therefore, as the Indus valley became overpopulated, the population drifted away to exploit new lands using the same low level techniques and organization. In Fairservis' words (p. 43) the Harappa culture was ". . . a civilization with cities but was not, at least politically, a state. Thus, it was neither Sumerian-like nor Egyptian-like but stands forth unique in its civilized character."

6. For a contrary view, see Damodar D. Kosambi, *An Introduction to the Study of Indian History* (Bombay, 1956), pp. 62–63. Kosambi does not believe that the Indus was wetter in Harappa times. Burned bricks, used in the Indus settlements, he feels could have been fired from fuel obtained in the upriver country.

7. Samuel N. Kramer, *The Sumerians* (Chicago, 1963), pp. 281–82, thinks that Dilmun was actually the Indus area. If, as Kramer feels, the "cedar land" of the Gilgamesh epic is Indus–Dilmun (rather than Lebanon) it means that the geographical horizons of the Sumerians were wider than usually assumed.

8. Kosambi, *Introduction*, pp. 55–56, identifies Mohenjo-Daro with the Meluhha of Sumerian and Akkadian times. Kramer, *Sumerians*, pp. 278–80, however, considers Meluhha to be Ethiopia.

From Meluhha came gold, silver, carnelian, fine woods, and large boats. It seems fairly clear that at least some of the products were seaborne but, of course, this would probably have been the case had they come from either the Indus or Ethiopia. The description of Meluhha as rich in trees, reeds, bulls, "dar birds," "haia birds," and sundry metals is not helpful, for it could apply to either region as could a reference to the "black Meluhhaites."

## IX Between the Euphrates and the Nile

1. Samuel N. Kramer, *The Sumerians* (Chicago, 1963), p. 292, suggests that a historic Abraham possibly came from Ur around 1700 B.C., introducing Sumerian mythic elements into the Hebrew religion. To me a more basic question might be phrased like this, "To what extent does Hebrew literature draw directly on Sumerian prototypes?" Surely in many, possibly most, cases Akkado-Babylonian or Assyrian stories were the models for the Hebrew writers.

2. Frankly, we do not know who Moses was; even his name is incomplete, being a form of the Egyptian *mose*, child of (another name added here). Sigmund Freud in *Moses and Monotheism* (New York, 1955) has, in fact, suggested that Moses was an Egyptian, a follower of the monotheistically inclined Pharaoh Akhenaton. After the king's death, Moses chose the Hebrew people to receive the message of the one God. This idea of Freud's is doubtful in the extreme, but the point is that Moses remains one of the enigmas of ancient times.

## X Crete

1. The wealth in gold of sixteenth century Mycenaean tombs suggests that the Greek mainland was already trading

with the Near East, especially with Egypt. We simply do not know if the trade was direct or through Cretan middlemen. If Mycenaean trade was direct it suggests a strong independent mainland. Certainly it is unlikely (though of course not impossible) that a thalassocratic Crete would allow her vassal states such maritime liberty. Parenthetically, we have few actual reports of Cretan trading ships in Egypt and there is a serious question as to whether those reported actually are Cretan. Torgny Säve-Söderbergh, *The Navy of the Eighteenth Egyptian Dynasty*, Uppsala Universitets, Årsskrift, No. 6 (1946), pp. 49–50, feels that the ships listed in the Tuthmosis III texts as *Kftjw* could have been Cilician. He further suggests that, whatever its origin, the term *Kftjw*, by Eighteenth Dynasty times, may have been the name of a special kind of Egyptian-built ship.

2. Leonard R. Palmer, *Mycenaeans and Minoans* (New York, 1962), pp. 26–28, believes that both Crete and the Greek mainland had Luvian speaking populations until Late Helladic times. Luvian (or Luwian) was an Indo-European tongue related to Hittite and was spoken in western Anatolia in the second millennium B.C. A peculiarity of Luvian is the substitution of an adjective form *assas* for the ordinary Indo-European genitive case. This is used a great deal in place names and thus may explain such names as Knossos. Palmer, *Mycenaeans*, p. 26, feels that Parnassos is "a perfectly transparent word"; from the Luvian *Parna* (temple), it simply means belonging to the (Delphic) temple. Cyrus H. Gordon, *Before the Bible* (New York, 1962), pp. 210–17 ff., however, believes that the pre-Greek Aegean world used a Semitic language. Again it is possible that we have more than one language involved.

3. The situation is complicated by the fact that many words (probably a majority) in the tablets are not recognizably Greek. Possibly more than one language was used in the Linear B documents. In this regard it should be again pointed out that Linear B derived from Linear A and the language of Linear A script is not Greek. For a discussion of this point, see G. S. Kirk, *The Songs of Homer* (London, 1962), pp. 23–28.

94
*Phaistos Disk*

The famous Phaistos Disk inscribed with what seemed to be pictographs may also be written in Greek and be a list of shrines or other sacred places. Benjamin Schwartz, "The Phaistos Disk," *Journal of Near Eastern Studies,* XVIII, No. 2 (1959), 105–12.

## xi Hittites and Greeks

1. A part of this discussion is based on O. R. Gurney, *The Hittites* (London, 1962) and on Seton Lloyd, *Early Anatolia* (London, 1956).

2. The "Peoples of the Sea" relief of Rameses III at Medinet Habu makes it clear that a massive invasion involving a confederacy had already destroyed the Hittites, the Arzawa Kingdom, and Cyprus (assuming that Alasiya is Cyprus). Sir Alan Gardiner, *Egypt of the Pharaohs* (Oxford, 1961), pp. 284–85.

3. V. Gordon Childe once claimed that iron smelting and alphabetic writing were the only two basic inventions that appeared between the beginning of the second millennium and the end of classic times.

4. Though archaeological evidence now suggests that the Cyclades may have been a diffusion point for cult figurines of the Mother Goddess and probably also of an associated religious dogma.

5. Recent Carbon-14 dates for the Balkan area and for Anatolia may make necessary a revision of this statement. See James Mellaart, "Anatolia and the Balkans," *Antiquity*, XXXIV (1960), 270–78.

6. A Neolithic site near Elateia (Drachmani) in central Greece has been dated by C-14 to about 5500–5100 B.C. for the earliest pottery phase. Saul S. Weinberg, "The Neolithic Period in Greece," *Current Anthropology*, Vol. 4, No. 4 (1963), 377.

7. For an extended discussion of the early Neolithic in the Aegean and its relations with other areas, see Christian Zervos, *Naissance de la civilisation en Grèce* (2 vols., Paris, 1962–63).

8. Lord William Taylour, *The Mycenaeans* (London, 1964), pp. 170–71, feels that Mycenae was in fact the dominant power of the Aegean at this time.

9. Leonard R. Palmer, *Mycenaean Greek Texts* (Oxford, 1963).

10. A few scholars still question the correctness of the Linear B translations and, in effect, deny that they are Greek. The majority view is well-summarized by G. S. Kirk, *The Songs of Homer* (London, 1962), p. 24. "That the decipherment as Greek is correct in essentials I do not seriously doubt; though there is still a chance or two in a thousand that it is not."

11. What we have are records on clay tablets of one year, a year that ended in disaster. The tablets were seemingly used by palace officials for interim rec-

ords which were later copied onto some other material, possibly papyrus, for a permanent record. Then the unbaked clay tablets were thrown away. We have only the last year (this is especially clear at Pylos) because invaders sacked and

95
*Portion of Linear B tablet, Pylos*

burned the palaces where the clay tablets were kept—incidentally partially firing the clay and helping preserve the records.

12. Machteld J. Mellink, "Anatolia: Old and New Perspectives," in *Archaeology: Horizons New and Old*, American Philosophical Society, Vol. 110, No. 2, (1966), 111–29, points out (pp. 125–26) that both the Miletus area and Rhodes had not only Mycenaean but also an earlier Minoan settlement.

13. Denys L. Page, *History and the Homeric Iliad* (Berkeley and Los Angeles, 1959), p. 15.

14. John Garstang and O. R. Gurney, *The Geography of the Hittite Empire*, British Institute of Archaeology at Ankara, Occasional Publication No. 5 (London, 1959), p. 81.

15. In a provocative book, Rhys Carpenter, *Discontinuity in Greek Civilization* (Cambridge, 1966), discounts the effects of a "Dorian invasion" and suggests that worsening climatic conditions in the eastern Mediterranean caused the breakup of Mycenaean civilization.

16. Though the poet and classic scholar Robert Graves makes the suggestion that the Homeric bards were in fact devotees of the Great Mother and were simply making fun of the Olympian gods.

17. It seems so to me from the evidence, but I should point out that this is one of the many problems connected with the Trojan war on which there is no general agreement among scholars.

18. The arguments of Page, *History*,

pp. 120 ff., that the catalogue was composed before the Dorian invasions are quite convincing.

19. Kirk, *Songs*, pp. 261–65, scoffs at this idea.

20. Carl W. Blegen, *Troy and the Trojans* (London, 1963), p. 16.

21. For many of these suggestions I am indebted to the brilliant though rather unorthodox ideas of Rhys Carpenter, *Folktale, Fiction and Saga in the Homeric Epics* (Berkeley and Los Angeles, 1956).

## xii The Western Mediterranean

1. Recent discoveries suggest that the great cave art may have a fairly vigorous life as far south as Sicily. See L. Bernabò Brea, *Sicily* (London, 1957), pp. 29–31; also P. Graziosi, *L'Arte dell' antica età della pietra* (Florence, 1956); and J. B. Marconi, "Arte repestre en la Cueva Addaura," *Ampurias*, XIV (1952), 168–71.

2. D. H. Trump, personal communication; cf. also D. H. Trump, *National Museum of Malta, Archaeological Section*, National Museum of Malta, Guides (London, n.d.).

3. Long a favorite weapon in the West. As late as the Second Punic War, the Carthaginians drew on contingents of slingers from the Balearic Islands.

4. For an extended discussion of this problem, see Sibylle von Cles-Reden, *The Realm of the Great Goddess* (Englewood Cliffs, N.J., 1962).

5. V. Gordon Childe, *The Dawn of European Civilization* (London, 1957), pp. 222–28.

6. J. F. S. Stone and L. C. Thomas, "The Use and Distribution of Faience in the Ancient East and Prehistoric Europe," *Proceedings of the Prehistoric Society*, n.s., Vol. XXII (London, 1956), 37–84.

7. Rhys Carpenter, *Beyond the Pillars of Heracles* (London, 1966), pp. 64–65, denies a Phoenician settlement at Cádiz

before the fifth century B.C. Carpenter believes that Greeks were in contact with the area by the late seventh century but were later forced out by Carthaginians.

8. From the Latin *Punicus* (Carthaginian). Punic also refers to the Canaanite dialect in the West.

9. This is the Jezebel of II Kings 9:30–33, killed in a popular uprising probably in the year 853.

10. A name based on an early erroneous idea that they are pile "lake dwellings" on dry land.

11. Carl Roebuck, *Ionian Trade and Colonization*, Archaeological Institute of America (New York, 1959), suggests that Emporion was founded as a port of call early in the sixth century and (quoting García y Bellido) that the city was settled directly from Phocaea.

12. For a good summary of Hanno's voyage, see M. Cary and E. H. Warmington, *The Ancient Explorers* (London, 1963), pp. 63–68. These authors are reluctant to place Hanno beyond Sierra Leone.

13. Marcus Porcius Cato, who according to legend ended all his Senate speeches with the words "Carthage must go."

14. Most of the material on this people is drawn from Massimo Pallottino, *The Etruscans*, trans. J. Cremona (London, 1955), Raymond Bloch, *The Etruscans* (London, 1958), and Emeline Richardson, *The Etruscans* (Chicago, 1964).

15. Named after the village of Villanova near Bologna where it was first discovered.

16. But for some of the problems in classifying Ligurian, see Ulrich Schmoll, "Il Ligure, Lingua Mediterranea o Dialetto Indo-europeo?" *Rivistado Studi Liguri*, XXV, No. 1–2 (1959), 132–38.

17. Examples include Tarchon, son or brother of Tyrrhenos who was the traditional founder of the Etruscan federation. Bloch, *Etruscans*, p. 55.

18. Tyrrhenoi or Tyreseni may in fact have its origin on the Anatolian Pla-

teau, perhaps derived from Tyrrha or Tyrra in Lydia. The word Rasena (Etruscan) is also found in various forms in Asia Minor.

19. Childe, *Dawn*, p. 262, suggests that these nuraghi are foci for clan villages and draws parallels from modern Nigeria. He also feels that the Sardinians of the nuraghi are the descendants of the Sh'rd'n' (perhaps the Shardana) of thirteenth and twelfth century Egyptian records. "They [the Sh'rd'n'] are depicted protected by horned helmets and round shields and armed with swords precisely like those of bronze statuettes from the Sardinian *nuraghi*."

20. Geometric style pottery copied from Greek models was being produced in Etruria before 700 B.C., while an Etruscan variety of the Corinthian Orientalizing style was in evidence by 700. These were grafted onto essentially Villanovan ceramic techniques. At some point in the eighth century the Villanovan-Etruscans adapted wheel-made pottery. R. M. Cook, *Greek Painted Pottery* (London, 1960), pp. 35, 147–52.

21. Pompeii had, at least in part, an Etruscan-speaking population by around 500 B.C.

22. Cook, *Pottery*, pp. 150–53, 190–93 ff. The krater is a deep bowl for mixing wines, hydria a water pot, oinochoe a general name for jug, pyxis a round cosmetic box, olpe a tall pot-bellied jug or pitcher, amphora a two-handled pot with slender neck, and kantharos a handled cup.

96
*Etruscan kantharos*

23. One account states that after the alleged discovery of the Madeiras by Carthaginians (*c.* 500 B.C.) the Etruscans wanted to found a colony on these islands. In spite of an alliance between the two powers, the Etruscans were discouraged by the Carthaginians who controlled the Straits of Gibraltar. Nothing came of the venture. (Cary and Warmington, *Explorers*, pp. 69–70.

24. And technical skills. A burial from the La Tène period in Bavaria, dated 200 B.C. or earlier, was found to contain surgical instruments: a probe, a trephining saw, and a combination snare and retractor. It has been suggested that these and other La Tène surgical implements were Greco-Roman in origin, but in view of the known skill of the Etruscans in medicine it seems more likely that they were Etruscan inspired. See J. M. de Navarro, "A Doctor's Grave of the Middle La Tène period from Bavaria," *Proceedings of the Prehistoric Society*, n.s. Vol. XXI (London, 1955), 231–48).

25. Part of this description of Etruscan life is drawn from Chandler Shaw, *Etruscan Perugia* (Baltimore, 1939).

26. Possibly, if the nineteenth century finds of Leone Nardoni on the Esquiline Hill are validly interpreted, there may have been a continuous occupation of Rome from the third millennium B.C. till the present. See Einer Gjerstad, "Legends and Facts of Early Roman History," *Scripta Minora* (Lund, 1960–61:2, 1962), pp. 6–7.

27. E. Sachs, "Some Notes on the Lupercalia," *American Journal of Philology*, Vol. LXXXIV (July, 1963), 266–79, suggests that the Lupercalia has native roots in Italic or pre-Roman Italy.

## XIII The Birth of China

1. See William Watson, *Archaeology in China* (London, 1960), p. 11, for a brief description of the southern Neo-

lithic tradition in China. Watson considers it one of the major culture traditions, on a par with Yang Shao and Lung Shan.

2. Affinities to Yang Shao pottery are found as far north as the Amur river in sites that probably date from the third millennium B.C. M. B. Levin and L. P. Potapov, eds., *The Peoples of Siberia* (Chicago, 1964), pp. 38–39.

3. Berthold Laufer, *Jade* (Pasadena, 1946), gives the full story of the Chinese obsession with this precious material.

4. Li Chi, *The Beginnings of Chinese Civilization* (Seattle, 1957), pp. 26–29.

5. However, a connection of this sort has been suggested by Robert von Heine-Geldern. For a discussion, see Miguel Covarrubias, *The Eagle, the Jaguar, and the Serpent* (New York, 1954), pp. 32–33 ff.

6. The deposits at the village of Hsiao-t'un in the vicinity of Anyang contained layers of Lung Shan, Early Shang (probably before Anyang became the capital) and Late Shang. Li Chi, *Beginnings*, p. 45.

7. An earlier capital may have been at Cheng-chou in northern Honan. Kwang-chih Chang, *The Archaeology of Ancient China* (New Haven, 1963), p. 146.

8. For a description of Shang carvings in marble and in jade, see Chêng Te-k'un, *Archaeology in China: Vol. II, Shang China* (Cambridge, 1960), pp. 102–8, 113–25.

9. For a detailed discussion of the script and the oracle writing, see Chêng, *Archaeology*, pp. 179–94; Herrlee G. Creel, *The Birth of China* (New York, 1954), pp. 158–73; and Watson, *China*, p. 101.

## xiv The American Way

1. This corn, from Tehuacán in southern Mexico, was wild, as the earliest specimens in Tamaulipas probably were. The date of domestication of the maize plant is unknown but it must have been quite early in time. See Paul C. Mangelsdorf, Richard S. MacNeish, and Walton C. Galinat, "Domestication of Corn," *Science*, Vol. 143 (1964), 538–45.

2. See Gordon R. Willey, "New World Archaeology in 1965," in *Archaeology: Horizons New and Old*, Proceedings of the American Philosophical Society, Vol. 110, No. 2 (1966), 140–45.

3. In addition, there is a remote possibility that maize reached Africa from America in pre-Columbian times. For discussion and bibliography, see the letter exchange between M. D. W. Jeffreys and Paul C. Mangelsdorf in *Science*, Vol. 145 (August 14, 1964), 659.

4. Irving Rouse, "Prehistory of the West Indies," *Science*, Vol. 144 (1964), 499–513, dates the beginning of agriculture on the lower Orinoco at about 1000 B.C.

5. The latter writers feel that Valdivia ceramics may have been introduced by Japanese travelers of the Jomon culture. Betty J. Meggers, Clifford Evans, and Emilio Estrada, *Early Formative Period of Coastal Ecuador* (Washington, D.C., 1965), pp. 157–78.

6. As this book went to press, three colleagues and I organized a symposium of anthropologists, botanists, geographers, and historians that met in Santa Fe, New Mexico, May 1968, to discuss the problems of Old World-New World pre-Columbian contacts. Many new ideas were presented, and a certain amount of new evidence. What I say in this book may eventually have to be modified on the basis of this continuing exchange of ideas. I must confess, however, that as of now the possibility of significant transoceanic pre-Columbian contacts seems to me unlikely.

## xv Mesoamerica

1. Much of this material has been drawn from the following works: Michael D. Coe, *Mexico* (London, 1960)

and *The Maya* (London, 1966); Eric R. Wolf, *Sons of the Shaking Earth* (Chicago, 1959); Miguel Covarrubias, *Indian Art of Mexico and Central America* (New York, 1957); George C. Vaillant, *The Aztecs of Mexico* (Garden City, N.Y., 1944); and Gordon R. Willey, *An Introduction to American Archaeology*, Vol. I, *North and Middle America* (Englewood Cliffs, N.J., 1966).

2. This is a tetraploid cotton (*Gossypium hirsutum*) and may have been domesticated even at this early date. C. Earle Smith, Jr. and Richard S. MacNeish, "Antiquity of American Polyploid Cotton," *Science*, Vol. 143 (1964), 675–76.

3. Recent work indicates that the great pyramid at La Venta is in fact a fluted conoidal frustum rather than a rectangular structure. See Robert F. Heizer and Philip Drucker, "The La Venta Fluted Pyramid," *Antiquity*, Vol. XLII, No. 165 (1968), pp. 52–56.

4. Augustín Delgado, "Infantile and Jaguar Traits in Olmec Sculpture," *Archaeology*, Vol. 18, No. 1 (1956), 55–62.

5. Canal irrigation was practiced in Oaxaca during Middle Formative times. See Kent V. Flannery, Anne V. T. Kirkby, Michael J. Kirkby, and Aubrey W. Williams, Jr., "Farming Systems and Political Growth in Ancient Oaxaca," *Science*, Vol. 158, (1967), 445–54.

6. This date is based on what is called the GMT (Goodman-Martinez-Thompson) correlation of Christian and Maya calendars. Another correlation, that of H. J. Spinden, makes all dates approximately two hundred and sixty years earlier.

7. For examples of such decoration, see Laurette Séjourné, *Un Palacio en la Ciudad de los Dioses, Teotihuacán* (México, 1959).

8. The Swiss architect and student of Frank Lloyd Wright, Franc Sidler pointed this out to me many years ago. Architecturally, Mesoamerica was about at the stage of Early Dynastic Mesopo-

tamia with the ziggurat and flat-roofed house. The Mesopotamians, however, had a knowledge (albeit limited) of the true arch, essentially missing in Mesoamerica.

9. William T. Sanders, *The Cultural Ecology of the Teotihuacán Valley* (University Park, Penn., 1965), pp. 199–200, feels that the indirect evidence for irrigation, terracing, and other advanced agricultural techniques in Classic Teotihuacán is very strong.

10. J. Charles Kelley and Ellen Abbott, "The Cultural Sequence on the North Central Frontier of Mesoamerica" (MS, Southern Illinois University, Museum, n.d.). Also Carroll L. Riley and Howard D. Winters, "The Prehistoric Tepehuan of Northern Mexico," *Southwestern Journal of Anthropology*, Vol. 19, No. 2 (1963), 177–85.

11. It could well be that certain tribes that were on a hunting-gathering "Chichimec" level at Conquest time once were within the borders of the northern fringes of civilization and had a more evolved culture. The possibility of this for the Pame and Otomían-speaking groups in Querétaro and Potosí has been suggested by Pedro Carrasco Pizana (*Los Otomíes*, Mexico, 1950), pp. 3–6 ff.

12. For a detailed discussion of the religious situation in Toltec times, see Basil C. Hedrick, *Quetzalcoatl*, Katunob, Occasional Publications in Mesoamerican Anthropology, No. 1 (1967).

13. See Carrasco, *Los Otomíes*, pp. 254–55 ff., for movements of Otomí speakers into the Valley of Mexico in the thirteenth century and earlier.

## xvi The Central Andes

1. This early flowering of developed architecture in Peru may necessitate re-evaluation of certain aspects of Peruvian prehistory. Recent work on this problem has been done by Frederic Engel, Seiichi Izumi, Edward P. Lanning, and Toshihiko Sono among others.

2. This is, of course, the general region of head shrinking as practiced by the present-day Jívaro Indians.

3. Wendell C. Bennett, *Chavín Stone Carving*, Yale Anthropological Studies, Vol. III (1942).

4. A. L. Kroeber, "Art" in *Handbook of South American Indians*, Vol. V, ed. J. Steward, BAE Bulletin 143 (Washington, 1949), pp. 417–20. But see John Howland Rowe, "Form and Meaning in Chavín Art," in *Peruvian Archaeology, Selected Readings*, eds. John Howland Rowe and Dorothy Menzel (Palo Alto, Calif., 1967), pp. 72–103.

5. Rafael Larco Hoyle, *Los Cupisniques* (Lima, 1941).

6. It must be pointed out, however, that in the Virú valley where detailed archaeological work has been done, there is no evidence for irrigation until Salinar times and no detailed evidence until Gallinazo. See Gordon R. Willey, *Prehistoric Settlement Patterns in the Virú Valley, Perú*, BAE Bulletin 155 (Washington, 1953), pp. 361–62.

7. The red-on-white pottery was made possible by a technical advance. Kilns capable of producing a hot "oxidizing" fire were being used instead of the lower-heat, half-smothered, "reducing" kilns. Negative painting on pottery surfaces is produced by covering certain areas of the pot with wax and then applying a paint or a slip to the pot. In firing, the wax melts leaving unpainted designs on the pot surface.

8. For a concise summary of the early periods in northern Peru, see Rafael Larco Hoyle, "A Culture Sequence for the North Coast of Peru," *Handbook of South American Indians*, Vol. II, ed. Julian Steward, BAE Bulletin 143 (1946), pp. 149–75.

9. As pointed out by G. H. S. Bushnell, *Peru*, rev. ed. (London, 1963), p. 29, the llama and alpaca are basically highland animals and their presence as domesticated animals on the coast involves highland-coast contacts.

10. Many anthropologists dislike the word Mochica because it also refers to a historic language of the North Coast which may or may not have been spoken by the archaeological Mochica people. Another term, "Early Chimu," has been largely discarded because of lack of clear cultural continuity from Mochica to the historic Chimu kingdoms. I shall continue to use the term Mochica but stress that the word has no linguistic implications in this context.

11. Rafael Larco Hoyle, *Los Mochicas* (2 vols.; Lima, 1938–39).

12. As Pedro Armillas, *Programa de Historia de América: Período Indígena*, Instituto Panamericano de Geografía e Historia (Mexico, 1963) pp. 52–53, points out ". . . es difícil decidir si [Tiahuanaco] llegó a constituirse alguna forma de imperio unificado, pero cualquiera que sea el caso esa expansión constituye un precedente de unificación —aunque fuera solamente en el plano ideológico—panandina y por tanto de la formación del imperio incaico."

13. Although relatively little fine masonry-work has been found at Huari, the other large Tiahuanaco site in the southern highlands.

14. One of the best short summaries of Inca culture is that of John H. Rowe, "Inca Culture at the Time of the Spanish Conquest," *Handbook of South American Indians*, Vol. II, ed. Julian Steward, BAE Bulletin 143 (1946), pp. 183–330.

## XVII From the Past the Future

1. The growth of these nuclear civilizations seems to follow the process for which the term "complex demand" was introduced by the author and Dr. Robert L. Rands some years ago. See Robert L. Rands and Carroll L. Riley, "Diffusion and Discontinuous Distribution," *American Anthropologist*, Vol. 60 (1958), 274–97.

2. This lucrative business still flourished in the tenth century A.D. as wit-

nessed by the importance of slave girls in the cargo of Norsemen traveling through Russia to the Near East. Johannes Brøndsted, *The Vikings* (London, 1965), pp. 264–66, quoting the writings of Ibn Fadlan who in 921–922 visited Norse traders on the Volga and recorded his impressions. Brøndsted (pp. 231, 267, 269) believes that fur and slaves were the two principal trade items exported to southern Europe and to the Islamic world.

3. The Australian aborigines, situated as they were in a peripheral, sealed off continent, never produced a civilization. They seem able enough, however, to participate in the European civilization introduced as a complex by nineteenth-century colonists.

4. For that matter, we have no legitimate grounds for assuming that the people who invented civilization were more intelligent than their contemporaries who did not—or even assume that innovation necessarily takes a high level of intelligence. It may be more of a response to a cultural situation or, indeed, to an emotional state of mind.

Mongoloid: racial type in Indus, 74; in China, 149–50
Monkeys: primates, 8
Monotheism: in Jewish thought, 92
Montaña, 163, 193, 203, 210
Monte Albán, 174, 185, 188
Montehuma: site of, 180
Montezuma I, 192
Montezuma II, 192
Mortar and pestle: in Mesolithic, 20
Moses, 58, 90, 222n2
Mother Goddess: in Indus, 74; in Crete, 99–100; at Mycenae, 116; *Iliad* lacks, 121, 224n16; in western Mediterranean, 126; in Malta, 127; at Carthage, 131; as Turan, 145; in Cyclades, 224n4
Motya, 134
Mouflon, 25
Mount Ida, 93
Mu, 167
Mummification. *See* Burial customs
Murex: used for dye, 134
Muwatallis: Hittite king, 108
Mycenae: script at, 85, 103, 116; wealth of, 116; identified with Ahhiyawa, 117; Schliemann worked at, 119
Mycenaean: elements in *Iliad*, 119–20
—influence: on Syria, 81; on Lipari Islands, 128; in Italy, 136
—period: religion in, 101; cities of, 115; mentioned, 83, 110, 118. *See also* Late Helladic
Myth: Egyptian parallel to Mesopotamian, 39, 53

Nahuatl, 171, 185, 187, 191. *See also* Language
Nakada (Naqada), 218n2
Nal, 63. *See also* Amri-Nal
Nanna. *See* Sin
Nardoni, Leone, 226n26
Narmer, 38, 219n4. *See also* Menes
Narmer palette, 38
Nasca (Nazca), 199, 200–201, 205
Natufian: location of, 18; compared, 21; food habits, 21; houses in, 21; tool use in, 21; at Jericho, 23, 86; agriculture in, 23, 216Vn2
Navajo Indians, 212
Navarro, J. M. de, 226n24
Naxos: in Theseus legend, 102

Neanderthal man, 13, 216IIIn1. *See also* Man
Negative painting, 229n7
Negev desert, 77
Negro Africa: language in, 4; civilization in, 209, 211
Negroes: in predynastic Egypt, 28; in Minoan Crete, 102–3
Nehemiah, 92. *See also* Prophets, Hebrew
Neolithic: definition of, 22; at Sialk, 61; at Bakun, 62; on Orontes, 76; in Crete, 93, 94; in Anatolia, 105; in Aegean, 113; in western Mediterranean, 125, 126; in China, 150, 151; in South America, 163; in Mesoamerica, 166
New Stone Age. *See* Neolithic
Nile valley: civilization in, 22; environment of, 33
Ningirsu, 58
Ninlil, 53
Nippur, 56
Noah, 52
Nola, 141
Nomes: in Amratian, 27–28; in Gerzean, 36; defined, 49; compared to Mochica, 203
Nubia, 34, 103
Nuraghi, 139, 226n19
Nut, 40

Oaxaca: Olmec period in, 174; calendar in, 175; Classic period of, 185. *See also* Monte Albán; Olmec
Obsidian: traded to Crete, 94
Oceania: first human occupation, 13
Odysseus, 119, 123
*Odyssey*, 119, 123, 124. *See also* Homer
Oinochoe, 141, 226n22
Old Kingdom, Egypt: dates of, 36; history begins in, 39; demise of, 44, 88. *See also* Dynastic Egypt
Old Stone Age. *See* Paleolithic
Old Testament, 91, 132
Olive tree, 80, 87, 98, 126
Olmec: Maya debt to, 180; possibly spoken Mayan, 185; compared to Chavín, 194; mentioned, 171, 172, 175. *See also* Middle Formative
Olpe, 141, 226n22
Olympian gods: in Homer, 121
Oranian culture, 18
*Oreopithecus*, 8
Orientalizing period, 123, 138

Orientalizing style: in Etruria, 226n20
Origin myth: Egyptian, 39; Sumerian, 53
Orinoco river: agriculture of, 162, 227XIVn4; early cultures of, 163
Orontes valley, 77–78, 79
*Oryza. See* Rice
Oscan: in Iron Age Italy, 137
Osiris, 39, 40, 44
Otomí: spoken in Classic Mesoamerica, 185; and Chichimecs, 191, 228n11
*Ovis musimon. See* Mouflon
*Ovis orientalis. See* Mouflon
*Ovis vignei. See* Urial

Pacamama, 206
Pachacuti: Inca emperor, 202; compared to Menes, 206
Pagans (Pagani), 3
Page, Denys L., 224n13, 224–25XIn18
Painted Pottery Culture. *See* Yang Shao
Pakistan, 61
Palaces: at Knossos, 96; in Middle Minoan, 101
Palaikastro, 95
Palenque, 181, 183
Paleo-Indians, 16, 161
Paleolithic: meaning of, 15; absent in Crete, 93
—Upper: in Europe, 15; end of, 17; in Mediterranean, 125; in China, 150; in America, 167; art in Sicily, 225n1. *See also* Paleo-Indians
Palettes: in predynastic Egypt, 27
Pallottino, Massimo, 225n14
Palmer, Leonard R., 104, 223Xn2, 224n9
Pame, 228n11
*Panicum miliaceum*: in early cultures, 216n3. *See also* Millet
Paracas: site of, 200
Paracas Cavernas, 199
Paracas Necropolis, 199
Paracas peninsula, 198
*Paranthropus*, 8, 215IIn1
Parnassos, 223Xn2
Patricians: in Etruria, 144
*Pekinensis*, 149. *See also* China
Peleset, 90. *See also* Philistines
Pendlebury, J. D. S., 102
Penis sheath. *See* Libyan sheath
Pentateuch, 92

Dynasty of, 59. *See also* Sumer

Urbanism: importance of, 3; in Mesopotamia, 32, 46; reasons for, 33; in Elam, 48; late in Egypt, 49. *See also* Cities.

Urial, 25. *See also* Sheep

Urnfield culture, 120, 136

Uruk culture: Sumerians present in, 32, 218n15; urbanization in, 32; pottery of, 45; life in, 46–47; and Jemdet Nasr, 48; temples in, 51; writing in, 54; dates for, 55; warfare in, 57; on Syrian coast, 79; in Amq, 80; mentioned, 46, 63

Uruk site: in Uruk period, 45; as Sumerian city, 56

Urukagina: king of Lagash, 58; law code of, 221n13

Usumacinta valley, 181

Utica, 129

Uxmal: corbeled vault, 181

Vaillant, George C., 228

Valdivia, 162

Valley of Mexico: Olmec period in, 173; in Late Formative, 174; in Classic, 175; language in Classic, 185; in Aztec period, 191, 192. *See also* Aztecs; Teotihuacán

Vasilike, 94

Vedic peoples, 67, 154. *See also* Aryans

Veii, 141

Venetic: in Iron Age Italy, 137

Ventris, M. G. F., 103

Venus figurines, 15, 27. *See also* Figurines

Vetulonia, 141

Viking period: slave trade in, 229–30XVIIn2

Villafranchian, 215IIn1

Villanova: site of, 137, 225n15

Villanovan culture: cremation practiced, 136; ancestor to Etruscan, 138; at site of Rome, 146; mentioned, 120, 137, 139

Viracocha, 207

Virú valley: irrigation in, 229n6

Volaterrae, 141

Volsinii, 141, 144

Volturnum, 141

Vulci, 141, 144

Warfare: in Merimdian, 27; of nomes, 38; in Uruk, 47, 57; in Dynastic Sumer, 57; lacking in Indus, 71–72; common in Palestine, 88, 90, 91, 92; rare in Crete, 95; between Hittites and Egyptians, 108; at Troy, 119; by Greeks, 134; between Carthage and Rome, 135; by Etruscans, 146; in Shang, 153; in Postclassic Maya, 186; Aztecs engage in, 191–92; in Chavín, 197; in Tiahuanaco, 197; by Inca, 202. *See also* Weapons

Warka. *See* Uruk

Warmington, E. H., 225n12, 226n23

Washburn, S. L., 215n3

Water buffalo, 156

Watson, William, 226n1

Weapons: Mesolithic, 19; Merimdian, 27; in predynastic Egypt, 38; at Sialk, 61; at Bakun, 62; Hittite, 112. *See also* Metallurgy; Warfare

Weaving: origin of, 24–25; in Tasian, 26; at Carthage, 134; in New World, 167; in Chavín, 195, 197; in Paracas, 199; in Nasca, 200–201; in Tiahuanaco, 201; by Inca, 204. *See also* Clothing; Clothmaking

Weights and measures: uniform in Indus, 74

Weinberg, Saul S., 224n6

Wessex, 128

West Africa: kingdoms of, 211

Wheat: early domesticate, 23

—found in: Egypt, 26, 27; Mesopotamia, 29; Indus, 70, 72; Crete, 98; western Mediterranean, 126; China, 151, 154

—varieties of: club (*Triticum compactum*), 23, 70; emmer (*T. dicoccum*), 23, 126; einkorn (*T. monococcum*), 27; bread wheats, 70. *See also* Agriculture; Einkorn; Emmer

Wheel: New World lacked, 165, 205

Wheeler, Mortimer, Sir, 75

White Mountains, 93

White-on-Red Culture, 199

White-on-red pottery: in Peru, 198

Willey, Gordon R., 218n14, 227XIVn2, 228n1, 229n6

Williams, Aubrey W., Jr., 228n5

Wilson, Allan C., 215–16n3

Wilson, John A., 218Vn13, 218VIn1, 219n3, n8

Wine: in Helladic trade, 114

Winters, Howard D., 216-IVn1, 228n10

Wisconsin glacial period, 13, 17

Wittfogel, Karl A., 219n3

Wolf, Eric R., 227–28n1

Woolley, Leonard, Sir, 47, 51, 101, 218n15, 220n2

Wormington, H. M., 216IVn2

Wright, Frank Lloyd, 228n8

Writing: in early Near East, 33; in Egypt, 37; in Mesopotamia, 41, 48, 54, 55; in Elam, 48; in Indus, 68, 73–74; in Minoan, 98, 103–4; at Boghazköy, 110; in Mycenaean, 116. *See also* Cuneiform; Hieroglyphic writing; Linear A; Linear B

—alphabetic: replaces other scripts, 86; Greeks learn from Phoenicians, 124; Etruscans use Greek alphabet, 137, 140. *See also* Alphabet

—in China: in Shang, 153, 158–59, 227n9; origins of, 154. *See also* Shang

—in New World: in Olmec, 174; at Teotihuacán, 178; in Maya, 181; central Andes lack, 203

Würm glacial period, 13, 14, 17, 125

Yahweh: God of Israel, 92

Yang: appears in Chou, 159. *See also* Yin

Yang Shao, 152, 156, 227XIIIn1, n2

Yazilikaya: sanctuary at, 111

Yellow river. *See* Hwang Ho

Yin: appears in Chou, 159

Yin period. *See* Shang

Yogi, 74

Zebu. *See Bos indicus*

Zervos, Christian, 216IIIn2, 224n7

Zeus, 100, 101, 121, 131

Zhob, 65, 66, 69

Ziggurat, 46, 56

*Zinjanthropus*, 8, 215IIn1

*Index*
243

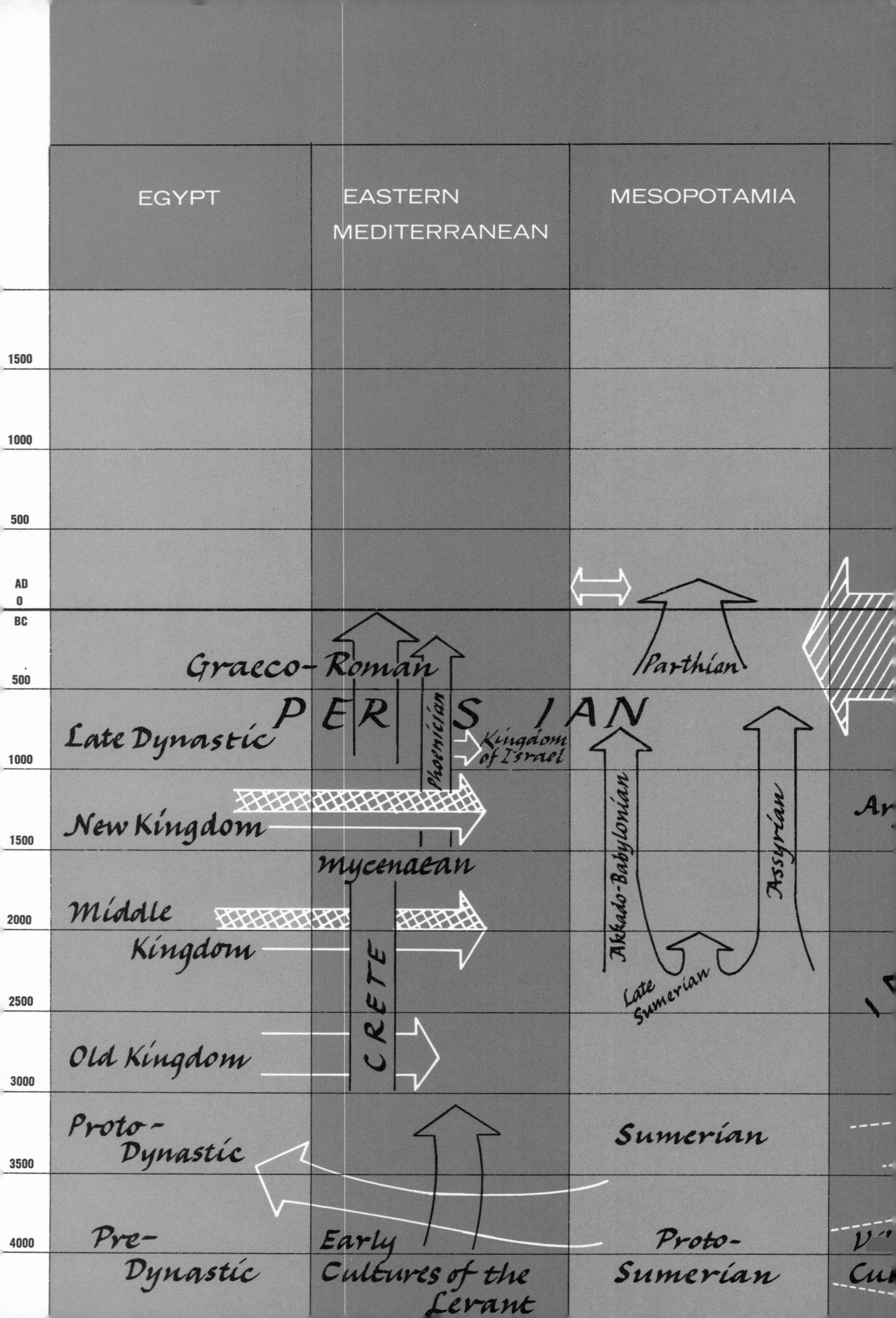

|  | EGYPT | EASTERN MEDITERRANEAN | MESOPOTAMIA |  |
|---|---|---|---|---|

1500

1000

500

AD
0
BC

500

*Graeco-Roman*

*P E R* *S I A N*

*Parthian*

*Late Dynastic*

*Phoenician*

*Kingdom of Israel*

1000

*New Kingdom*

*Akkado-Babylonian*

*Assyrian*

*Ar*

1500

*Mycenaean*

*Middle Kingdom*

*C R E T E*

*Late Sumerian*

2000

2500

*Old Kingdom*

3000

*Proto-Dynastic*

*Sumerian*

3500

*Pre-Dynastic*

*Early Cultures of the Levant*

*Proto-Sumerian*

*V* *Cu*

4000